65
BRUNSWICK
ROAD

65
BRUNSWICK ROAD

Shirley Thompson

BREWIN BOOKS

First published by
Brewin Books Ltd, 56 Alcester Road,
Studley, Warwickshire B80 7LG in 2017
www.brewinbooks.com

ISBN: 978-1-85858-577-2

A Cataloguing in Publication Record
for this title is available from the British Library.

Typeset in New Baskerville
Printed in Great Britain by
Hobbs The Printers Ltd.

CONTENTS

APPENDICES

ACKNOWLEDGEMENTS

The authors are indebted to the following people, companies and organisations, for their invaluable contributions, various favours and support, which have been of great assistance in the publication of this book.

Family:
My husband, David Thompson, for his outstanding patience and support, during the production of 12 books, over a twenty-year period… and for his advice in historical and political matters.

Wareing Family Members:
Harry's family: Eileen Wareing (née Upton) – Harry's wife.

Two surviving daughters: Caroline Palfrey and Julie Vincent (the author's sisters).

Also, my deceased sister, Yvonne Wilson – (contribution recorded in 2008).

b) Madge's family: Jackie Mason (daughter); Gary Dexter (her son) and his wife, Linda.

c) Reg's family: Pat Ward (his daughter); Carolyn McCoy (granddaughter); see note below about Ward Family.

d) Bernard's family: Kenneth Wareing (son).

e) Laurie's family (aka Larry): Dennis Wareing (son). Lilian McMillan and Caroline Carroll (his daughters). **A special mention for Dennis, for his additional years of painstaking research.**

f) Audrey's family: Steven Rogers.

g) Ida's family: Rita Cotterill and her son, Geoffrey

The Upton Family:
Minister Steven Upton, Michael Upton and Aunt Sylvia (now deceased); Eileen Upton – (see also Wareing Family).

The Curtis Family:
Jaqueline Curtis (Jackie) – Nellie Upton's grand-daughter).

The Ward (Baylis) **Family:**
Reg Baylis, the oldest, half-brother;
his daughter, Pat Ward and granddaughter, Carolyn McCoy.

Special thanks to comedian, raconteur, writer and Papal Knight, Don Maclean, for an inspired Foreword and additional, insightful material, in several other chapters.

Balsall Heath Local History Society:
Val Hart, Phil McMullen and Chris Sutton.

Former Balsall Heath Residents, Shopkeepers etc.
Lily Bullen; Kate Cook (née Roony); Pat Hands (née Stevens); Ken Malin; Don Maclean: (see also special mention above); Ken Miller; Steve and Josie Treanor; Trevor and Lorraine Williams.

The Claines/Worcester Connection:
Vivienne Jones: former resident of the village.
Elgar: various sources.

Ebenezer Baylis & Co and Worcester: Internationally acclaimed author Helen McCabe.

Other Companies and Associations:
Publishers: Alan and Alistair Brewin of *Brewin Books Ltd.*

St Chad's Cathedral: the Dean and Chapter, for permission to include three internal photographs of the Cathedral.

FOREWORD

My Lords, Ladies and Gentlemen; I come before you as the Chairman of Music Hall in bygone days. What qualifications do I have for performing this exacting role? Well, as you see, I am a picture of sartorial elegance, I have recently swallowed a copy of Roget's Thesaurus and I have a gavel, which I wield with alacrity, accuracy and malicious intent.

The more discerning amongst you who have paid their thruppence to sit in the Orchestra Fauteils – an insignificant amount I hear you cry, but not when you consider that ale is being sold tonight at a penny a pint – you will realise your money is well spent, when I reveal to you tonight's stars, foremost among which is Lilian Baylis, chanteuse – that's a singer to you madam – and tickler of the ivories; nay not a tormentor of elephants, rather a virtuoso of the piano-forte.

She will be followed by her son and daughter, protégé and protégée extraordinaire. Harry Wareing, who began playing the violin at the tender age of three and his sister, Madge, whose lilting soprano vocalisation could charm the dickie birds from the trees. But that's not all we have to divert you discerning theatregoers this fine evening; in addition you will be treated to a piece of melodrama, light on the mellow and heavy on the drama, entitled 'Mayhem in Brunswick Road'. Guaranteed to bring a tear to even the most hard-hearted amongst you, it has not one but two evil villains: William James Wareing; philanderer and bigamist (allegedly) and his son, Harry Wareing Senior: despite winning a grammar school scholarship, Harry's life spiralled downwards. Bedevilled by lust, alcohol, a short temper and the traumas of the Great War, he abandoned two of his youngest children to an orphanage.

Do we have a hero who will save these waifs from a life of poverty and despair? How better to find out than to stride briskly along Ladypool Road, turn right into Brunswick Road and open the door to number sixty-five.

Shirley Thompson is a writer who loves the great and glorious city of Birmingham and its inhabitants. A true Brummie herself, she adores Brummies and so she should, we're a smashing lot! Having written biographies of various people who have been movers and shakers in the

City, she now embarks on a saga of ordinary… and not so ordinary folk, the salt of the earth that made us great.

I know every brick and paving stone of the area this novel inhabits; I grew up in Ombersley Road, just off 'The Lane', as we locals called Ladypool Road. I attended Clifton Road Primary School and paid my tuppence on a Saturday, to sit with several hundred other kids, in the Olympia Picture House. I knew people exactly like the inhabitants of Brunswick Road and when you've read Shirley's epic novel – you will know them too.

Don Maclean

PROLOGUE

It's a beautiful Saturday morning in May, in Claines, Worcester – and we're going on a picnic. Grandma Griffith and mother are taking me... what a treat! Mother bangs our front door shut, then out of our gate and into the garden next door – to Grandma Mary Ann's. She doesn't like us walking across her front garden.

"Rat-a-tat-tat!" goes the heavy brass knocker at Number 10. Grandma comes to the door, dragging a heavy wicker picnic basket behind her ... looks very promising!

Northfield Street is lined with cherry and almond trees, as far as the eye can see: their delicate pink and white blossoms fill the air with a heavenly fragrance. I'm still too small to be of much help with the hamper, so Kate and Mary Ann carry it between them, as I skip happily behind.

Crossing the road, we pass East Street to our right; then the *Arboretum Inn*, where Father is often to be found. He and the landlord, Edward Tilbrook, are really good friends: he does so love his whisky!

"Such a pity that Eustace can't be with us Kate," remarks Grandma.

"They've called him to inspect a school in Lower Broadheath this morning," Mother explains. "Damp walls and silver fish I shouldn't wonder. He'll probably take a look at the Attendance Registers too, while he has the chance."

On past the bright-red Letter Box, we reach Eliza Nunney's store, where Mother and I often shop. Straight on down Barry Street – my little legs can only just keep up with the grown-ups!

Finally, we've reached my favourite place – the Worcester to Birmingham Canal. I love watching the pretty, painted narrowboats… imagining where they might take me, if I could only hop on board. Do you think anyone would notice? The canal's murky waters are magically transformed today: motes of golden sunlight sparkle, like thousands of jewels.

Mr Tompkins is polishing his barge with a chequered cloth, just to the left of our picnic spot. Now's my chance – but Grandma's asking me about school – so I'm not going to get away with it!

Lunch is very satisfying, but my eyelids grow heavy in the warm sunshine – and holidaymakers' voices grow more distant...

There's an old canal cottage... and a little girl in a green gymslip, squatting on the edge of a slippery towpath, bordered by brambles. She's trying to sail some kind of toy boat... but it's drifting away from her. She's reaching out for it now – oh, please, do be careful!!

Suddenly, her face becomes mine. I'm thrashing about, as water gushes into my nose and throat. I'm choking on foul-smelling, slimy weeds... sucked down into a bottomless world. Everything's going dark – and *icy* cold. Water filling my lungs ... I'm going to die!

There's much shouting above me, as I bob up to the surface for a second time. An old lady – who looks nothing like *my* Grandma – is rushing in terror along the towpath, screaming for help!

But the girl is no longer me. I'm hovering up above, in the fluffy white clouds, like an eagle... looking down on the scene below. She's stretched out on the towpath, her head cushioned by someone's jacket. A man in a light-grey soldier's uniform, bends over the schoolgirl's lifeless body: trying, desperately, over and over again, to breathe life back into her.

If only they can save her. Please help, someone, anyone... you'll *have* to call a doctor!

But suddenly, my eyes blink open... I'm lying on *our* canal bank; Mother and Grandma are still chatting. A blackbird is singing... and the hamper has tipped over, onto its side...

DEDICATION

This book is dedicated to the memory of my paternal grandmother, Lilian Gertrude Wareing (née Baylis); to her youngest son, Harry Nash Wareing, my father, and his youngest sister Madge.

Also, to all of my relatives, listed in the Acknowledgements, who have given generously of their time, effort and love, to supply so many missing pieces of our family jigsaw.

God bless every one of them.

*   *   *   *

As my mother, Eileen Wareing's life draws to a close, at 92 years of age, in her Nursing Home, we take comfort from the fact that she remained well for long enough to reunite with the family… and to take part in the telling of our story.

```````````````````````````````````

# Lilian

*If you could walk beside me*
*And take me by the hand*
*Down to the Worcester-Brum Canal*
*Oh, wouldn't that be grand?!*

*For down from leafy Northfield Street*
*It only takes five minutes*
*Dappled sunlight glistening on the Cut*
*Bright narrowboats moored in it.*

*On grassy banks, with hamper*
*'Neath skies of powder blue*
*And you'd relate such wondrous tales –*
*The Gran I never knew.*

```````````````````````````````````

Shirley Thompson © 2017

"Why is it that the children must always pay for the sins of their fathers?"
'Death Comes To Pemberley' – by P.D. James
(screenplay, Juliette Towhidi).

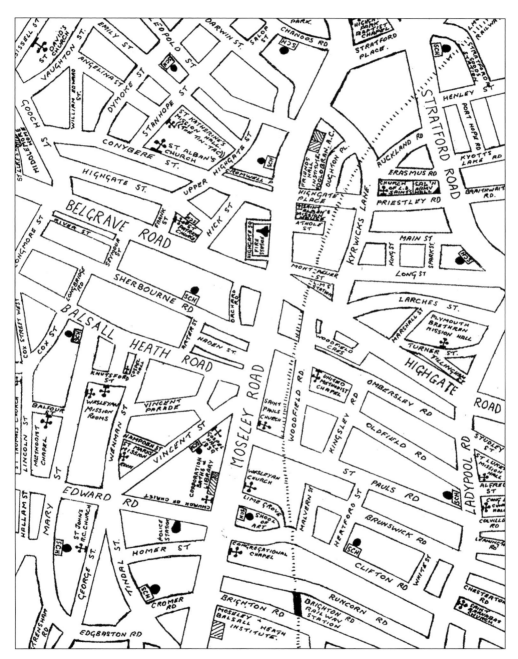

Churches, Chapels, Schools and other Public Buildings in The Balsall Heath Area c1925.
By kind permission of Balsall Heath Local History Society.

Chapter One

SALUT D'AMOUR

A spectacular show awaits us, behind the red velvet curtains. We suspect that you've not seen anything quite like this before!

The stalwarts amongst you may purchase an elegant – nay extraordinary – book of gilt-edged tickets, divided into twenty sections: enabling you to view every one of these unique performances.

We must demand extraordinary versatility from our Theatre Orchestra, for each show has its own musical title – a song or a piece of music – which they are obliged to play for you. They have been chosen to reflect the theme of each act or 'chapter', but they are not in any rigid chronological order.

Scuffling sounds are heard on stage, as the curtain is about to go up.

So… Music… Maestro…please!

Violins play the opening bars of Sir Edward Elgar's haunting *Salut D'Amour*.

Two schoolboys are walking on the Malvern Hills, calling cheerily to each other.

Edward is three years older than his companion, Eustace, who is running, to keep up. Edward strides out ahead of his young friend, clutching some sheet music, which has just arrived at his father William's music shop, at 10 High Street, Worcester.

Eustace's father owns a printing works, *Baylis, Lewis & Company*, at 5 New Street Worcester, just a short walk away from Elgar's Music Shop, so the boys often see each other. Commenting recently on the Elgar/Eustace link, our cousin, Pat, Reg's daughter confirmed: "Everyone in the family has been told that. Grandfather, Eustace, first told my father, Reg, about those treasured walks, when he was a young boy – and Reg was never a fanciful person."

William Elgar is a piano tuner, organist and purveyor of a variety of musical instruments, to order, as well as sheet music. Eustace's father, Alfred Baylis is a respected local councillor and proprietor of his family printing

1

business, so he would turn in his grave if he realised that their former family home would eventually become a Bar called *Sin!*

Both boys hail from ambitious entrepreneurial families; from the cradle, much has been expected of them and their siblings; perhaps that's why they get on so well?!

Edward walks more slowly now, humming an unfamiliar tune to himself. When Eustace requests the name of the melody, his friend confides, "There is music in the air, music all around us; the world is full of it – you simply take as much as you require!" That thought fills Eustace with tremendous joy... which remains with him throughout the day. Edward possesses such depth of feeling – like an invisible, warm aura surrounding him...and those who spend time in his company.

The following day being a Sunday, William Elgar will be playing the organ at Saint George's Church, at the end of Sansome Walk. Several members of the Elgar and Baylis families will be attending.

Once Edward and Eustace leave school, at the age of fifteen, they will go their separate ways: Edward, to embark on a musical career, despite being self-taught, which will take him to the pinnacle of success: becoming a baronet, through compositions destined to establish his reputation, as one of the best-loved English composers of all time.

Eustace, having no interest in the family printing business, much prefers administrative roles: Public Health Inspector for a range of government establishments – and Registrar of Births and Deaths, are just two of the roles that he will fulfil. But we're getting ahead of ourselves!

Even in his twilight years, Eustace took great pleasure in recounting his adventures with Edward, to his eight grandchildren. Other members of both families remained in touch with each other during the years that were to follow ... as we shall discover...

Eustace's home, at 5 New Street Worcester, was above the factory, owned by his parents – Alfred Michael and Lucy Baylis. Alfred's brother, Ebenezer, was the younger of the two. A third brother, Joseph Edwin Baylis, owned a glove factory, in Devon, near Barnstaple. Having no children, Joseph later bequeathed his factory to his niece, Marion Reavell (née Baylis).

At one time the Baylis family owned a tavern. When Ebenezer was a boy they lived in Park Place, Worcester. The *Park Tavern* was run by Ebenezer's eldest brother, Josiah Baylis, who was a publican and a printer.

Josiah went into business with Alfred Michael Baylis, as printers. So *Baylis Brothers, Printers* was the start of their printing business. It was situated at 5, New Street, where Eustace was born.

His Uncle Ebenezer was born in Worcester, then moved to Birmingham for a while, marrying his first wife, Sarah Lane, in Edgbaston. Their daughter, Marion Jesse, was born in Birmingham. Later, they returned to Worcester, where their son, Frank Edwin, (1869-1935) was born.

Ebenezer Baylis & Son Ltd Printing Works, was established at 27 The Tythings; from there he moved to larger premises, at 22, The Cross. Ebenezer was married three times. His first wife, Sarah, from Birmingham, had seven children, then died around 1870. He then married a widow, by the name of Smith. She was also from Birmingham, but they lived in Worcester. When she died, he signed the firm over to his son, Frank Edwin, and then left Worcester, about 1915. Local records for Worcester, reveal that the *Ebenezer Baylis Company* moved out to the London Road.

Born in 1834, by the time Ebenezer married his third wife in 1916, he was 82! That was in the Christchurch Registration District, somewhere around Bournemouth. The couple moved to North London – where Ebenezer died, in 1920. According to his obituary, he was very popular with the ladies!

Frank Edwin's son was Frank Russell Baylis; then his son was Russell Baylis. The male line dies out with Russell, because, to the best of our knowledge, he has no children. According to Russell's handwritten family tree there's a Clifford Baylis too.

Enter my cousin, Dennis Wareing, taking centre stage.

Dennis has been researching material for our show, for many years, so will be making frequent appearances with me. Various other cousins will be combination-hosting with me, during our weekly shows. They'll be in at least two shows each – some, considerably more!

Our three principal characters are our mutual Grandmother, Lilian, my father, Harry and his younger sister, Madge.

My words will be shown in normal font. Anyone else's contribution will be within speech marks. Any photos or other illustrations that we'd like to show you, will, for the most part, be displayed on two screens, near the front of the stage, on the right and left hand sides. Occasionally, these make take the form of posters – or something similar.

So, now, without further ado – over to you Dennis!

"Eustace's father, Alfred Michael Baylis, had remained a Liberal Councillor, at the time of his death. I hold in my hand a report of his burial, in Worcester, ladies and gentlemen. At one time, Alfred's business changed from a printing, to a sewing machine works, called *Busy Bees*. Then it reverted to a printing works, when his brother, Ebenezer, took over.

Eustace's eldest sister Laura Joseland, lived next door to Elgar's sister and her husband."

Dennis continues, "I'm holding up a picture, also displayed on your overhead screens, of 4 Field Terrace, Bath Road, Worcester, which is where Lucy Elgar and her husband, Charles Pipe, a provisions merchant, lived; around 1880, Elgar lodged with Lucy and Charles. Eustace and Kate Griffiths were married in July of that same year, in Droitwich.

Laura Joseland, Eustace's sister, lived at number 2 Field Terrace, between 1883-1889: she was married to William Joseland, a grocer, so those two professions were linked. We also know that the two families socialised with one another.

"Frank Elgar, Edward's brother, knew Lewis Baylis, Eustace's brother," Dennis continues. "Lewis took over, the family printing firm, at 5 New Street, which became *Lewis Baylis & Co.*"

The following article, featuring several of the aforementioned, appeared in the 27 October 1900 edition of the *Worcestershire Chronicle*:

Complimentary Dinner to Mr Frank Elgar, A most pleasant gathering took place at the Crown Hotel on Tuesday evening, the occasion being a welcome accorded to Mr Frank Elgar by the Civil Military Band, who invited him to a dinner. Mr Tarrens ably filled the Chair and several visitors who are interested in the work of the band, which has become so popular in Worcester and the neighbourhood, were present.

Edward Elgar also wrote many other pieces for military bands. Moving on to the toasts:

To Mr Frank Elgar. The other toasts were 'The Visitors'. Given from the Vice-chair, to which Mr Lewis Baylis, Mr C.E. Pipe, and others, responded.' 'Success to the Band' – by Mr W Mann-Dyson, with which Mr Hubbard's Honorary Secretary name was coupled.

During the evening, Messrs C.E. Pipe, H. Bishop, G.E. Porter and the brothers Locke, contributed to the programme, their efforts being much appreciated.

"So again – there's the link to Charles Pipe. Those mentioned in that last list play musical instruments, in some form of band, perhaps even singing, because they're talking about a rehearsal and a meeting since its formation, five years ago.

"The Tythings, where the Ebenezer Baylis and Elgar shops were situated were further up, near the Corn Market. There's also King Charles Street, so named because one of the houses is supposed to be where King Charles stayed, whilst fleeing from Cromwell's army. So that part looks quite medieval."

Dennis continues: "A copy of the Worcester section of British Phone Books, for 1937 lists, *Baylis, Ebenezer & Son*, the Trinity Press. It also lists

Baylis Lewis & Co, Printers, New Street, residence 41 Lansdowne Road, so this was Eustace's eldest brother, Lewis Baylis, I've also noticed that it lists Baylis, Miss MD, Christchurch Road, that's Russell's Great Aunt, Marion, Dora. There's Mrs R.E. Baylis, *The Three Horseshoes Inn,* But the Baylis Tavern was a century earlier than this, owned by Josiah Baylis, Ebenezer's eldest brother."

And I've got a copy of the firm's magazine, Dennis, the *Baylis Bugle.* It was my deceased sister, Yvonne, who started the Baylis research. I visited Russell Baylis several years ago; he kindly gave me additional information.

As Dennis exits, internationally acclaimed writer, Helen McCabe, takes his place as the first of two special guests. Helen's mother, Mary, was the main proof reader for *Ebenezer Baylis & Co, Printers.* The stage is yours Helen!

"My mother Mary worked in an entrance that went off the Cross then went down and joined the end of the Shambles. Queen Elizabeth's House is there, which is a very small black-and-white house. That's where Queen Elizabeth I stayed, when she was on one of her progresses.

"There's an alleyway, with a stationery shop down there; I think it's still there. I can't remember what that's called, but it's definitely very near to Nat West Bank, down the side of it, by the Cross, and that is where Mum worked – it's like a bridge over the road."

When I visited Russell some years ago, Helen, there was a painting on the wall, showing that exact location with the road bridge, which you've described.

"Well certainly, if you find the alleyway, by the Nat West, it goes down and joins the other end of the Shambles. It's not actually the Shambles; it's a street leading up the Shambles, so it comes off the Cross."

There's still a leather goods shop close by, Helen, which was owned by Mr Durrant, whether it's still in the hands of the family we don't know. It's on Meal Cheapen Street, on the right-hand side. He used to know Edward Elgar, who was called 'Teddy Elgar'. But do carry on.

"Well, between the 1930s-1980s, with a few breaks, because of the Wars, my mother, Mary Frances Goodbody (née Young) worked for *Ebenezer Baylis & Co.* in an office, with three glass sides. The actual offices were above that, so she worked on the shop floor below, where all the machines were. The reason she came to be employed by them, in the first place is quite a strange story.

"She really wanted to be a teacher originally, because she was very bright, but her parents, my grandparents, couldn't really afford to send her to

Helen's mother, Mary Frances, with her dog, Paddy. Helen became the main proof reader for Ebenezer Baylis & Co. By kind permission of Helen McCabe.

college. So she was very disappointed; this was in the time of the recession. She actually got the job, but she had no idea how she got it!

"Her father said, 'You've got an interview at Baylis's.' She knew nothing about them, but she went into a room which was full of people, waiting to be interviewed for that job – mainly men of course. She just sailed in and got the job, having no idea how she got it. The next week, she started working there.

"She was extremely clever and won lots of prizes at school. She was very much a favourite of Lucy Galton of the Galton Family. She didn't know anything about printing, but she was extremely well read.

"Our family always lived in a canal-side cottage. My grandfather bought his house on the Galton Estate. He came down from Manchester, to work on the Estate. My grandmother was milliner to the Galtons, so she made hats for the ladies of the house. They'd send a coach and horses for her every morning, to take her up to the main entrance. My mother used to go in the coach, when she was a baby. It was a brougham carriage, with a horse, which took them up to the house. There is a photograph of my grandma on the front row, with members of the aristocracy.

"My Grandfather bought the cottage in my painting in 1910, for approximately £100. He was the Crossing Keeper at Oddingley Crossing, which is the only crossing that is still manned; there are only two in England, It's a railway crossing and you have to ring a bell – the Crossing Keeper comes out and opens the gates for you – day and night. It's best not to go at night, because you have to get them out of bed! That's where he was, all of his life.

"My cottage is in Dunhampstead, but the crossing is at Oddingley: up the canal and the next bridge along. So we lived by the bridge, almost opposite the *Fir Tree Inn* – they were our neighbours. Actually opposite us was a blacksmith's forge, which belonged to the owner of the *Fir Tree*.

"I started writing in 1949, at the age of seven. It was the grandson of the family, who I knew well – whom they called 'Young Jack', because his father was a Jack. He was Russell's father.

"Jack was very much liked on the shop floor – everybody liked him. He was a bit of a champion for the workers, because, allegedly, his father, Russell, was a bit of a martinet – I think he called him 'The Old Man'."

Just like my Grandfather, Harry Senior, Helen, for the same reason!

"Jack was very blond – very good looking; he wasn't very tall. He always used to talk to me, because I'd be there in my school uniform, every day! I became a bit of a mascot for the firm. I was at St Mary's School at that time.

Helen's maternal grandmother, Sarah Ellen Young, outside the family cottage in Dunhampstead, c. 1935. By kind permission of Helen McCabe.

After I was eleven I transferred to the Convent, after I'd won my scholarship and continued to go up to Baylis's every day. Vivienne Jones, who'll be helping to present the next show, went to the same school.

"I occasionally saw Jack's wife, Diane: she was very blonde and very glamorous. Everybody used to call her 'Mrs Jack'. My main memories, as a child and as a teenager, were that Jack used to make quite a fuss of me. And we'd go to the dances. He used to lift me up at the end, when it was the Last Waltz. He'd put me on the stage and I'd sing into the microphone. I remember having a green ball-gown, which was marvellous! I remember trying to get into it, because it was a bit tight. As I pulled the zip up I caught myself in it. They were marvellous, these dances.

"The Baylis family held them annually, for the staff. My mother used to go on quite a lot of trips, of course; they went all over the place. Somewhere in my cupboards, I've got a card, with details of those trips.

"As Mum worked for Baylis's I used to go there in the holidays as well. I wasn't allowed in the factory for safety reasons – dangerous machinery – so I'd spend a lot of time in the canteen. I'd take the tea round to all the machines. It was very interesting, because I saw how the printing worked. It was quite a messy job in those days: putting the type in – amazing! I remember when they started not doing that – litho printing they call it – and everybody was worried about it.

"I also remember union meetings. Anyone who spoke stood on the Speaker's Stone, right in the middle of the factory. They had apprentices and all kinds of people there. They had a strike once and my mother was off work for about two or three weeks.

It was a good time for us, because my brother and I had her at home. In fact, they went fruit picking and things like that during the strike, to make some money. They were only paid a small amount by the union. I think it was a National Strike. I was about 14 when that happened, so that makes it around 1956. I've got a friend whose family owns *North Wales Newspapers*. She remembers a strike, but only from the bosses' point of view.

"Jack and Diane, ladies and gentlemen, lived in the Lenches, but I don't know which one; it was a thatched cottage, between Evesham and Worcester… a beautiful place.

"The Guild Hall is where the Baylis dances were held – on the first floor there. Worcester was a city that was faithful to the King, so Cromwell's face is over the door at the Guild Hall, so that they had an effigy of him to stick pins into! It's just been restored and has a 'Semper Fidelis' inscription:

'Always Faithful'. So the whole city is imbued with the Civil War. If you go down to the Commandery – that was the hospital."

Ebenezer lived at Park Place, Helen, but Joseph Baylis and Ann Lewis, Eustace's grandparents, lived near the Commandery.

"Charles escaped from a house not very far from Queen Elizabeth's House, in the Corn Market there's a black-and-white house on the corner, which is now a Garden Shop: that's where he escaped from during the Battle of Worcester and then he went down to Herefordshire and, allegedly, hid in the Boscobel Oak. So the whole of Worcester is Civil War territory.

"My school, St Mary's Convent, was built on Battle Road, so the battle was fought underneath the school! On those grounds... and then you go out to Powick Hams. So I know a lot about the history of the city. But certainly, the ballroom was on the first floor. They've got a café there now. Following in his father, William's footsteps, Edward Elgar also used to play in St George's Church, Sansome Square, by Sansome Walk."

That's where Eustace moved the family to Helen, from Northfield Street... 2 Norwood Villas, Sansome Walk.

Internationally best-selling authoress Helen McCabe, signing books from her 'Piper' series, at Waterstone's Princess Street, Edinburgh, as part of a National Tour for the store. By kind permission of Helen McCabe.

"Our audience might like to know that the organ that they use in the church is the same organ that Elgar used. From what I understand, he played there as a boy: he used to run along there as a child. I don't know whether any of you are from Worcester. Oh look – a few hands are going up! Many of his works were later played at the Grand Concert Hall in that city. I was actually born in Britannia Square myself… at Springfield," Helen concludes.

Were you? Because Lilian's maternal grandparents lived there too. Malvern is a doubly relevant part of the story too, because my Dad's ashes are scattered close to a bench in Malvern, overlooking a church, It's a favourite spot for my parents, where they used to go courting. I expect Mum's ashes will eventually be scattered there too. (Helen exits stage left, to tremendous applause).

Lewis Baylis's wife, Ida Doward, was a renowned teacher and performer of the pianoforte, as one of our later shows will reveal. She taught Grandmother Lilian to play the piano; grandma named one of her daughters after her. We're following that musical connection throughout the shows.

Most of the cousins on the Baylis side are musical, including Jackie Mason, Carolyn and myself; Jackie and I have performed in and/or directed musical shows and sung solos. Carolyn and her sister, Liz, both sing in choirs. We're calling it the 'Lilian Gene', because our cousin Pat, who doesn't identify herself very much with the Wareings, said, "It's not the Wareing Gene!" She reckons it's the Baylis Gene – she plays the piano as well!

So, to conclude our first show, allow me to introduce you to Pat's daughter, my second cousin, Carolyn McCoy!

"I used to work in a Nursing Home, ladies and gentlemen, in a village called Redmarley, just outside Ledbury, on the edge of the Malvern Hills. It was called Phera Hall; it's something else now. At that time it was a very smart Nursing Home. That's the house where Elgar's wife lived. After they'd run away they came back and were married.

"There was a beautiful dining room where we worked. We called it the Reconciliation Room, because that's where she went back and met her parents. I understand that Elgar was Diane Baylis' music teacher.

"Elgar originally met his young wife in this same house in Redmarley, when he went to the house as her music teacher. From the garden of her house, you look straight across to Great Malvern. When I was working as a nurse at the house, we would watch pilots training. They came from an

11

aerodrome in the Cotswolds. The pilot would fly across from there, through the valley between the house and the Malvern Hills, across to Wales; he would be flying west. We would be looking down the valley, watching these pilots training.

"Elgar's wife, Caroline Alice, was seven years older than him. In 1888, the year of their engagement, he wrote *Salut d'amour* (our chapter title) which he dedicated to her. They had a daughter, Carice Irene Elgar, born 14 August 1890. Her name was derived, in a typically quirky Elgarian way, from her mother's full name. The book this information is taken from is *'Dear Carice...'* postcards from Edward Elgar to his daughter. (See Bibliography). The family lived at 'Plas Gwyn' in Herefordshire.

"A member of the Baylis family owned that nursing home where I worked," continues Carolyn. "The lady that I worked for was Paula Baylis. Her husband, Donald, was there all the time. That was in the 1980s. They also had two boys who went to *Kings School.* Donald was several years older than Paula. He must have been around fifty in the eighties, which means that he would have been born in the 1930s. I know he was from Worcester and her mother had a very strong accent. Paula trained as a nurse and then became a Ward Sister at the Queen Elizabeth Hospital in Birmingham," Carolyn concludes.

So, thanks to my co-presenter cousins, Dennis and Carolyn and to international writer, Helen McCabe. Don't forget to join us for Show Number Two – *Gathering Primroses.*

Tickets are now available in the Box Office, if you haven't already purchased your special book of twenty tickets, in advance.

Have a safe journey home.

Chapter Two

GATHERING PRIMROSES

Welcome back, ladies and gentlemen, to the second show in our '65 Brunswick Road' extravaganza! (Behind the curtain, someone is playing 'Gathering Primroses'.)

As the curtain rises, the mezzo-soprano pianist begins to sing:

Gathering primroses down in the dells
Making fine posies, mixed up with bluebells.
Walking through Claines, on a hot summer's day
Pretty pink bonnet, to lighten my way…

She is dressed in Edwardian costume. Turning her head slightly, towards the audience, she continues the song. She is playing entirely from memory, with no sheet music in front of her. The spotlight catches the red and gold highlights, of her elegantly coiffured auburn hair.

As she completes the performance, she remarks wistfully, "My husband used to so enjoy that song!"

The lights gradually dim. When they are turned up again, a rural backdrop of a canal is revealed, complete with narrowboat, but the lady has completely disappeared…

The Baylis family lived at 12 Northfield Street, Claines, during Lilian's early childhood.

The Griffiths family lived in the same street. That was probably how Eustace and his wife, Kate, met. The Griffiths family had a company, like the Baylis's. Eustace and Kate had to marry, because she was pregnant; but they had a daughter who died, before Lilian.

Shirley steps forward to the front of the stage, to address the audience, as the curtains close.

One of the opening pages in your programme, bearing the title Prologue, describes an episode in Lilian's early life, when her grandmother and mother took her for a picnic, down by the canal. This will provide you with further background information, ladies and gentlemen, because in this second episode of our story, we are attempting to recreate Lilian's early years.

Vivienne Jones, the Convent School friend whom Helen McCabe mentioned in the previous chapter, also lived in the Claines district of Worcester, albeit half a century after Lilian. But we are hoping that she can shed some light on the kind of experiences that she and Lilian may have shared.

(Vivienne enters, front of stage right, seating herself adjacent to Shirley, at a green wrought iron table – both facing the audience.)

Welcome Vivienne. I understand that you hold some childhood experiences in common with my grandmother, Lilian. We're trying to imagine what those early years would have been like for her.

"I'll do my best to recall some of them, Shirley, although she lived much closer to the City Centre, so we can also contrast it with my more rural way of life.

"I was born at 368 Ombersley Road. I remember my mother saying that she didn't have a local midwife; there was a lady around the corner, in Cornmeadow Lane. My father cycled round there and fetched her.

"My parents came from London in 1932. My father was a production engineer in a factory called *Williamson's* of Providence Street, which after the war was taken over by the *Metal Box*. My mother worked hard, bringing up seven children. For education, my brother and I went to Claines School, but the rest of my siblings had to go to the school attached to St Stephen's, which is mentioned in the Barbourne Book.

Birth Certificate of Lilian Gertrude Baylis, the Wareing Family's Paternal Grandmother – one of the three main characters in our book.

Vivienne Jones' family lived at 368, Ombersley Road, Claines, Worcestershire, from 1943-1962. Her mother, Ellen Jones (née Doyle) with her children, Vivienne and David. By kind permission of Vivienne Jones.

Vivienne, outside The Mug House, during a day trip around Worcester, with Shirley. The pub is only one of two UK pubs, to be accessed via a churchyard! Photographer Shirley Thompson.

"I went out into the country because I had double-pneumonia. I had to go into the Worcester Infirmary. I was very poorly and the doctor recommended that I went out to school in the country, where we could have fresh milk from the farm. It was also delivered to our house in a horse and cart, with churns hanging off the back.

"My brothers had fun with other boys, at Oak Farm, owned by the Sansome Family. They helped with the haymaking and so on. I had older siblings and my Mum used to pack up picnics and off we would go to the river. At Northwick there was a sandy beach called the Slip and we used to paddle there and walk along the river. We'd cut the Willow branches and make bows-and-arrows. Lilian may have visited that area too.

"Being number six in the family, one of my earliest memories is that, when I was three, I didn't have many clothes, so Mum bought me this beautiful little pink outfit, with bonnet, leggings and a little coat. Of course, walking along, I fell into a cowpat! My sister, who was ten years older than me, was in charge.

"Initially, my Mum took me to school, aged five, along the country lane. The school was about a mile away; we walked along footpaths, across the field. We didn't have a car. I came home for lunch as well, then back again.

"The school was in what is now a little institute. Again we had our milk delivered, but I went off it in the summer, because it was warm. We had no refrigerators.

"The Rag-and-Bone Man came with a horse and cart and would stand at the gate. On Mother's Day, we would gather primroses and bluebells, to make posies; we thought nothing of walking three or four miles. One of my brothers told me that he used to tie little bundles up to a beanpole and carry it over his shoulder, selling these posies.

"We had an orchard next door where we played and built dens. We had free access to the fruit as well, which was lovely. It belonged to a local farmer, who always hoped to sell this plot of land. It was between our house and the pub called *The New Inn*.

"Another enterprising thing that we would do was to go into the pub garden and collect the empty bottles, because you would get a penny back on each one. There was a bar for people who didn't go into the pub; you would take your jug for your glass of beer there, so children were actually allowed into this little entrance at the pub; you tapped on the window and there was a pull-up hatch.

"It wasn't a community because our house was built in the 1930s and people felt the need to shut themselves behind their doors. But there were allotments down the road and there the Dads would grow vegetables, so there was a community atmosphere down there.

"There was a local cinema down the road called the *Northwick*. As children, we would go there to watch a Charlie Chaplin film and also Norman Wisdom. But then on Coronation Day, in 1953, we had street parties.

"One of my big memories was in 1952. We were in the little Institute School. Someone came in and said that King George VI had died. We gathered up and went across into Clayton Church, said the 'Our Father' and sang *All Things Bright and Beautiful.* By then, my brother was at the school with me. He's the one in the photograph. As we walked home we sang the National Anthem. Can you imagine children doing that today?!

"Most journeys were walking, as they would have been for Lilian, but we did have double-decker buses going past, which went from Worcester to Kidderminster. In Lilian's day, it was probably horse and cart, or trams.

"For outings, we would go at least twice, in the long hot summer, down to Worcester and take the paddle steamer, up the river. That was great fun; you could go up as far as Stourport and you'd wave to all the people along the bank, who were having picnics.

"The river was a big focus of life, as it probably was for Lilian… and walking along by the racecourse. I'm not sure if the racecourse had been opened when Lilian was young, but Pitchcroft was there and Victoria's Diamond and Golden Jubilee Celebrations were held there.

"Like your grandmother, when I started school we had slates and chalk; I still recall the smell of the chalk now! Our teachers were extremely strict: you didn't speak in class at all. We all sat very close together and we had inkwells.

"My mother took us down regularly to the library. We didn't have many books. I remember I was about seven before I owned my first book. Lilian would have gone to the library in Worcester because that was the old Library next to the Shire Hall; that would have been her nearest library to where she was living in Northfield Street. Of course, it was silence in the library!" Vivienne concludes, then exits via the auditorium.

When my cousin, Dennis, was in Worcester, in the 1990s, he found Northfield Street, where Lilian was born.

My cousin, Dennis enters. Taking Vivienne's former place at the table, he addresses the audience:

"I approached Northfield Street through Sansome Street, Sansome Place, where Lilian's grandmother lived – Lucy Baylis. There are some lovely Georgian Townhouses. She lived there as a widow, when she died, around 1900.

"Then I came out of Sansome Walk or Sansome Place – this is at the back of the Shire Hall," Dennis continues. "There was this real country feel to it, ladies and gentlemen. There were some lovely old houses, which were more like cottages and a garden, so they would have been older than the Georgian Townhouses. I didn't find her exact, second house in Sansome Place, but we do know that Eustace had moved his family to 2 Norwood Villas, in Sansome Walk, by 1892.

"Then I came into this even more countrified area – the cottages and old English country gardens. On the other side of the road was the Shire Hall, which is where you go into the Civic Area. This is where I asked someone for directions, because there's Arboretum Road and they said that Northfield Street was the next street," Dennis recalls.

"Lilian's birthplace – number 12 Northfield Street – was on the right-hand side. Her mother's family lived next door – the Griffiths. I think it was Number 10. I found on the Census that she actually had an older sister, Lucy Kate, who died as a baby, about a year before Lilian was born. She was named after the grandmother. Four more years passed after Lilian was born and then Horace Eustace was born in 1885. In the 1890s Herbert George was born, but he died of diphtheria.

"One of Ebenezer Baylis' daughters was Ruth Lilian Gertrude, so that's probably where Lilian's middle name, Gertrude, came from."

I explored the area just a few months ago, Dennis, taking photos of the various landmarks, such as the two houses – 10 and 12 Northfield Street, the *Arboretum Pub*, across the road and the modern version of the original General Stores. It was such a pleasant surprise to find that they lived so close to such a picturesque, canal-side setting!

Some of these photographs can be found in your *65 Brunswick Road Programme*, ladies and gentlemen.

As you know Dennis, most of our Wareing ancestors did really well, but there seem to be two 'Black Sheep' in this book: Harry Senior and William James Wareing.

But Lilian's father, Eustace, had contradictory sides to his nature too. He was a local dignitary, a Sanitary Inspector, but whisky seems to have been his Achilles Heel!

We're now a little closer to establishing exactly what the link was, between Lilian and her performing musical ancestors, whom our Aunt Elsie, our fathers' older sister, used to talk about.

Dennis elaborates: "Ida Baylis, Eustace's sister-in-law, who married his older brother, Alfred Lewis Baylis, played the pianoforte at concerts. Her maiden name was Ida Doward. She was also Lilian's piano teacher. We think she may have been at least one of the theatre/music hall links.

"The first reference to her is in the *Worcestershire Chronicle*, Wednesday 10 July 1872. It's the marriage of Baylis/Doward on July 2nd at St Peter's Church, by the Reverend E. Robinson:

Alfred Lewis Baylis, eldest son of Mr and Mrs A.N. Baylis, New Street, to Ida, eldest daughter of Mr Charles Redgrave-Doward, Edgar Street, both of the City.

"The second reference to Ida is from the *Worcester Journal* Saturday 13 July 1872:

A testimonial of a most gratifying nature has been given by some of the most influential residents in the City and the choir of St Clements, to Miss Ida Doward, a member of the choir and daughter of the organist of that church.

Miss Doward has efficiently presided at the pianoforte, for several seasons, at the popular concerts, given by the choir and their friends.

"So Ida played pianoforte for popular concerts, Shirley; her father was the Church organist, like Elgar. The Doward Family were from St Peter's, Wisbech, Cambridgeshire. There's a maternal link with a Scottish printing and bookselling family called 'Walker'. Neil Walker was the maternal grandfather of Ida Doward. He was a bookseller and publisher from Scotland. She had an uncle, Bernard Walker, who was a Printer/Compositor. Neil Walker was born in Scotland, but they moved to Wisbech, in Cambridgeshire, in the 1860s."

Madge had heard from Elsie that one of Lilian's ancestors sang at Birmingham's *Royal Theatre*. That's why she had her voice trained – to follow in the family tradition.

I looked on both websites, Dennis, under both theatre titles, but couldn't find an entertainer with the surname 'Baylis'.

"Well, the *Royal Theatre* opened in the 1850s, around the time that Charles Dickens was writing. In 1861 he actually gave a reading there of *A Christmas Carol.* Shortly afterwards it became the *Prince of Wales Theatre* when Queen Victoria's son married Princess Alexandra of Denmark – so that was in the 1860s," Dennis continues.

"In Chapter 6, Lily Bullen, who was born in 1920 and lived in Brunswick Road for most of her life, describes how she used to see shows, at that very theatre, with her mother.

"According to the *Worcester Academies and Public School* records,

"Ida's mother ran a ladies school in Worcester. Her surname was Walker. They were the Scottish Publisher/Printers. I remember Dad talking about the Scottish connection in the family. As Lilian named one of her daughters after her music teacher, Ida, maybe there was a special relationship between the two women?"

So, ladies and gentlemen, as we're remembering that music hall period, from around the 1850s onwards, here for your delectation and delight, are our very own company of singers, accompanied by our inimitable orchestra, with a rendition of Harry Clifton's much-loved song, *Polly Perkins of Paddington Green!*

The curtain rises again, this time with a 'Streets of London' backdrop, as the performance begins:

She was as… bee – eye – utiful as a butterfly and as proud as a queen
T'was pretty little Polly Perkins of Paddington Green…

Chapter Three

TREBLE CONNECTION

Don's back as your MC again, explaining the link between St Chad's Cathedral Birmingham and the Wareing family. Particularly appropriate because of his distinguished connections with the Catholic Church – (Papal Knight et cetera). He'll then pass the narration to myself and my cousin, Dennis, who has discovered a fascinating connection between Emily Bronte and our paternal Great Grandmother, Sarah Patchett.

So we'll present all of this, batting it back and forwards between us!

Although several of our chapters are in Music Hall Mode, other chapters may have a different format, such as various narrators appearing on stage, (as in this chapter) or scenarios being acted out, in front of you.

At the start of each Show or Chapter, ladies and gentlemen, we will identify the format we are using. Please note that some of the photos you will hear about in our shows are not in the book version of our story. Over to you Don...

"Bishop William Wareing was George Wareing's brother – the George who is buried in the crypt at St Chad's. He also presided at Pugin's funeral in Ramsgate, Kent during September 1852.

"I'm looking at the William Wareing page that Dennis researched. There's a coat-of-arms, with Mary and baby Jesus on the left of the shield, and the coat-of-arms for St Mary's, Oscott, which is in Erdington, so that's very close to home. But the other three sections: the two deer, the three hunting horns and the single deer below, are the arms of the Wareings of Shrewsbury, who were landed gentry.

"Dennis also discovered that Bishop William Wareing was baptised in the Sardinian Chapel," Don continues. "Apparently, back in the late 18th Century, a lot of Catholics in London lived in Covent Garden. There were several embassies in that area, each with their own Embassy Chapels. The Sardinian Chapel was one of them, so if you went to that chapel you were, technically, no longer in England; you could be a practising Catholic without any problems if you worshipped there. There was also the Bavarian

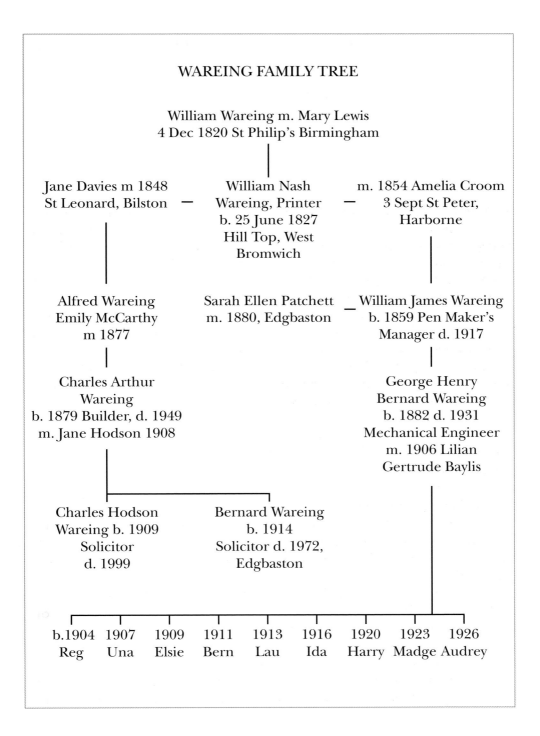

WAREING FAMILY TREE

William Wareing m. Mary Lewis
4 Dec 1820 St Philip's Birmingham

Jane Davies m 1848
St Leonard, Bilston —

William Nash
Wareing, Printer
b. 25 June 1827
Hill Top, West
Bromwich

— m. 1854 Amelia Croom
3 Sept St Peter,
Harborne

Alfred Wareing
Emily McCarthy
m 1877

Sarah Ellen Patchett
m. 1880, Edgbaston —

William James Wareing
b. 1859 Pen Maker's
Manager d. 1917

Charles Arthur
Wareing
b. 1879 Builder, d. 1949
m. Jane Hodson 1908

George Henry
Bernard Wareing
b. 1882 d. 1931
Mechanical Engineer
m. 1906 Lilian
Gertrude Baylis

Charles Hodson
Wareing b. 1909
Solicitor
d. 1999

Bernard Wareing
b. 1914
Solicitor d. 1972,
Edgbaston

b.1904	1907	1909	1911	1913	1916	1920	1923	1926
Reg	Una	Elsie	Bern	Lau	Ida	Harry	Madge	Audrey

Embassy Chapel in Warwick Street, Soho, which is still there. The outside of the building is quite plain: you wouldn't know it was a church!

"There were various anti-Catholic riots at the time, such as the Gordon Riots. Once you enter the Embassy Chapel, you realise that you're in an old 18th Century chapel! So that's why William was baptised in the Sardinian Chapel. Dennis' information about Bishop William also mentions Moseley, in Staffordshire. Then Alton, as in Alton Towers: he was in that area as well.

"William Wareing was born in London on 16 February 1791, the son of David Wareing and Mary Winter," Don explains. "He had at least three brothers, George, John and James and two sisters, Mary and Teresa. William's family became related to the Hardman family: Lydia Wareing was the second wife of John Hardman, button maker and medallist, of Birmingham.

"George, William's eldest brother, collapsed while attending Mass, on Palm Sunday 1843, in Saint Chad's Cathedral and died in Bishop's House. He is commemorated in the window in the south aisle. He was also listed, in the trade directories, as a tailor at 30 Paradise Street, from about 1815 onwards. During George's lifetime the city was expanding, with people moving to live on new estates, in areas such as Balsall Heath. Let's talk about the branch of the Wareing Family, George and James Wareing tailors from London's Covent Garden, who became benefactors of St Chad's."

South Aisle, 3rd window, given in 1850, by Mary Wareing, in memory of her husband, George Wareing, who died in the Cathedral during Mass, on Palm Sunday, 24 March 1844. The window, designed by Pugin, shows Our Lady and St George and at the bottom, a depiction of George's death, in the presence of his wife and twelve children.

Dennis explains: "They had a shop on New Street Birmingham. The Corporation were looking to build Corporation Street. George's shop was right on that junction, between Corporation Street and New Street, so the Council bought them out; that's how they made quite a lot of money.

"I think they had several shops; at least one shop on the High Street. George had several sons, like James. I believe he was a tailor in Snow Hill as well… Near St Chad's. Henry Wareing was a clothier on the High Street," Dennis continues.

"George's father was David Wareing: he came from London. He was born in Preston, but they moved to London for business purposes. There was a Eustace Bernard Wareing, who was a journalist. He wrote for *The Spectator*.

"Eustace was Bernard the jeweller's son, and was the *Times & Telegraph* War Correspondent too. He's mentioned in *Pat Roach's Birmingham*. I found his obituary on *Ancestry*. Eustace Bernard wrote about their ancestors, near Preston. They had a farm there – with God in the title; there were Wareings there, going back centuries.

"It seems like this London connection goes back a long way. Their home was Lancashire, but they travelled down to London; there were family connection in London too.

"David Wareing was a Covent Garden tailor – but he's not the first – it goes back generations. In the Ancestry Archives there are lists of people who were supposed to pay money towards the Poor Rates. These lists give the addresses, names and occupations, going back to the 1840s. You'll find George Wareing, or at least his family, there. Because they were quite a big family," Dennis concludes.

"Chris Sutton of the *Balsall Heath Society* has researched Chamberlain and the development of Corporation Street," continues Don, "including details about Birmingham City Council buying one of George Wareing's tailor's shops, situated at the junction where New Street met; what was to become the new Corporation Street."

"Many of those people whom Chamberlain rehoused from the city slums ended up in places such as Balsall Heath," Chris explained. "By replacing all those houses in the area around what became Corporation Street, he also effectively increased the amount of rates, which the council collected. So although he was a social reformer, he covered both bases."

"Dennis also discovered that Bishop Wareing would have known Cardinal Newman, quite early in Newman's life, before he became a Cardinal and converted to Catholicism. William Wareing was much older that John Henry Newman," Don continues.

"*Birmingham Post* records confirm that Bernard Wareing was an Old Boy of St Phillips and an Honours Graduate from Birmingham University. I remember that when Ray Zacaroli qualified as a solicitor, Bernard Wareing employed him, because, like myself, he was an Old Boy of St Phillips. Bernard's addresses were 192 Gravelly Hill, Erdington and 60 Newhall Street."

Thank you Don. The Wolverhampton Wareings were based in Penn, Staffordshire. I'm looking at six different coats-of-arms, for the different branches of the Wareings. The Wareing spelt with an 'e' is the Lancashire version of the name; the one without the e is more general.

Bernard Wareing, the solicitor to whom Don was referring, was born in Aston, Warwickshire, in January 1914. A Family Tree from the *Ancestry* website, *Nicky's Tree 2012*, gives the Ancestry for Bernard Wareing. According to that Tree, Bernard died in 1973.

The Wareing firm then merged with *Stephen Gately & Sons*, solicitors, becoming *Gately Wareing*. Bernard the solicitor was one of the children of Charles Arthur Wareing (1879-1949). Charles Arthur's father, Alfred Wareing, was born in Lentwardine, Herefordshire, in 1849. His mother was Jane Davis. In 1851 Alfred was living in Lentwardine, with his mother and grandmother... but no father.

Alfred married Emily Florence McCarthy in Birmingham, in 1877. Her family, the McCarthys, together with the Devilles and Cliftons, toured the provincial theatres, particularly in Yorkshire. On the marriage certificate Alfred gave his father's name as Alfred Wareing, but, allegedly, his father

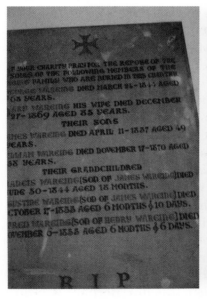

Left: Memorial plaque in Crypt, confirming George's death and details about other members of the Wareing Family. Right: St James's Chapel Crypt; family buried somewhere below the blue and terracotta floor tiles; plaque out of sight, on far left of the white wall. All three photos taken by Shirley, during a private tour for the Wareing Family, arranged at the kind invitation of St Chad's Cathedral. Images used by kind permission of the Dean and Chapter, St Chad's Cathedral.

was William Nash Wareing. This William Nash Wareing is our ancestor – our great great grandfather… the printer.

So William Nash Wareing is the key – the connector – who joins both sides of the Family Tree together! His first wife was Jane Davis: they married in Bilston, but by 1851, when his wife and child were in Lentwardine, he was back living with his mother in Hope Street, in the Jewellery Quarter, Hockley.

William classed himself as 'single' at that point. Then in 1854 he married a second time to Amelia Croom, in Harborne. According to this certificate he was single, not a widower. It's not clear what became of Jane Davis, or their son, Alfred – until he turned up, years later, when he married Emily McCarthy, in Birmingham. Back to you Dennis.

"Amelia Croom was born in Wollaston, in the Forest of Dean. Then she came to Birmingham, married William Nash Wareing and they had a family of their own, although he'd got this son, by his previous marriage to Jane Davis.

"Amelia later moved up to Manchester, with her daughter and son-in-law. She died in 1910, in Prestwich, Manchester," continues Dennis. "For a woman of her times, 1830s, she moved around quite a lot. So we've got that Gloucestershire connection; the Lancashire/Yorkshire connection, through Sarah Patchett and then the Worcestershire connection, through the Baylis Family… the family connections are quite spread out," he concludes.

I'm looking at the Ancestry File on William James Wareing, to tie in with what Dennis has just told us. So our paternal Great Grandfather, William James Wareing, was the son of William Nash Wareing. His mother, Amelia, is William Nash Wareing's second wife. Until 1901, they were living in Ladywood, in Friston Street. I can't find him after that. W.N. was born 1827 in West Bromwich, so he would have been in his seventies then.

On Alfred Wareing's marriage certificate he said that his father was Alfred Wareing (farmer) deceased. But his father, as we've previously explained, was William Nash Wareing and his mother was Jane Davis. So William Nash had two wives – and this is the connection with the solicitors, Bernard and Charles. They were second cousins to Dennis' Dad, Larry, and my Dad, Harry. Alfred Wareing and William James Wareing were therefore two half-brothers. So Harry Senior, our Grandfather, would have been a first cousin of Charles Arthur Wareing

This is collateral, it isn't direct, but Emily McCarthy was actually of Jewish descent, on her mother's side: probably Irish on her father's side. Then we've got Ellen Sarah Patchett, wife of William James.

Looking at William Nash's file, they had a daughter who died when she was three. They married in Harborne in 1854. He was born in Hilltop, West

Bromwich. Amelia was born in 1830, in Wollaston, Gloucestershire. She came to Birmingham to work as a Domestic, in Monument Road, Edgbaston.

Twenty years later, Bernard Wareing the jeweller, was living in Monument Road. Bernard ran his own business in the Jewellery Quarter for fifty years, from 1877 to c.1927. *Bernard Wareing Ltd* was located at 70-76 Northwood Street; on the right-hand side, just past the Caroline Street junction. In 1881 he and his family were living in Acocks Green, he employed three workmen and two reps.

But there was the Oratory connection in Edgbaston. Our Dads' great grandfather... William Nash Wareing, my father's namesake, knew Cardinal Newman apparently. Dennis' Dad, Larry, referred to William Nash as 'George'; he worked as a bank porter. But they lived at the back of the Oratory, Morville Street/Crystal Street, so he may have met Cardinal Newman, simply because they lived in the Parish.

So William Nash's father (aka George) was another William Wareing, and apart from his marriage – he married Mary Lewis in 1820, at St Phillip's Colmore Row – we don't know what became of him then – he's not on the 1841 Census. He was born about 1770, in Alvechurch. We've got Mary Lewis' Death Certificate – the mother of William Nash Wareing.

There was a Charles Wareing, probably a brother, who is on the 1841 Census. He was christened in Alvechurch, in 1822. There were Wareings in Alvechurch, going back quite a long way. So possibly, Mary's husband William Wareing, was from Alvechurch too – otherwise it seems a bit of a coincidence! There was an older Charles Wareing in that same area, who moved to West Bromwich and had a pub there. But then Uncle Larry said they came from Shropshire.

The family branched out more and more as time passed. Amelia and William Nash also had a daughter, Marion. My Aunt Elsie's second name was Marion: (Dad's older sister – also my Godmother).

Marion was born in 1870. Then she married someone named Taylor. Our Canadian branch of the Wareings includes Helen Ayres, whom I met during a private Wareing Tour of Saint Chad's. Helen discovered that going back as far as the 1500s, the Wareings had always been Catholics; it's only in the last century or so that some of them branched off into Church of England and other denominations.

We've joined up the two sides of the family now, because we found that William Nash Wareing linked the two branches together; he lived at Top Hill Farm West Bromwich.

Bernard Wareing, the solicitor, who died in 1972 – his firm *Bernard Wareing Ltd* merged with *Steven Gately & Sons* to become *Gately Wareing,*

Solicitors. The Gately's link up with St Chad's and there's also a link, further back, to Stephen Gately's niece, Edith Gately, who married Bernard George Wareing – they lived in Olton. We are trying to find a precise link between the Olton Wareings and Bernard Wareing the solicitor... and hence us – because we're all descended from William Nash Wareing! We've included a Wareing Family Tree in this book, to simplify things.

Dennis received an email in 2009, which also included a photograph. Back to you Dennis.

"It was from a relative of the Hodson family: a relative of Charles's wife; a niece or a great niece. But she actually KNEW Bernard, the solicitor... Dyan was her name... she lived in Birmingham. The man in the centre of the photo that she provided is Charles Arthur Wareing, Harry Senior's first cousin.

"Bernard the solicitor might actually be in the photo, because they had four sons. It could be that these are the four sons, in the background. There was a photo on *Ancestry*, of Bernard the Solicitor."

And I included a photo of Bernard the Jeweller, in my book, *Pat Roach's Birmingham*, Dennis.

"Bernard the Jeweller was the father-in-law of Edith Gately. So there seem to be connections, but we can't prove any of them conclusively, Shirley.

"What we can do is present our evidence – and let people draw their own conclusions: 'This is what we know – make of it what you will!'"

"Dad said that we were related or connected to Lloyds Bank, which was started in Digbeth by the Taylor Family as Lloyds and Taylor. The 'Taylor' was a John Taylor from London, back in the 18th Century. So I'm wondering if he was an ancestor of this same, Lambeth Taylor family.

"Then there's the D.H. Lawrence connection, Shirley. D.H. Lawrence was born in Nottingham, but according to Dad, the Lawrence family came from Birmingham. His Grandfather Lawrence was from Digbeth; going further back, his Grandfather or father lived on New Street. I found them in the Registration of Marriages for Birmingham... still on the paternal line.

"So this goes back to the 1820s as well. I haven't found the direct connections, but it seems that you had these families: the Wareings, the Lawrences, and the Hailstones – all in the same area of Birmingham, at that time."

And with the Wareings being businessmen/entrepreneurs, they are more than likely to have met each other in some capacity.

"Also, ladies and gentlemen, I had a DNA Test done recently, through *Ancestry*," explains Dennis. "It gives you links, which go back five or six generations. One of the possible links was a guy whose surname was Boulton. One of his ancestors was a Daniel Wareing, from Chorley, Lancashire. Then there's an Ann Wareing, which leads into the Boulton Family. I found this myself, from looking at his Family Tree on *Ancestry*.

"So it's likely that we share our DNA, at least through a Lancashire connection and that Daniel Wareing is a mutual ancestor. Overall, my DNA Test said that I'm 59% British: 28% Irish; 4% Scandinavian; 3% Finnish; 1% South Asian; 1% Caucasus Region; 2% Iberian Peninsula. My DNA Test indicates that our direct Wareing line came from the Chorley area of Lancashire, which is just down the road from Preston.

"I can't find Daniel Wareing's baptism. If he was C of E there probably would have been one. But he married into the C of E so this could have been when some of the Wareings changed from Catholics to the Church of England.

"We've got two Bernard Wareings: the more recent one who died in 1973 – he was a solicitor. He was living in the Hagley Road area, when he died."

That must be the one who went to St Phillip's Grammar School, whom Don Maclean knew. He was my Dad and your Dad's second cousin, Dennis.

"The story, which I heard from David, (Kenny would certainly have heard about this as well) is that they were related to the Wareings of Olton. These Wareings of Solihull link back to the St Chad's Wareings – they're all the same line, coming originally from Preston. That's the Jeweller's line too.

"So we're missing one or two generations, Shirley, because the DNA link confirms that our paternal DNA goes back to Lancashire, so the connection with the St Chad's Wareings is somewhere back in Lancashire… the Preston/Chorley area.

"But I still can't conclusively prove that Eustace Wareing the *Times/Telegraph* War Correspondent, who was Bernard the Jeweller' son, is directly linked to us, although it's more than likely that he is. At present it's only anecdotal. But we're certainly related to the Gately/Wareing solicitors… and Charles Hodson Wareing.

"And that links with Stephen Gately. After Bernard Wareing's death, the firm was taken over by another Bernard, with an Italian surname. The Stephen Gatelys are old Catholics as well, from Erdington.

"So the Saint Chad's Wareings who were the jewellers and tailors in Covent Garden, and later benefactors of St Chad's, are where the connection to Bernard the Jeweller, can also be found. If someone can clarify, once and for all, the connection between ourselves and the Wareing Jeweller branch of the family, we'd be most grateful!

"I spoke to Bernard the Solicitor's brother, Bob Wareing, years ago and he knew about this link to the Olton Wareings as well. They lived on St Bernard's Road. Bernard George who married Edith Gately – their family lived there: 1920s-1940s – that generation: our Dad's generation," explains Dennis.

"But just before our show closes, I've found an even more fascinating link, between Emily Bronte's *Wuthering Heights* and Harry Senior's mother, Sarah Patchett.

"His Great Grandfather, James Patchett 1796-1839, a carpenter of Mytholmroyd, Halifax, was first cousin of the misses Maria and Elizabeth Patchett, who ran *Law Hill*, a young ladies academy. They employed Emily Bronte as a teacher, from September 1838 – March 1839," explains Dennis.

"In 2016 Alan Titterington published his ancestor, John Titterington's biography, *Saint John in the Wilderness*. It includes a section about the *White Lion Inn*, which was run by Henry Patchett and Abigail Titterington. Henry's brother, James, is the grandfather of Sarah Wareing née Patchett, our paternal great grandmother. The book also confirms that the Titteringtons were in-laws of the *White Lion* Patchetts in Halifax, where Branwell Bronte drank with John Titterington.

"There's speculation that *Wuthering Heights* was based on nearby *Old Sunderland Hall* and that the character of Heathcliff might be based on the builder of *Law Hill House*, a real life revengeful cuckoo in the nest, called Jack Sharp, whom Bronte would have learnt about from the Patchett sisters," continues Dennis.

"Catherine Earnshaw may even have been based, in part on Elizabeth Patchett, who was remembered as tall and beautiful and an excellent horsewoman. The cousins were certainly close: the funerals of Elizabeth's mother and brother, Mary and John Patchett, were carried out in 1835, by William Patchett, joiner and undertaker. He was the Great-Uncle of Harry Senior's mother, Sarah Patchett. If you want to learn more read *The Patchetts of Warley 1350-1900* – by John H. Patchett MA."

Thank you Dennis. I hope you've been following all of this ladies and gentlemen. Branwell Bronte was not only an artist/writer (some of the darkest parts of *Wuthering Heights* are thought to have been written by him) but a notorious drinker… so I think it has to be double whiskies all round for everyone in the audience, after digesting that little lot!

Don't miss our next show… it should be much more straightforward!

Chapter Four

THE GIRL FROM ASTON HALL

If you go east from Aston Hall
Down by the Lichfield Road....
Etc.

The red velvet curtains roll back, to reveal the opening of our 4th Brunswick Show, as our orchestra and chorus perform this much-loved song.

The scene is a Midland Red Omnibus Office. A young clerk, auburn-haired Lilian Baylis, is working diligently on a ledger, at a raised oak desk. Seated behind her, a glass screen, dividing them, is the office manager.

Lilian's son, Reginald, who is now an adult, is watching the scene from afar – rather like a character in a Charles Dicken's play, watching the scene unfold, like an invisible narrator.

Reg, (to the audience):

"Mother looks rather tired, don't you think? My real father was already married, with a family… that's him behind the screen. He would invite me over sometimes, while I was growing up… took an interest in me – by no means ignored me. So I had two families.

"Mother realises at this stage, that she is pregnant. She has also just learned that she is to spend her confinement at a Surrey Nursing Home; by removing her from the area it avoided any embarrassment. It's quite likely that my biological father arranged to pay for the nursing care. It's unlikely that her father, Eustace could have afforded it!

"Many years later, this biological father of mine wrote a letter of introduction for me… addressed to someone in Personnel at the Midland Red – my daughter, Pat, still has it.

"But it's written in the Third Person, which makes it awkward to read. He could never openly acknowledge our true relationship, but there's no doubt that his letters and advice were invaluable, on several occasions.

"My brothers, Larry and Harry's children, my nephew and niece, Dennis and Shirley, have spent years researching our family history, long after I had departed!

"Before we continue with my mother, Lilian's part in our story, Dennis and Shirley are about to reveal parts of our family's history, which have remained hidden for years!"

(Curtains close on the office scene).

Shirley and Dennis enter (seating themselves alongside each other, at the front of the stage). For most of the time they both address the audience, but occasionally turn towards each other.

As usual, ladies and gentlemen, my co-presenter's words are enclosed within occasional speech marks; as usual, mine aren't!

"The Wareing and Baylis families were both living in Aston, at the same time," Dennis begins. "The Baylis family lived up by Aston Hall. There's the centre of Aston – the Cross – where *Ansells Brewery* was. If you go north from there, that's going up towards *Aston Hall...* the Villa Ground. Then if you go east from there, you're going along the Lichfield Road. The Wareings lived along the Lichfield Road part and the Baylis family were by Aston Hall, the Aston Park end. Elsie remembers that her father, Harry Senior, used to sing in the church choir, in Church Road, Aston, probably the Church of St Peter and Saint Paul.

"Horace Eustace Baylis, Lilian's brother, died in 1899 (that was the manslaughter case). In 1901 I can't find Eustace or his wife, Kate, on the census. Lilian is living in Aston that year and she's working in a munitions factory. She had been living in Aston Park Road, with her parents, which was the better end of Aston; by 1901 she's living in a more down-market part of Aston, near the brewery – 39 Parliament Street. She was lodging with the Ward family.

"By that same date, her parents had moved from 24 Bevington Road, probably to 366 Lodge Road, where Lucy eventually died, in August 1920.

"So Harry Senior would have been sixteen at that time, maybe still attending King Edward's Grammar School. Lilian would have been seventeen; possibly she moved from munitions, to work as a clerk at the Midland Red Bus Depot, around 1902-3.

"But it's quite likely that the two families would have known each other as they lived in the same area. Harry Senior would certainly have read about the Manslaughter Case: Eustace and his son Horace, in the local press," observes Dennis.

Do you think that Harry Senior and Eustace may have met at a local pub Dennis?

"Well there was the big pub, the *Aston Cross*; they may have drunk in the same pub."

Also, Harry Senior became a driver when he left school and Lilian was working at the *Midland Red*, so they could have met that way. We're not revealing the identity of Reg's biological father – but he might have known them too.

However, I've now discovered a much stronger connection between Lilian and Harry Senior, centred on Bevington Road, Aston. We know the Baylis family were at 24 Bevington Road, in August/December 1899, as this was where Horace died.

"In 1901 at 57 Bevington Road lived Charles Edwin Landon, dispenser of medicine and his family, including son, Harold Edwin, an art student," continues Dennis. "In 1910 he married Annie Alberta Patchett, cousin of Harry Wareing, daughter of his uncle, James Patchett. So it's very likely that the Baylis and Landon families were neighbours in 1899!"

It's interesting that Harold Edwin Landon later became a well-known silversmith, commissioned by Winston Churchill. He worked in New Street, Lancaster.

He and Annie Alberta lived in a beautiful home, called *Thortindale Cottage*, on the Lancaster Canal at Bolton Le Sands. It seems her parents, James and Alice Patchett lived with them and their son, Norman Landon. Tragically, in 1929, Annie Alberta drowned in the Lancaster Canal and her son, Norman, went into a lunatic asylum, where he spent the rest of his life.

"Harold Edwin remarried to a clergyman's daughter from Morecambe, Isabella Bosanquet Vivian, She was a violinist and performed in an orchestra. She died in 1937, giving birth to a son. Her funeral, at Lancaster Priory, mentions a wreath from 'Mr Patchett' (Grandad Thortindale), so it seemed Uncle James Patchett continued living there as a retired Building Surveyor, until his death in 1943, aged 95.

"Harry and Lilian, our paternal grandparents, married in May 1906. Harry was living in Cowley, by that time, but Lilian was living in Ladywood, so they married in a Birmingham Registry Office, in Newhall Street," Dennis explains. "But she was lodging with a Landlord there, whose name was Frederick Rose. He was one of the witnesses at the wedding.

"Harry was born in Ladywood and his grandparents lived there. So however Lilian got from Aston to Ladywood – maybe Harry found somewhere for her to live – in Ladywood?"

I wonder how old Harry Senior was when his Dad left his mother, Sarah?

"His Dad is on the 1891 Census, in Washwood Heath Road. William James must have left the family before 1901, because by that time Harry's older sister, Elspeth, is living with their mother, Sarah, in Lichfield Road, just the two of them. He's listed in a Directory, in the 1890s, so he'd left somewhere between the mid-1890s and 1901. Una and Harry would have been teenagers when he left. So by the time Harry Senior met Lilian, his Dad had already gone.

"The Baylis family came to Birmingham somewhere between 1895 and 1899," Dennis continues. "Probably around the time that Harry's Dad left. Lilian probably didn't know her father-in-law, although she would have known her mother-in-law, from Kidlington.

"The family first lived in Green Road Cowley, which is where Una was born. A couple of years later they were in Kidlington, where Elsie was born. Sarah lived in Lyne Road, Kidlington, although I don't know which road Elsie was born in. She stayed there after Harry and Lilian returned to Birmingham."

During a recent visit to Oxford, Dennis discovered Una's Green Road birthplace, in a sought-after location, across the bridge from the University Botanical Gardens. The frontage of the William Morris Garage is preserved, opposite the Magdalen College grounds: idyllic – and a long way from Balsall Heath! "I also found a christening for Aunt Una, the oldest daughter, for 1907, at Saint Peter and Saint Paul's Aston, but they were living at 28 Cowley Road, Oxford, at that time: a four-bedroomed terraced house, just a few minutes' walk across Magdalen Bridge, to Longwall Street and the William Morris garage.

"She was christened Una, Elspeth, Kathleen Wareing. But it was strange, because she should have been christened in the parish where she was born – in the Anglo-Catholic church in Cowley.

"Now that St Paul's Parish was the old man's parish – he'd moved there in his teens. I remember Dad saying that Lilian was Anglo-Catholic, but Harry Senior didn't like that, whereas he was just Broad Church of England. So maybe that's why Una was christened in Aston?"

Harry S worked at the Morris Oxford factory in Cowley. Was he working on the Morris Oxford cars, Dennis?

"No, he was more likely to have been producing motorbikes than cars; it was just a garage at that time, because William Morris was just starting out. Harry S was there in 1906, when he married Lilian. They're back in Birmingham by 1911.

"Una and Elsie had no childhood recollections of Sarah, but Elsie went to Kidlington years later, and met her grandmother there. She was living on her own, in a cottage. Sarah was a dressmaker in Aston first, then later in Kidlington."

So, up until 1895, our Grandfather, Eustace's career was going well, Dennis.

"Yes, here's the reference to the *Jubilee Ball* at Worcester. Saturday 16 April 1887, *Worcestershire Chronicle,* there's a long list of attendees at the Lord Mayor's Ball, including Mr and Mrs Eustace Baylis, so this was for Queen Victoria's Jubilee 1887.

"Also attending were Mr and Mrs H Brookes; Mr and Mrs Eustace Baylis; Mr G Bennett; Mr and Mrs F Corbyn – a long list of local dignitaries; people of influence, for one reason or another. So that's evidence of how they lived when they were in Worcester. Eustace was also on the *Droitwich Board of Guardians,*" explains Dennis.

"They were responsible for the orphanages, schools and various other institutions. He was also an 'Inspector of Nuisances'. His father Alfred was on the Boards too...and he was a local councillor.

"This is from the *British Newspaper Archives*. There's a lot here about Eustace's role as Sanitary Inspector. He was also Registrar of Births and Deaths. He's registered in passing here, in Census, on 21 March 1891.

From the *Worcester Journal:*

'Eustace Baylis is Registrar in the sub-district of South Claines, in South-west Worcester.'"

That's in the St Martin's District, Dennis. They held many Public Celebrations on *Worcester Sports Ground*: Vivienne Jones showed me where that is.

He was on the *Board of Guardians* as well. There's a list of them, under the Heading 'Worcester Board of Guardians.

And he was also a School Attendance Officer:

'A letter was read from the Local Government Board, approving of the appointment for twelve months, of Mr Eustace Baylis, as School Attendance Officer'. This is the *Worcester Journal* 21 May 1892.

"Eustace seems to be in a good position during these earlier stages in his life. So something must definitely have changed him, around 1895, when disastrous events began to happen to him.

"He eventually went to Derbyshire – and worked there as a Sanitary Inspector, but he was arrested, because the landlady at the house, where he was living in Derby, said he had threatened her! He refused to appear in court, when he was summonsed for the offence, so I don't know what happened after that.

The *Derby Telegraph* describes the incident:

'A Sanitary Inspector of Etwall, Eustace Baylis, was charged on a warrant, with using threats towards Emily E.N. Tomlinson, on September 30th 1895. Mr Whites (Whykes?) appeared for the prosecution. Mrs Tomlinson said that prisoner lived next door to her and on September 30th he said he would break her – neck!

He had been using threats to her all the summer and the witness was frightened that he would do her some bodily harm. The prisoner pleaded Guilty and was bound over in the sum of £10.00, to keep the peace for three months. He was also ordered also ordered to pay the costs – £1.15shillings or fourteen days imprisonment.'

Today's Police News, Monday 14 October 1895, Derby Daily Telegraph.

"Etwall is just west of Derby. But it's interesting that she was afraid that he would commit actual bodily harm! And then four years later, he was charged with murdering his son. Years later, in 1911, in total contrast, Eustace was Secretary of the *Birmingham Liberal Party*."

"Eustace lived with Lilian and the 'Old Man', at 65 Brunswick Road, after his wife, Kate, died of heart failure, in 1920, at their home address, 366 Lodge Road, the same year that Dad was born.

"So he had this lovely house in Claines, as a young man – the one in our *Prologue*, but he gradually went downhill and became an alcoholic.

"In 1894, there's a reference to the birth of Eustace's youngest child. 'Baylis June 3rd, at 3, St Mary's Terrace, Arboretum, Worcester. The wife of Eustace Baylis, the birth of a son.' It doesn't name him there, but he was Herbert George Baylis, who died a year later, in infancy. So there were three children, ladies and gentlemen, apart from Lilian: an older sister, Lucy, who died at birth; Horace Eustace – and Herbert George, who died in infancy in 1895.

"Then Eustace loses his job as a Sanitary Inspector in 1895 and moves up to Derby. That year seems to be the point at which things begin to go badly wrong for him."

Perhaps he started drinking more, after Herbert died? It's sounding that way, Dennis.

"Yes, could well be. There was a terrible tragedy in his family, as well. I hope this won't shock you ladies and gentlemen, but Lilian had a brother – Horace Eustace. They were living in Aston at that time. When Horace was thirteen, Eustace was actually arrested for the manslaughter of his son, because young Horace Eustace died, in 1899!"

Oh my life Dennis – I thought the situation was bad enough already!

"I found Horace's name by chance, when I was researching. The boy was born in Worcester. I've got all the newspaper reports about that. So

Eustace was charged and the Inquest was held at Warwick Assizes. But they found him Not Guilty.

"Some of the evidence suggested that both Eustace and his wife were drunk at the time. Lilian gave evidence in court, about her Dad; at seventeen she was the oldest child. The case involved a broom and a broom head. Apparently, the broom head flew off and hit young Horace on the crown. So it was an accident, but it took him a couple of days to die. They were living near to Aston Park. There was a surgeon who lived across the road from them.

"I wonder if Horace Eustace had started King Edward's? He died when he was thirteen. So there are possibilities: they were both in Aston in the 1890s. Harry Senior was a couple of years older than Horace."

So eventually, Lilian was the only survivor wasn't she? Having to live through all of that, and eventually the court case, must have really toughened her up!

"When Lilian's mother, Kate, gives evidence, in the Court Case, she says that she's been married for eighteen years and has one surviving daughter. She doesn't actually give any further details, but as we now know, she'd given birth to four children. The date of the court case is 25 August 1899. It was held at Warwick Assizes.

"Originally, Eustace was arrested and he was locked up in Aston," Dennis continues. "The police station was in the centre of Aston, so that would be Aston Cross. The important thing about the particular article that I copied was that you *hear* Lilian, because she gives evidence. Her personality comes through but.... it also gives you a feel for the family. Some of it is quite disturbing to read. One of the neighbours said that Mr and Mrs Baylis drank – and there were always rows at the weekend and they could hear the daughter screaming!"

That sounds as if there was some violence involved, which might throw some light on what happened to Horace Eustace. Do you think his death was accidental Dennis?

"Well that's the thing, ladies and gentlemen. Some of the neighbours giving evidence, said that they weren't surprised that the boy died!"

They'd be classed as an 'At risk Family' now, wouldn't they? Which is amazing, because you'd think that with Eustace's background and occupations, he'd be more respectable. It's sad that he, Harry Senior and our Great Grandfather, WJ Wareing, all had flaws that brought them down. So Lilian's parents were drunks and she married a drunk! I wonder if she realised, when she married him. It's very sad. From an early age she would have witnessed that kind of drunken behaviour, so she may have had issues, as a result, that we don't know about.

"Our Grandmother was seventeen when her brother, Horace Eustace's death occurred. She stated in her evidence that she left the house, so she wasn't home when her brother was hurt. She had gone out with a friend. But she came back later and found Horace. He was saying, 'Oh my head does hurt!' It sounds like a concussion – it happened in the back kitchen.

"Lilian further states that her father was very fond of them, as children. Her parents weren't drinking that day; also, that her brother was cheeky.

"Her mother Kate's evidence was dismissed by the court because it was too confused – too rambling. She said that her son was at the end of the hallway and that the top of the broom flew off and hit him on the head! Something that didn't make sense, because the broom head couldn't have travelled that distance, from the hall to the back kitchen! But Lilian comes across as a very together person. She obviously had a story, to protect her father. When his son died, Eustace was working for *Singers*, the sewing machine company. We've got a later reference here, to the death of his son, in Warwick Assizes: that he was charged, but later acquitted:

'Eustace Baylis, aged 39, Commission Agent, was charged with feloniously killing and slaying Horace Baylis – 9 December 1899 *Leamington Spa Courier*. He was also a member of the Worcester District of Oddfellows'… a kind of Freemason organisation. So that could explain why he got off – because of who he knew! There were other people at the same time, at the same court, who were sentenced to Hard Labour for theft and other far less serious charges!"

What I can't understand Dennis, is that our Great Grandfather is offered responsible jobs and is invited to special civic events, but in his personal life everything's going 'pear-shaped'!

"Yes, he seems to be sabotaging it really."

When she first met Harry Senior Lilian must have thought that he was a saint – compared with her father!

"So this happened in 1899, but I couldn't find Eustace and his wife, Kate, on the 1901 Census," Dennis continues. "But Kate is buried in the Jewellery Quarter, following her death in 1920. There are two cemeteries: one for Non-Conformists, which is where Kate is buried – Key Hill; the other for Church of England people – that's where the Patchetts are buried: they are Harry Senior's mother's family. Sarah went to live in Kidlington, Oxfordshire, near Woodstock."

This is about William James Wareing, the Old Man's father: trying to work out how his desertion of his family impacted on Grandad's life.

"William James married Sarah Ellen Patchett in 1880 at the Congregationalist Church, Francis Road, Edgbaston. At the time, Sarah was living in Albion Street. Harry Senior was born in 1882. Eustace and Kate Griffith, coincidentally, married just a few months before their first child was born, in Worcester.

"So Sarah Patchett married from Albion Street in Hockley, where her mother and brother were also living. They are buried in the Jewellery Quarter – that's Key Hill Cemetery, where Lilian's mother is buried. The Patchetts were buried in the Church of England Cemetery, where the catacombs are.

"The Patchetts are there, but the headstones have gone, because some of them were removed. Sarah Patchett was born in Bacup, Rochdale, near Burnley. Her father, Abraham Patchett, was still living up there, although he died a few years before.

"But her mother, brothers and Sarah came down to Birmingham, during the 1860s. Sarah was born 1858. In 1871 they were living in Ladywood. She was a dressmaker. Sarah would have met William James, because before they moved to Albion Street, they lived in Rushton Street, Ladywood, just off Friston Street and Morville Street, where the Wareings lived.

"Having this Lancashire connection, the Wareings having come from Lancashire a couple of generations previously, maybe there was that kind of identity too? Whereby the two families already knew about each other?

"However, when William James moved to London, then remarried – he was, allegedly, a bigamist! He married Annie Pilgrim in 1907 in Southwark – Lambeth way. She was a widow, formerly married to George Pilgrim.

"Annie's family name was Hailstone. They were living in East Square. Annie Pilgrim was born Jane Ann Hailstone. Tracing the Hailstones back, they actually came from Birmingham then moved to London. In the 1820s they had a pub in Birmingham City Centre, called *The Bell Inn*. At that time 'Birmingham' just covered the central area."

I wonder why William James met Annie Pilgrim, who was from Southwark, when he was managing a Pen Factory in Birmingham?

"There's a family connection – through a family called Taylor. They lived in Ladywood, practically next door to the Wareings, in Friston Street. William James had a brother and sister: Frederick and Marion (Elsie's middle name). They each married members of this Taylor family: a brother and sister married a brother and sister.

"These Taylors were originally from Lambeth, near Southwark," Dennis explains. "They were next-but-one-door neighbours to the Hailstones – the family of William James' second wife. So it all fits. His first wife, Sarah, Great Aunt Una's mother, was totally outside of all that; they were Patchetts from Lancashire. But it sounds as though, with his second wife, she was almost an 'in-law'!"

I think Sarah may have gone to America, when her husband William deserted her. My Godmother, Elsie, mentioned something about that. So she must have returned to England in her later years. I thought: 'Good for her!' Because he went off to London.

"That's right Shirley – I found him! And his second wife – my Dad used to call William James 'Bill'.

"He died in 1917, in the Epsom Registration District, Surrey. Then his second wife died a few months later. She left a will, of three hundred-and-something pounds. Sarah, on the other hand, lived until 1942.

"Elsie, used to describe a Great Aunt Sarah as 'a bit of a character'… probably this same Sarah Patchett, who had been married to William James Wareing. He left Grandad (aka 'The Old Man'), when he was nineteen – and his sisters; we've found his new address in London, where he moved to."

That's brilliant – another piece of the jigsaw Dennis! What I can't understand is why a lad who was that intelligent and won a scholarship to King Edward's turned out the way he did. I mean, that's intriguing isn't it? Whether it was because his own father, William James also deserted his family, I'm not sure.

"I've found Harry Senior's sign-up papers for the First World War – 1915 – I've got them on *Ancestry*. He gives the name of his wife – and the children: up to that point, so that includes my Dad, Larry, who was born in 1913. The only thing that isn't factual on those papers is that he gives his date of marriage as May 1904, which was six months before Reg was born. Whereas in fact they married in May 1906, at Newhall Street Registry Office."

I heard that Harry Senior had one of the first sports cars in Birmingham.

"I heard that too. Elsie was born in Kidlington, where the Grandmother lived – Sarah Patchett. Sarah had a brother, James Patchett. There's a building in Digbeth, just opposite St Martin's, which James designed: he was an architect. It looks as if he went back up to Lancaster; his family were originally from Bacup in Lancashire. But I've lost track of him now."

I found it particularly interesting that, because Sarah's husband, William James left them, his younger daughter, Elspeth didn't marry Sydney Wilson until she was well into her thirties, Dennis. I wondered whether that was because her father absconding put her right off marriage. She was a member

William James Wareing was manager of a pen factory in the Jewellery Quarter. Grandfather Harry Senior is on the left, his sister, Elspeth on the right. With older sister Una, she later owned a tailoring business, like several family members. Other Wareings were Birmingham jewellers and solicitors. By permission of Eileen Wareing.

of the *Birchfield Harriers* and won a gold medal for sprinting. Elsie gave the medal to Mum – she still has it – because they share the same initials – E.W. Our cousin Pat, remembers her, in a later show.

Elspeth was born in Harborne, Greenfield Road. Una, the older sister, was a dressmaker, as was her mother – so presumably their mother taught them the trade?

"The family moved around a bit. Their mother, Sarah, had a shop too. They started out in Morville Street, Ladywood. Then Greenfield Road Harborne, in 1884, where Elspeth was born, followed by Washwood Heath Road, which would have been quite fashionable at the time; not like it is now. They were there on the 1891 Census.

"But then a bit later, they were in Lichfield Road Aston, which is where they had a house and shop. They probably lived over the shop. So this was Sarah's dressmaking business.

"This was the last place where she and William James were still together. Then he disappears... and she's still there... for a while – and then *she* disappears – and turns up in Kidlington," Dennis continues.

"But going back to her brother, James Patchett, his daughter, Annie, Alberta, later Annie Landon, was born in Woodstock, in the 1880s, so possibly this was the connection with Kidlington. And Sarah remained a dressmaker, in later years too – in Lyne Road, Kidlington. Elsie was born in Kidlington but not in the same house.

"From there, Lilian and Harry Senior moved to Aston, living in a house near the Villa Ground, in Witton Road. Then they moved to Tame Road, where Bernard was born, in May 1911. A couple of years later, in 1912 they moved to Brunswick Road, because that's where my father, Larry (aka Laurie) was born, in 1913.

"My Dad, Larry, said that Lilian was interested in Anglo-Catholicism, which is the High Church part of the Church of England, ladies and gentlemen. When Harry and Lilian first married they lived in Cowley, because Harry worked at the William Morris factory. They lived on Cowley Road, so our Aunt Una was born there, although she was christened in Aston.

"But the local church in Cowley is a very old Anglo-Catholic church, so I'm wondering if that might have sparked her interest? It's a very theatrical kind of religion and very musical, with the choirs and chants."

There seems to have been a marked personality difference, between Lilian and her daughter, Madge. Madge was unpredictable and found it difficult to sustain personal relationships; the picture I have of Lilian is that

Baby Ida's Christening. Lilian with Reg, standing; 3-year-old Larry (aka Laurie) in front.

she was a much a more balanced individual… although she always seems quite sad in photographs.

If you look at the Group Photo, that we're showing on the screen now, ladies and gentlemen – of Lilian and the three children, you can see that they were very well looked after. The other thing that strikes me is that as the flash went off, she was prepared for it…. and held the baby in with her hand, in case it scared her. She's holding her hand against the baby, to keep her steady, so she was prepared for that – it's actually Ida's christening picture! She was born in March 1916 and died in 1984.

Also, the fact that she had a daughter like Elsie, my Godmother, who always seemed to be in control of situations; I imagine that there was something of that character in Lilian too. Elsie must have got it from somewhere, unless it was from her Dad. But her older sister Una, was more reserved.

Looking at this next photo on your screens, of Grandad and his sisters: they're dressed rather formally – and Harry's wearing a velvet suit. Chris Sutton tells me that the photographers, *Bristol Street Studios*, were on the left-hand side of Town, as you come out, going towards Northfield; the whole row of shops, just past the Holloway Circus Island, is where the photographer's shop was. The *Odeon Queensway*, Birmingham, used to be on the corner.

One or two people have asked why on earth Lilian married Harry Senior – she was a lady – she'd had a good education and so on. Surely she could have done better for herself? But of course, she was pregnant at the time, which in those days had much more of a stigma attached to it. So Harry Senior may have thought that he was doing her a favour.

Chapter Five

THE GREAT WAR AND BEYOND

The year is 1913, ladies and gentlemen, just before the outbreak of the First World War. The Wareing family have recently moved in to 65 Brunswick Road – but there is a sense of dread in the air.

The Birmingham Repertory Theatre opens its doors for the first time, 'Sons and Lovers' by D.H. Lawrence, first sees the light of day (as we've explained, there is a family connection!) and Stravinsky's ballet 'The Rite of Spring', has its first performance.

The orchestra strikes up one of the central themes from the ballet, as the curtain rises, on a street scene. It is spring…

(Your Presenters, as the show begins, are my 92-year-old Mum, Eileen Wareing, my cousin, Dennis Wareing and myself).

Dennis begins: "My Dad was born on 4 September 1913. In order of birth it was Reg – 1904, Una – 1907, Elsie – 1909, Bernard – 1911, Laurie – 1913, Ida – 1916, Harry – 1920, Madge – 1923 and Audrey – 1926. But the four youngest, from Ida onwards, are yet to be born.

The Upton family lived just across the road, at Number 70; their sons would soon be marching away to glory – or certain death – for Germany will be declaring war on Russia, on August 1st of the following year.

Eileen recalls: "Nellie, my father, George Upton's sister, lived at 51 Brunswick Road. The Wareings lived seven houses up, on the same side, at 65 Brunswick Road, so Nellie and Stan Curtis were close neighbours of the Wareings. Auntie Nellie's house was on the opposite side of the road; your Dad's family lived a few doors away, on the same side as the Curtis Family. But it would be six years before Harry was born.

"My brother, Dennis Upton, was very young, when he and my parents lived with my Auntie Nellie, when they were first married, because they didn't have a house," Eileen continues. "Mum (Irene Upton) didn't like Auntie Nellie and neither did I, when I met her later. Auntie Emily was the oldest, Nellie was the next one, then there was Hilda Margaret (Auntie

Maternal Grandma, Irene Varney, College Road School, seated 2nd from left, c.1913.

Maggie); then Dad (George) and Uncle Jim who was the youngest. Jim was called John James, after his mother's brother, John James Nealon, in Ireland. My Dad had just come out of the army when they went to live with Auntie Nellie. Then they moved to Yardley, to a house at 40 Purefoy Road.

"My Grandmother Annie's first child, Florence, died as an infant; then there was Doris Varney; then Mum – Irene Winifred; after that there was Victor Leslie (Uncle Les)."

"Returning to our side of the family, Eileen, at number 65, the Baylis Family were Liberals and the Wareings were Tories. Our grandfather, Harry Senior, was a staunch Tory. I think his parents were too," explains Dennis.

"Lilian's best friend, Amy Cockerill, who lived next door, put a 'Vote for Labour' poster in her front window, years later. Harry was outside number 65, his house, on a ladder, painting. He ordered her to take the Labour Party poster out of her own window! She refused to do so, so he tipped the tin of paint over her! Harry Senior had fought in the First World War, but he was in his thirties – 34 – when he joined up. He must have been one of the first."

"My husband, Harry, did the same during World War II, Dennis," Eileen interjects, "because he was in the RAF Cadets, or something similar."

"Well Harry Senior volunteered as a driver. My Mum, Sheila, remembered the Brunswick Road houses, from living in nearby St Paul's Road. She said they were like the house that we lived in, in St Paul's Road. We were tenants and the landlord lived there as well. It was bay-fronted. There was a long hallway, which was very dark. There was a Front Room as you went in, then the staircase; then the Living Room, which was our room. Then the kitchen.

"All these features, in the St Paul's Road houses, were in a straight line with each other, with the kitchen at the end of the hall. All the rooms were on the right, as you went in. We had a bathroom upstairs. Before those houses had bathrooms, people would use Moseley Road Baths. My Dad, Laurie, (or Larry as we called him) used them, because they were just across the road. Upstairs there were three bedrooms.

"The children weren't allowed in the Front Parlour. I suppose that's where Lilian's piano would have been. I remember Reg saying that he was a half-brother – and they never let Lilian forget that… the Wareing side of the family… Harry Senior and his sisters."

"For Harry to marry an unmarried mother, he must have been a free agent; but there was money in the background too, so that could have provided an incentive," Dennis continues.

"Regarding the layout of 65 Brunswick Road, there was an entry by the side of the house. The back entry would be shared with a few houses. They were bigger houses than the row in this photo that you're looking at, ladies and gentlemen – not average terraced houses.

"You went through a gate and there was quite a small front garden and a long back garden with a tree in it. The ball from the school playground of Clifton Road School used to come over the fence, into the garden of Number 65; we know that they had to keep throwing it back!"

There was the Depression too. This next photo shows Margaret Nealon in the middle. On the left is her daughter Emily; on the right is Nellie, Jackie's grandmother.

Now we're looking at a photo taken in the back garden of 70 Brunswick Road.

"Looking at it from this angle, the privy is there and then that wall with a pipe, but there's another wall there – before the sash window. That's where the kitchen was. This is very similar to the house we lived in for a time in St Paul's Road," recalls Dennis.

"We have Thomas George Upton and Margaret Nealon's Irish Wedding Certificate. Thomas' father's occupation is shown as Working Brewer. Her father was Patrick J Nealon: farmer. They were married in the Church of Ireland, so that must have been her religion. It's not the Catholic Church, it's Anglican."

Lilian's Colmore Row postcard sent to her eldest daughter, Una.

The postcard (top) was posted to Una at the Chequers Inn (above), Friar's Wash, Flamstead, Dunstable. Chequers Hill was nearby.

This next document, on your screen, is written on parchment. Thomas Upton – it's his discharge from the army.

"Have you seen the Ancestry document about Harry Senior, Shirley? He was in the army in 1915 – during the First World War. It gives a description of him. He's 5 foot 8 and he'd got a scar on his left eye."

Kelly's Directory provides details of tradesmen in the area; we also have a letter of recommendation for my Great Uncle Joe, from a baker in Brunswick Road.

"Audrey mentioned a postcard from our grandmother, sent to Una or Elsie, from Colmore Row. Lilian was going to visit someone, so I imagine she was going from New Street to Snow Hill Station. Our grandmother's writing is on it."

"Would you believe, I've just found it, amongst all my papers, after all these years," interjects Eileen. "You'll find a photo of it in your programme!"

Here's a Pavilion photo of a family wedding. Do you recognise this as being somewhere in the Bournville area?

"I don't know if it is, but it reminds me of the park near Bournville Infants School; or it could be in the grounds of *Cadbury's* – and there's a park over the road…. then you've got the Infants School," adds Dennis.

We'll be meeting Trevor and Lorraine Williams in Show-chapter 17. They ran an Outdoor in Balsall Heath. Trevor told me: "We used to have an old lady come into the shop – a Mrs Giles. She told me that when she was young, if she was walking down Princess or Varna Road with her friends and they were making a noise, the servants would be out to clip them round the ear. That's how much the area had changed! She said the houses were owned by wealthy doctors and lawyers at that time," Trevor explains.

(Mum exits the stage, aided by her walking stick, but Dennis remains. Our cousins Pat and Carolyn, join us, together with Dennis' sisters, Lilian and Caroline.)

Lilian recalls, "Dad said that it was very hard, growing up at Number 65. He obviously thought a lot of his mother, but that his Dad was violent towards her. He was also very severe with the children."

I know that Harry Senior was the typical Edwardian father: if any of the children spoke at mealtimes they were sent to their room. Can you remember anything that Larry told you Caroline?

"He used to talk about Eustace a lot… his Grandad. He talked more about Eustace than his own Dad, especially when I was pregnant with Kerry, because she was the first grandchild. If it was a boy, he wanted me to call it Eustace, so I was thinking: 'please don't let it be a boy!' That's one of the reasons I think he liked Eustace; he never suggested calling him after his father, Harry. He didn't even suggest that we call it Lilian, if it was a girl, but he probably thought it would be a boy," recalls Caroline.

I'm trying to build up a picture of Lilian: in some ways she seems to have been a very resourceful and talented woman: bringing up, what would eventually be, eight children; being so musically-gifted and refined; helping to get Eustace acquitted through her crucial evidence, when she was in her teens; taking a wartime job and totally refurbishing the house. On the other hand, Harry Senior seems to have been a violent and exploitative husband, so she had to endure all of that – and worse was to follow!

"She could play the piano 'by ear' – she had a photographic memory for music. Dad said that Harry liked to listen to her playing the piano and he loved her long, auburn hair. At one time she had it cut – and he went absolutely mad about it," explains Lilian.

Our cousin, Pat, interjects: "Reg told me that in the war time, when Harry Senior was away in 1915, Lilian got herself a job – and went out to work – and he was a Telegraph Boy, with a little pillbox hat on! With her earnings Lilian refurbished the house and got all new furnishings. When Harry Senior came home he didn't try to get any work; eventually, he sold every stick in the house! My Dad told me most of these things when I was about sixteen. He thought it was a terrible thing that he was illegitimate – in those days it was!"

Reginald William Baylis was born in 1904, ladies and gentlemen, at Queens Road, Mortlake, Richmond, Surrey. Ironically, the fact that his Dad was a well-educated man, gave Reg quite an advantage.

"Shirley told me that his biological father used to take Reg out, to various places, with his family. I'm amazed that he did that. Grandad never told me about it. He must have had a very broad-minded wife!" exclaims Carolyn.

"I know that his real father had two boys. My father, Reg, told me that unfortunately, he didn't get a lot of schooling," Pat recalls. "For various reasons: I think, mainly, helping his mother look after all these babies she was having! When they moved into Brunswick Road, Reg was nine, so he should have been going to Clifton Road School, shouldn't he? He may have gone there, but not as often as he should have. If he'd had had full schooling, he'd have done a lot more. Reg was three years younger than my mother, Nellie.

"Your Dad's sister, Una, used to visit us from time to time. I always thought that Elsie was the oldest sister, because she was more extrovert – and she brought her baby sister, Audrey, up."

"This is a photo of my Dad's caravan at Ingomells – and Una and my Dad," Pat continues.

That's Madge with Gary… and Elsie and Phil on the beach. This a photo of all of the Wareing brothers and sisters, possibly at someone's birthday.

"Well they used to just get together from time to time," Pat recalls, "not because it was someone's birthday."

My other Presenters exit, apart from Dennis, as another cousin, Steven Upton, Spiritualist Healer and Minister, enters. Steven remembers visiting 70 Brunswick Road.

"It was a typical two-up, two-down terrace. I don't remember the front room at all – I think I was shown it once. That would be the parlour. You weren't allowed to go in there," Steven begins.

"I remember the back room quite clearly. There was a dark wood table in the middle, covered with a table cloth – a heavy darkish colour. I remember the picture on the wall opposite the window clearly too, because I used to call it a rocket – it was actually a lighthouse! It was on rocks, with the sea bashing at the side of it.

"I was born in 1956, so this would have to be around 1960 or '61; I would have been four or five years old.

"If we were in that room, looking towards the back, there was a window and a door to the kitchen, on the left of the window, looking towards the back. So the passageway was on the right-hand side of the house. As I turned to look towards the front, the doorway was to the right side of the room so you'd go through there to the back door; stairs to the right; front room to the left; front door in front of you.

"If you went out of your front door," Steven continues, "underneath the front window is where you'd tip the coal in… on the street side. The coal holes were usually underneath the front window."

Our cousin, Jacky Curtis, said there was a door that you opened, with some steps leading to the cellar. I think that was under the stairs. Jacky said that seemed quite magical to her – the fact that Maggie and Jim's house had a cellar, because they didn't have one in their house!

"Well, if you went in through the front door (which I never did – you always went in through the back) I can't remember whether we went down the alley then turned left or right. I've got a photograph of the back garden and another one of the pigeon coops – looking down the back garden," explains Steven.

"From the back of the house, the kitchen was to the right, so therefore the alleyway would be to the left. Inside, looking towards the back garden, there's a window there and then the kitchen doors over here. So you go through the kitchen door and turn right to get out of the house. Auntie Maggie and Uncle Jim were living there when I visited. It was years before I knew they were brother and sister you know! I just assumed... they seemed small, compared to my father."

Jacky Curtis said that Jim used to grow chrysanthemums. She said he called the yellow variety, "Them big yelleruns." Also, that Jim was very shy: she gave him a kiss once when she was a little girl – and he went bright pink!

"There was a quite a large square table in the middle of the room, taking up half the room, with some chairs around it. The table was built of big, heavy dark wood," Steven continues. "If you were facing the back window, to your right was an open fireplace, with a grate – a fairly small fire. Behind me, against the back wall, opposite the window, was a dresser of some sort; dark wood and just drawers; big, old-fashioned heavy furniture. I was six years old at the time, so the table seemed quite high; to an adult it would be normal height.

"I remember being shown into the front room, or parlour, once, but not allowed to sit down. It was for special occasions. There were some armchairs and other furniture. Net curtains and that front window looking straight out onto the pavement. It was front door, pavement, and road. I can't recall any front gardens. The back room was the living room and the kitchen was behind that – like an extension coming out from the main house."

We're looking at a photo of three Uptons: Thomas George in the middle, flanked by his two sons, ladies and gentlemen. My grandfather, according to his uniform, must already be a sergeant, even though he was only about eighteen. But his brother, Uncle Jim, is still a private here, but he's got two wound stripes on his sleeve.

"Like Harry Senior, Uncle Jim was also in Gallipoli," explains Steven, "so they'd have been there at around the same time. Jim was wounded there. He joined up when he was under age. On the outbreak of war, he was about fifteen and was in the Territorials, in 1913. Uncle Jim went to join up on the outbreak of war. They asked him how old he was and they said, 'Come back tomorrow, when you are eighteen,' – but in reality he was only fifteen!"

There's something like over a quarter of a million, in the army, who joined up under the age of eighteen, for the First World War. The army would have collapsed without them, so they kept it quiet! There was a big controversy about it and questions were asked in the House, but the army couldn't afford to lose them.

"Jim was in the trenches in Gallipoli, at the age of sixteen – and the stripes on his uniform tell you that he was wounded twice," Steven continues. "That's the West Yorkshire Regiment cap badge, that Jim's wearing (horse symbol) but George Upton, his brother, was in the Royal Warwickshire Regiment (heart symbol). I've got Jim's cap badge at home.

"Our Great Grandad, Thomas George Upton, was born in 1861, which means that he would have been forty years old at the time of the Boer War. He could have gone, but he might have been a bit too old," Steven conjectures.

This is a picture of Grandad George seated, with Jim to the side of him; that's got to be around 1908, hasn't it? As a boy, George looks rather like your Dad, my Uncle Dennis, doesn't he? But that changed as he grew older. This next photo is of Mum and Dennis.

"As he was born in 1923, that's got to be around 1930 hasn't it?" observes Steven.

This is Dad's younger sister, Madge, the one who endured real traumas. The sad thing is that she tore up all the family photos, so I've promised Jackie Mason, her daughter, that she can have some of mine when the book's finished.

"I seem to have a memory about Uncle Jim, that somewhere after the First World War, in the 1920s, he went in the RAF and had something to do with airships... when the RAF were experimenting with them," continues Steven.

This is a photo of Danny, holding Evie, as a baby. I'm including a whole section about Yvonne in the book – in memory of her. There's your Dad at Purefoy c. 1928.

"At one time they all cycled to France – do you know about that? Grandad and Irene, my father and your mother, all went on holiday there," remembers Steven. "Probably around the mid-1930s. Who does that nowadays?!"

I've had all the family medals put together in one frame: Grandad's, Steven's Uncle Jim, and the John Nealon one, from the 1880s: India General Service Medal with the bar for the Burma Expedition of 1888. John Nealon was killed in action. What's interesting is the action he was killed, the Burma Expedition of 1888, was during the same action that someone in his regiment won a Victoria Cross – and it was the last Victoria Cross actually presented by Queen Victoria. That makes John's medal very valuable, because most people during that expedition died from disease; not many were killed in action!

The three Uptons. Great Grandfather, Thomas George (seated), Great Uncle Jim on the left; my maternal Grandfather, George Upton, on the right.

"This photo of Grandad has a band on his right arm... Regimental Police. First World War. During the Second World War he was a driver on Home Service with the Royal Artillery.

"Here's the one of Grandad in his Great Coat. He's a Lance-Corporal there, so this is 1916, possibly early '17. Round about the time he was in the Somme," Steven continues.

"We're looking at a photo of my father (now deceased) – your Uncle Dennis, in a little folder. He was a Lance-Bombardier, in the Artillery. I took him back to Normandy in 1995, for the 50th Anniversary. We found the exact spot where his Battery was dug in at a village called Choux (pronounced 'Shoe').

"We went to a nearby cemetery and found the graves of some of his friends," Steven recalls. "He explained to me how they were killed. He was in this dug-out with them. They sent him to get something from another dug-out, but a shell went straight into the dug-out where he'd been, so all of his friends were killed and he survived! It was one of those chances of war, where he went off to get something and everyone else was killed."

That's like my Dad, when they were loading bombs. He'd just gone to the Naffi. Someone dropped a bomb and his friends' heads were blown off!

"John Nealon's pay book goes back to when he joined the army, in the early 1880s," Steven recalls. "John puts his sister Margaret as next-of-kin, with a family address in Limerick. I found the house, which is still there and now belongs to a firm of High Street solicitors. But the doorway and the entrance still has the original Victorian stained glass and floor tiles. I suspect she was in Service there, because you would have had to be quite wealthy to live there."

One of the Upton sisters worked in a house on the Moseley Road and on her Marriage Certificate she was allowed to give the address of her employment. That would be one of Margaret's daughters.

When I visited Croom, the original Nealon family's home, I just had a quick glance around the graveyard and the village, but like when you visited, Steven, it was raining.

Steven exits.

Steven's step-mother, Sylvia Upton is, sadly, recently deceased. But I'd like to read her recollections to you:

"Maggie did have a boyfriend, but I'm not sure what happened. She never bothered with anyone else. I think he may have died during the First World War. A lot of that happened didn't it?

"Grandad not only had a webbed-fingered hand but it was also shorter than his other arm. But he always kept it out of view – especially in photos."

56

"Jim was very nice. I went to see him one day and he said, 'I've got something for you.' And he gave me a really big aspidistra, because he knew I liked plants," Sylvia concluded.

"During the First World War, the 'Old Man' was conscripted as a Driver/Mechanic in the Transport Division. He was posted to the Dardanelles/Gallipoli in 1915, as a combination of mechanic and driver. He caught meningitis, during the First World War," Dennis adds. "Audrey told me that; when he came back he started drinking much more heavily than before. Meningitis is an inflammation of the brain tissue."

My publisher Alan Brewin, who's quite an expert on military history, said that the fact that Grandad actually survived the Dardanelles was an achievement in itself, because the majority of soldiers who were posted over there died of disease, rather than in combat!

"Yes, they were basically left to their fate: it was terrible! But some of the sick were shipped home, so possibly Harry Senior was. I remember reading that there was Malaria in the camps at the Dardanelles. Dad used to talk about the Australian troops – the Anzacs – Churchill wanted to go through Turkey to Germany, but they didn't get that far.

"Dad said that Churchill was responsible for what happened. I remember Churchill's funeral in 1965. My Dad watched it on TV: it was very unusual to have the TV on in the daytime then," Dennis concludes. "Everyone kept the 1 or 2-minute silence."

In our next show, more Wareing children appear on the scene!

Chapter Six

THE BREWHOUSE AND DUNGEON

Down the Brewhouse and Dungeon
Went Lily, we know
A-doing the washing
Through rain and through snow.

Clink, clank in the Dungeon
As the tubes shot straight through.
Wine, women and song
And a violin too!

Chorus; *The Brewhouse and Dungeon*
As Lily will tell –
In the basement of Lewis's
Cheese there as well.

Et cetera…

The theatre orchestra and singers begin performing this song on stage, including the first two verses above and a chorus. On the second time through, the singers, dressed in Edwardian street costume, dance down the steps, encouraging audience members to dance hand-in-hand with them, back up onto the stage. Remaining audience stand, link arms and join in the merriment. The performance continues for a full ten minutes!

(Shirley takes centre stage as the audience returns to their seats)

Brunswick Road, ladies and gentlemen, had, by 1913, become home to five branches of my family: the Wareings, Uptons, Curtises, Baylises and Nealons.

When the First World War ended two more children were born to Lilian and Harry Senior: my father, Harry, in 1920 and Madge in 1923 – Ida having already been born, during the war (1916).

Higher up the road, at number 91, lived the Bullen family. Their young daughter, Lily, was born in 1920, the same year as my father, Harry.

96 years later, Lily can still recall life 20th Century in Brunswick Road, making her totally unique in our story!

The curtains remain up, against the backdrop of an Edwardian parlour. Lily enters from the right. She and Shirley seat themselves at the table, as Shirley pours tea for the two of them, from a silver teapot, into delicate china cups.

I understand that you lived at 91 Brunswick Road for most of your life, Lily, also that you were born in 1920 – the same year as my father? It's absolutely *wonderful* that we've found you! Tell me about the living conditions at that time.

"At the back of 91 Brunswick Road you came up an entry and then there were houses there… back-to-back. You just had one room. As you went in the house you came to the stair. Just before the stair there was a little door where they came through what you would call your lounge today… and dropped the coal.

We shared the Brewhouse with other families. My husband used to light the Brewhouse fire, under the copper boiler. It was a coke fire. Each family had their own day for using the Brewhouse. He lit it very early in the morning, before he went to work: I could never do it.

My Brewhouse day was Monday: it didn't matter whether it was raining or not. You had a washing line across a big square, which separated the first lot of four back-to-back houses, from the second lot of back-to-back. Everybody used that line in turn. You took your washing in of a night-time, because the children from the houses played there; it was a big area.

Next to the Brewhouse was a toilet, which was a wooden seat with a hole in. It was shared between two families. The man who lived next door, worked at a cinema. I scrubbed the toilet because he wasn't there in the daytime, to do it. If you wanted to go to the toilet of a night-time, you had to come out of your house and walk down quite a way, past your neighbour's house; through the square, down a little passageway and then round; it would take you a good five minutes to walk there. That is why you had, what they called in those days, 'pos', under your bed."

They were often called 'guzunders', weren't they Lily, because they went under the bed! Was it the same set-up for all of the houses: they all had these squares?

"Yes, for the middle section of Brunswick Road, where we were, but not all the way up the street. Brunswick Road was divided into three sections:

the section at the bottom of the road came off Stoney Lane. You came up that first section; then across the middle of that first one came Ladypool Road, where there was a *Westwood's* Greengrocers: part in Ladypool Road and part in Brunswick Road.

You'd cross the road in Ladypool Road to get to the middle section of Brunswick Road. On the corner of Brunswick and Ladypool there was a little pub. You came a little bit further up Brunswick, then there was a small road on the right called White Street. In White Street there used to be a Bookies: in those days you weren't supposed to have bets or anything, so they were illegal. You'd have a man on the corner of White Street and Brunswick Road, watching out for the police."

The Stoney Lane end of Brunswick Road is what you're calling 'the bottom end'. Tell me about that.

"I never went down there very much, but a girl lived down there and they used to call her 'Silly Lil', because she wasn't quite with it. This was when I was a child, so it was well before the Second World War. I assume that she was born that way. She used to run around and be silly; by the age of ten she used to shout at you, so that was one of the reasons that you didn't go down Brunswick Road at the bottom end! Right at the bottom end, just across from Stoney Lane, there was a chemist: that's where all the mothers used to go – and take the children when they were ill.

Mr Mayer the chemist gave you medicine, to save you having to pay 2/6d to the doctors. It was called *Mayer's*. I think people will remember it because it had the blue glass bottle shape on the front of the shop, which chemist's shops used to have."

I remember those: our chemist's bottle shape was red. We're looking at a photo of *George Mason's* (also hanging as a poster, for the audience to see).

"My mother used to shop there; it was a very clean shop – sold everything really that you'd need from a grocer's shop. I'd go shopping sometimes with my mother.

I remember an 'up-market' sweet shop in Ladypool Road. At Easter Time all the children would be looking in the window, because they couldn't afford to go in! It had the most beautiful Easter Egg, in the middle of the display, that I can ever remember; you'd never see anything like it today!

It was about a foot high, all carved out in different coloured chocolate; with bunny rabbits – and all sorts of things to do with Easter. It was opened up so that you could see what was going on inside: little children rabbits, berries: all sorts of beautiful things. So that used to be the highlight of our Easter. I can remember it to this day and I wonder what the children of today would think about that. Because all they do now is wrap them up in silver paper – there's no presentation."

The next poster, being lowered now, shows the trams in Mary Street.

"We used to walk up Brunswick Road, when I worked at *Lewis's*, in Town, down Hertford Street, up Clifton Road – and get the bus at the top of the road there – after crossing it. The depot was Trafalgar Tram Depot, on the Moseley Road. You could actually see it, from the top of Clifton Road... and you could see the trams coming out of the depot.

I remember the trams because I was always one of those people who were late! Having to run up the road – and in those days, you could run along the tram, if it had only just started. Then you'd jump on, holding the rail in the middle. The conductor would curse you, but he'd help you on. If my parents had seen me do that I don't know what they would have thought!

Of course, from Clifton Road School, in the Juniors and from the Boys' School, they used to go to Moseley Road Baths. I helped them when they made a booklet about that. I was in a reserved occupation in the war, you had to do something, so I'd go to Moseley Road Baths on Monday nights, with Doctor Cronin, who used to be in St Paul's Road: he'd show us how to put slings on and things like that, in case there were any casualties. We'd be there all night; there were bunk beds for us to sleep on. The actual baths were covered over for the war, so that made a kind of floor.

If we had a disturbed night, with people coming in for help, you'd then walk into work the following morning, from the Baths."

In Annie Murray's *Chocolate Girls*, two of the main characters are actually helping to drive around, collect the wounded, and then drive them back to the First Aid Centre, Lily. There are fantastic descriptions of the street scenes, with the bombing's in full swing, as they're rescuing people.

When you mentioned bikes, did you mean motorbikes? There was a motorbike shop in Taunton Road. I wondered if you knew it, as your Dad was in the Trade?

"Not really, because he used to make parts for *OK Bicycles* and for *George Brough's* – who were the Rolls Royce of motor bikes. He didn't supply any of the local shops.

My father would come from work of a night, have his tea, then when I was older he'd send me across the road, with a jug, for some bitter and he'd sit there, on a wooden chair, with his leg tucked underneath him, read a book all night, then go to bed.

My mother used to work upstairs, on a Singer sewing machine, making trousers, which a Mr Corberg, a Jewish person, would collect. He'd bring the trousers to her, cut and ready to sew. My mother would often work from nine o'clock in the morning until nine o'clock at night, sewing these trousers. Sometimes, if he wanted something special done, she had to sew the coats by hand: she got a little bit more money for doing that. She got a penny for doing a pair of trousers and threepence or four-pence for doing something by hand.

Mr Corberg would tell her what day he wanted a service, for example, a pair of trousers for a customer, but he always came on a Saturday, to collect everything else.

My Dad worked in Long Street, behind his mother's house, which was quite large. It was next door to a public house, the *Victoria*. She had a long back garden, with a brick building built on. He'd walk into my grandmother's kitchen, then through another door, straight into the Works, which was an engineering place. He had two or three very young people working for him, making parts for *George Brough Motorbikes* and the *OK Supreme Bicycle Company*."

We have another link too, Lily, because you remember going to the *Prince of Wales Theatre* on Broad Street Birmingham. (Poster is lowered)

"Yes, I suppose we had got a little bit more money than other people, even if it was only a few pence, so occasionally, my mother, who was always singing, (she sang really well) would take me to the *Prince of Wales Theatre*. My father would never go to anything like that.

We'd sit up in the 'Gods'; we saw the *Student Prince,* the *Desert Song* and things like that. Another place we went to was the *Empire Theatre,* just off the Stratford Road, Sparkbrook, going towards Birmingham City Centre, on the left-hand side as you went into Town. There were more variety shows there, rather than classic. I was only a child when I went there."

It's possible that Lilian's ancestor singer performed there too.

"I was fourteen on March 6th 1934. I went to work at *Lewis's,*" Lily recalls. "Although I left school on the Friday, at the July end of term, I'd already got a job. I wanted to work as an assistant, on the shop floor, but you had to take an exam. Because I was exceptionally good at Arithmetic, I was put down in a department that took the money from the shoot and tube system, and sent back the correct change.

We called it the 'Dungeon', because it was two floors down, in the basement, where they sold the cheese. You weren't allowed to use the lift, so two floors down, there were seats along a very long desk, with twelve-to-fourteen people seated there.

These tubes with the money in would come along a shoot at the back, then down to each person; unfortunately I was the last one, so if everybody shut the top off, with a lever, because they'd got to many tubes coming down, mine would pile up! Plus the fact that in every tube you opened was a half-a-crown, or two-shilling piece, wrapped up in some paper, making an indentation in the paper. I was nineteen when the war started."

Take a look at the Wareing Family Tree, (opens album). This is my Dad, with his brothers and sisters, in age order: Reg, Una, Bernard, Laurie, Elsie, Ida, Harry, Madge and Audrey.

Elsie said that other branches of the family had money; the only reason that they themselves were poor, was because her father didn't behave as he should have done. She said that her Dad was very good looking and he used to get off with the women.

Before their mother died, when Elsie was a teenager, her father worked at the *Boot Pub* in Catherine-de-Barnes, part-time. The barmaid there was his mistress, but he used to keep a 'sharp eye' on his two oldest daughters, Una and Elsie, when he took them there!

"Your grandfather sounds a very complicated man. Thank you so much for the tea Shirley, but I must be going now."

And thank *you* for providing so much detail about what life was like for my family in Brunswick Road all those years ago, Lily. I can't believe the serendipity of our finding you, purely by chance, just at the right time – and simply because Audrey's son Steven is your gardener. How lucky is that?!!

(Dennis enters stage right).

You're just the man I want to see – and just in time – I'm about to make more tea … and we have a cherry cake! Lilian Bullen and I have just been talking about our Grandad – the 'Old Man'!

There was the home life, but then outside of that he was a free agent. It seems to me that he was almost like a Jekyll-and-Hyde. A strict Edwardian father at home – with the responsibility of all these kids to keep in order – but that he broke free once he was outside of the house: it was his own time.

"Yes and he was always working on the car, outside the house; always under the bonnet – tinkering about with it. Then at mealtimes, the children had to be totally quiet: if they said a word they were sent up to bed – they had to leave the table – very strict."

That doesn't explain the heartless things that he did though Dennis – particularly regarding Dad and Madge, but it does explain the 'breaking free' side of it. It's a strange dichotomy: a very strict father versus a scoundrel.

"And his Dad, WJ was, allegedly, something of the same. There's a lot about prostitutes in there too – he was 'Wine, women and song'. That's what Reg said about him. He used to take Reg on long-distance lorry trips; he got him to drive a lorry, at one time. Being only a boy he was petrified! He said: 'I can't, I can't!' Harry said: 'There's no such word as can't!' That was his 'phrase'. He and Eustace got on well; it's likely they went drinking together – although Eustace was a whisky drinker."

We also know that in 1920, Eustace and his wife, Kate Baylis, a Draper's Clerk, were living at 366 Lodge Road. Sadly, just four months before Dad was born, Kate died of heart failure. Eustace registered her death on 18 August 1920. We know that shortly afterwards, Eustace moved into 65 Brunswick Road, with his daughter, Lilian and all the family. He must have been devastated; Kate was only sixty years old, Dennis. You may recall that she and her mother are taking Lilian on a canal-side picnic, as our show opens.

Your sister, Lilian, remembers your Dad, Larry, saying that Grandmother Lilian looked after Grandad, further confirmation that he didn't want to live on his own.

Three years later, Dad had begun to play the violin. I remember him telling me that, as a small boy, he used to work the bellows for the organist in St Paul's Church on the Moseley Road, which was by that time, established as the Wareing family's regular church, as opposed to St Peter and St Paul's in Aston, which Harry Senior attended years earlier.

According to Madge's birth certificate, she was born on 1st January 1923, sub-district of Balsall Heath, at that time under the Kings Norton area. Madge Gertrude, same middle name as Lilian, her mother, and lived at 65 Brunswick Road. Her father's occupation is shown as Motor Fitter. Her birth was registered on February 13th 1923.

Her younger sister, Audrey, recalled that Harry Senior had various 'sayings'. Her son, Steve Rogers, is about to enlighten us. Do join our tea party Steve.

"Yes, I'll have a slice of cake, if that's ok? Another of the 'Old Man's' sayings was 'Time waits for no man.' Ken could tell you more of them – Bernard used to say them – he copied them from his father, Harry Senior. I can just imagine them all, sitting round the table…like we are now!"

Except that they weren't allowed to talk. On the other hand, he had several mistresses over a period of time. He'd even take Una and Elsie with him, when he visited a certain caravan site in Shirley. I've often wondered if that's why Una and Elsie married relatively late – being determined that no man would ever be unfaithful to them, like Harry was to Lilian.

By all accounts, he led her a very hard life. So he obviously had a double-standard. Whether that was a kind of safety valve, because of the responsibility of bringing up eight children, I'm not sure. We also know that he had a really bad temper.

Ken Wareing recalls that his father, Bernard Eustace Wareing, was named after their Grandfather. My Dad, Harry, remembers Eustace sitting by the fire. He'd probably had a glass or two; Dad was often worried that his Grandad would fall in the fire, because he looked as if he was going to keel over!

Elsie used to tell Ken, about his father, Bernard: "He was a little tough boy, when he was growing up. I can vouch for that, in my early teens. I understand that his father, Harry Senior, was very strict – and I think that's where my father got it from!"

Harry Senior, was a strange contradiction, personality-wise. When he took Elsie and Una with him sometimes, to the pub: they'd have maybe a lemonade and a packet of crisps – if such things existed then! But if any men started trying to chat them up, he was the Victorian father again – straight away: "That's my daughter – on your way!"

But, he was flirting with all these women and having affairs, so figure that one out!

Pat told me that her father, Reg, was put off religion for life, because Lilian was so fanatical about it.

"If she was a convert to Anglo-Catholicism they were often fanatical, so that would make sense," observes Dennis. "But Harry Senior didn't approve of it: there's a church in Highgate – St Alban's – which is High Church, but he wouldn't let her go there. According to my Dad, he wouldn't let Lilian go out; he made her stay at home. She must have 'escaped' occasionally."

I've invited one of the Upton side of our family over for tea too. I hope you don't mind fellas. It's my third cousin, Jacky Curtis.

(Voice from off-stage): "Hello there – anyone at home? May I come in?"

Jacky enters, stage left. She is holding a document case in her right hand.

As Jacky and I discuss our family history, we face outwards, addressing the audience throughout, as they are included in our conversation too.

Whenever a photograph is referred to, as before, a larger poster-type version is lowered, for the audience to see; we decided to have a change from the overhead screens, for this particular show.

Tell me, Jacky, about the difference between Mum's cousin, your father – and his brother, Joe. Here's a poster- photo of the two of them together.

"My Dad Jim was very serious, philosophical, quite a thinker. He was interested in yoga, poetry and gardening – which was quite advanced for those days… and very careful what he ate. Quite a studious nature, whereas my Uncle Joe was rather jovial – 'one the boys'. He liked a drop of whisky and he smoked a pipe. He was very cheerful; a bit more of a laugh. But Joe was a travelling salesman, for *Twyning's Tea Company*, which suited his personality," explains Jacky.

"My Dad was an electrical engineer; he was in REME in the army and eventually worked for *Lucas's*, in Shaftsmoor Lane, Hall Green – and Marston Green. Although the brothers were fond of each other, I don't think they really understood each other. They were quite different, although they shared a love of gardening and animals.

(*She empties contents of a case onto the table.*)

"Dad was older than Joe, but Doris was the oldest of the three – that's Peggy."

How about Great Auntie Maggie and Great Uncle Jim, who were brother and sister?

Nellie & Stan Curtis' Wedding 1915, 70 Brunswick Road. Back row l-r: Grandad, George Upton, 16 years of age; brother James; Great Grandma Margaret Upton (née Nealon); her husband, Thomas George; Auntie Emily; to Stan's left is his brother. Front row: two Curtis ladies including bridesmaid; Auntie Maggie – the second bridesmaid, seated in front of her father. The old lady is possibly also a Curtis. By kind permission of Jacky Curtis.

World War ll photo, taken at 51 Brunswick Road: Jim, Joe and Peggy Curtis, with my Grandad, George Upton and his son, my Uncle Dennis. By kind permission of Jacky Curtis.

"I always found my Dad's side of the family were quite formal in their mannerisms. They were very 'Proper', very respectable. Even when I was a little girl – they used to shake hands with me! I remember the first time I gave my Uncle Jim a cuddle, he giggled – and went pink! Neither he nor Maggie was married. He was a young man in the First World War – in the trenches."

My early memories of Jim and Maggie were that they were both quite shy.

"He was, he was very phlegmatic as well; we'd talk to him about the war, but he's say, 'Oh that's past!' He had no time for it at all. I was told that in the Second World War he used to cook for the Americans. He also kept canaries when I was a little girl."

I remember that too, Jacky, when I went round to Brunswick Road, as a little girl. I believe he had pigeons before that. Thomas George Upton, his father, (born Moseley c. 1861), also kept birds. According to my notes, both Jim and Joe were in the Retreat at Dunkirk.

"Well Dad certainly was; I can't remember what Joe did. They were both in the Territorials, before War broke out. That's why they were called up so quickly. Dad was in the 8th Army, in the Desert, at one time; in Egypt – Cairo and he was at Dunkirk; they also went to Belgium at some point."

According to Mum, they were in the first stage of the Little Ships – when small fishing vessels rescued them from the French beaches.

"Dad said that he was brought back by a military ship, called the *Lord Howe.*"

(*Shirley selects another document*): Your father's Jim's birth certificate confirms that he lived at 51 Brunswick Road, with his parents, Nellie and Stan Curtis. Nellie was Grandad's sister; Joe and Peggy were their two other children.

"Great Uncle Jim, died from a longstanding injury to the left leg and gangrene of the right foot: those are both injuries that he sustained in the First World War. Like his brother, George, your Grandad, he was in the trenches too."

We're looking at Maggie's death certificate now, I understand that Selly Oak Hospital used to be the old Workhouse. So that's quite an interesting link as well.

Both Maggie and her brother, Jim, were in hospital when they died, but their place of residence was Wickets Tower in Edgbaston. I remember visiting them there Jacky.

Great Uncle Jim's Birth Certificate is interesting, because it gives his birth date, 27 March 1898. It says Kings Norton, but that must have been Balsall Heath, as it came under Kings Norton at that time. He was nine years younger than Maggie.

Have a sandwich Jacky. My cousin, Steven Upton, told me about 70 Brunswick Road, where the Uptons lived? What do you remember about it?

"It had a front parlour, which was very 'proper' – very old-fashioned – and it was kept as a parlour: nobody used it. Then you walked through to a little, middle room, which was a dining room and living room. Then there was a back kitchen and an outside toilet."

It sounds a lot like 65 Brunswick – don't you think Dennis?

"Yes it does, but I must go now Shirley. Thanks for the tea," – (*exits stage right, together with our cousin, Steven Rogers*).

"I remember the backyard of 70 Brunswick being all tiled, in Staffordshire Blue Brick. Around the edges of the garden they put the bricks in sideways, so that they looked like a little pointed fence….that's where the pigeon coops were," continues Jacky.

"And Great Uncle Jim grew chrysanthemums. They'd got a cellar, which I was fascinated by – I thought it was wonderful! The door to it was off the living room and I presume it was the coal cellar, because there was a hole for coal on the pavement, outside the cellar, so that all the coal could be tipped down it."

I know who the Brunswick Road coalman was – a Mr Johnson – because his wife used to look after Audrey, while Una and Elsie were at work.

"I thought number 70 was the best house in the world, ladies and gentlemen, because we hadn't got a cellar. So as a child that was magical. Also, they kept the canaries on the landing!!" Jacky continues.

"I left 10 May Lane in Kings Heath when I was about two, where we lived with my Nan; my Grandad had died previously, so they transferred the lease to her – it was a private landlord. But he wouldn't transfer it to my parents; although when my Nan died, we only had about a fortnight to move. But the house I'm comparing Maggie and Jim's to was 5 Wyche Avenue, Kings Heath, which we then moved to. I'm still living there now, after all these years!

"I remember my Dad had a motorbike and sidecar. When we moved I sat on Mum's lap, in the sidecar – and I was holding a goldfish bowl! Here's something even more special ladies and gentlemen!"

This is absolutely wonderful: it's the Marriage Certificate between Thomas George Upton and Margaret Neiland, which took place in Ireland. The name was later changed to Nealon, from an original Irish O'Nealon family name, which goes back into the mists of time. The church where their Irish wedding took place was in the Parish of St Mary and the wedding was on May 21st 1883.

We also have a testimonial letter here for Great Uncle Jim, written by L. Hollis, who was a baker, living in Brunswick Road. It's dated 15 July 1887. We are *so* lucky that you were given this invaluable collection of documents by Great Uncle Jim, after his death, Jacky. Were they kept in his flat at Wickets Tower?

"Yes, they must have been moved from Brunswick Road."

These are real gems – to say the least! *(Reaching across table)*: We also have Great Auntie Maggie's Death Certificate. She was 73. It came under the Aston District, at that time.

Here is Nellie and Stan Curtis' Marriage Certificate, *(holding it up)*. Stan was resident in Nechells, at 6 Park Place. Nellie was a domestic servant. The address it gives, 25 Park Hill Moseley, was the address of her employer. In those days women in service were allowed to give their employers address on legal certificates like this.

"I believe that was also why they were allowed to use that particular church for their service: St Anne's in Moseley. It came under Worcester in those days; the boundaries moved later. It also confirms that her father, Thomas Upton, was a Carter, which tallies with the information I have from a Census for their family. Stanley Curtis' father, Charles Cedric Curtis, is shown as a Baker: that occupation seems to be going through at least two generations," Jacky explains.

"In Moseley, the house of the residents around the Park Hill area, backed onto a private park – it's still there: if you're a resident you have a key to the gate. I worked in Moseley for a year, ladies and gentlemen – and our office had a key to the gate – I went in and took my Dad: it was wonderful!"

That also fits in with the early histories of Balsall Heath and Moseley, Jacky, which I've been looking at. When they started to develop Balsall Heath (this tallies with what you were saying about that park area) they wanted to build a second Edgbaston. But it didn't have the protection of the Calthorpe Estate, like certain parts of Edgbaston had. So they started building grand houses on the Moseley and Wake Green Roads, but later introduced terraced houses in order to make more profit. So that's a good link between the type of house where Nellie was in service, as compared with the one she was living in – 70 Brunswick Road.

Now your Grandmother, Nellie, was the first child of Margaret Nealon and Thomas Upton. Her birth took place in Ireland – Carrigoline, in Kinsale. She was their first child, although the names given on the birth certificate are Gertrude Sarah, which are her second and third names. Her father, our great grandfather, Thomas George Upton was stationed at Camden Barracks at that time. That's another fantastic document!

Tell us more about your father, Jim Curtis.

"Dad always loved his gardening. He had an allotment when we lived in May Lane. When we moved to Wyche Lane, Kings Heath, he had one at Brandwood End, by the cemetery. I've got a very old photograph of him with a lawnmower, or roller, when he was a boy – he always loved his garden. He taught me how to love a garden too. Here's a photo of him at Hidcote Gardens."

Sylvia and Uncle Dennis loved to go there too Jacky. My Dad, and myself were also keen gardeners.

"Now this next photo that we're showing you, is of the back yard at Brunswick Road. It's Auntie Nellie's wedding, in 1915. These are her

Jim Curtis at Hidcote Gardens. By kind permission of Jacky Curtis.

parents, my great grandmother and great grandfather. The groom would be Uncle Stan."

It's more than likely to be 70 Brunswick Road, because that was the family home. Doesn't Auntie Maggie look different there? It's the first photo I've seen of her as a young woman.

"I don't know whether the old lady is a relative, or a neighbour. I'm not sure whether Auntie Maud is on the photo, because she died before the others. In the right, in the background are my Great Granny and Grandad. She looks rather severe!"

They are the couple standing to his left, as you look at the poster; we have the Blunns and the Uptons on the right.

"The only thing about this old lady is that she looks like a family member. She's got my Dad's eyes! So she could be a Curtis."

This is Nellie and Stan's wedding day again – just the two of them. The next poster features a Lorry Rally of vans from different companies, all assembled in Cannon Hill Park. It's a competition to see which van is best

Lorry Rally at Cannon Hill Park. By kind permission of Jacky Curtis.

presented. There are *Vim* and *Rinso* lorries – and we think this is Great Uncle Jim here, on the photo above, fifth from the left. It's a real historical piece this!

Now we're looking at a picture of Joe and Jim, around the time they were called up, in World War Two. From left to right in the foreground we have Peggy and Nellie. On the back row left we have Joe, then Stanley in the centre (Jacky's father) then Jim. That would be taken at the back of 51 Brunswick Road – you can see the entry.

There's a lovely sepia photo of Emily, with Daisy and George – her two children, who died young. Taken at a studio.

"Joe, Jim's brother, lived in Harpers Road, Hollywood. Joe and Anne's son, Chris, lived in. Out of all my Dad's family, my Great Uncle Jim and Auntie Maggie are the two people I was closest to," Jacky continues. "Me and my Dad used to go and see them almost every week, when they lived in Balsall Heath. Sometimes they'd come to us, of a Sunday here at Wyche Avenue and give me threepence or a sixpenny piece. I'm getting very emotional at the thought of it now!

They were very plain people; very quiet – unassuming; took what life threw at them. They were kind – good-hearted – and I thought the world of them. Auntie Maggie made the best Victoria Sponge that I've ever had in my life! She was a good cook – she was in service, you see. Uncle Jim cooked for the Americans, during the war."

I remember going to Aunt Emily's house. She'd been in service too – and everything was beautifully presented: hand-crocheted seat covers, lace doylies. The way she served afternoon tea with a silver tea service, was like an art form, Jacky.

"Auntie Emily used to send me into the garden to play, ladies and gentlemen, because she thought that children should be 'seen and not heard'! So I'd collect the little hard green apples that had fallen off the tree. She had a lovely garden.

It was on different levels. It started high at the top, with terracing work and steps. There were balustrades so that you could walk up. I think it was

Family Group – Harpers Road Hollywood, Wythall, the back garden of Joe Curtis, Jim's brother. From l-r: Jacky Curtis, Great Aunt Emily; Joe – and Billy the dog; Joe's son, Christopher; Auntie Maggie, Auntie Peggy (from Canada). Great Uncle Jim; Jackie's Mum, Claire.

48 Ashill Road, Rubery. So if you went up the main road, past the Austin and then turned right; it was a road off to the left there.

"Although she was living on her own, she had some very good friends who looked after her," Jacky recalls. "She was a bit more strict and proper. Auntie Maggie and Uncle Jim were always more relaxed than that. Maybe it was because Emily had brought up children?

"I can smell the house even now – because it was the old furniture, with all the curlicues – on it – the old dark polish. Beautiful china and anti-Macassars. I have one memory of Uncle Ern, who I believe had asthma, lying on a blanket in the front room, wearing a little pullover, with a blanket pulled over him. Auntie Maggie gave me a little Victorian gold ring, with rubies and pearls; she made me ask my mother if I had permission to wear a gold ring."

I think Jackie knew Maggie better than I did, ladies and gentlemen. On the rare occasions when I saw her, she looked quite serious.

"I was sixteen at the time, Shirley. She didn't tell me who gave her the ring, but I think it might have been a young man."

Yes, both Mum and my Aunt Sylvia said that they were sure there was someone. It's the same with Great Uncle Jim really. He was a good-looking guy when he was younger.

"But he was involved in two World Wars and he was injured. A lot of people didn't marry then because of circumstances. Not all young women found young men to marry.

Jim was injured in the leg, but I never remember him walking badly because of it. It never really healed very well though. We used to visit him in hospital; his leg was very badly ulcerated, which is why the gangrene set in. They were quite fascinated by what might have caused the damage; whether it was some kind of explosion or gas, I don't know."

Rather like my Grandad George Upton, born 1895. He had lung complications from the gas. Talking about what happened when that particular generation came home from the war, I'm sure many of you, ladies and gentlemen, will remember stories like that, within your own families.

"A lot of the young women didn't marry because their young men had been killed," adds Jacky. "The young men were often involved in both World Wars and had problems finding jobs too. I think that whole generation was blighted!"

There was the Depression too. Here is a fantastic photo showing Margaret Nealon in the middle. On the left is her daughter Emily; on the right is Nellie, Jacky's grandmother.

And this is one of the photos that I've taken of bay-windowed terraced houses in Brunswick Road.

"Yes, there was a step, which they used to polish, the little window above the door – I remember that; the front room. You walked straight into it. It was the parlour – it was very posh! Like the one we're sitting in now. May I have some more tea Shirley? All of this talking is making me really thirsty!

Auntie Maggie had an aspidistra in there, like the one we have here (**indicates a plant on the sideboard**) and couches; things like coffin stools. I had it for years but it grew too big, so I gave it to a friend of mine. There were alleyways every few houses. I think one of the purposes of those was to access the back gardens – for dustbins and delivery and so on, because the houses didn't have front gardens. They had blue brick down them."

So the house where your family lived, 51, was probably smaller than the ones on the opposite side?

"On the opposite side to my family, where 70 Brunswick Road was, there were two main rooms downstairs: the parlour, then you walked straight through to the living room, then the kitchen; there was a door through to the backyard. You had the door at the front of the house; the window on the right-hand side. The stairs – it may even have been the same door that went to the cellar. There was a landing across the top – like a T shape. There'd be a bedroom on either side of it. They didn't have a bathroom."

I imagine that the houses on the Wareing side (65) must have been bigger, because they had 10 people to accommodate.

"Yes, what I can't remember is whether Maggie and Jim had a third floor – a little garret room. When I visited them, the road was so quiet – you hardly ever saw traffic up there, or saw anyone else passing. Very quiet – very respectable. But it had a nice homely old-fashioned feel about it. It was also very smart: people took a great pride in their houses. There were lace curtains at every window.

Mum's family went to chapel and the preachers could be quite severe. Mum was a sensitive little girl and used to cry – she thought they were shouting at her. Dad's family were church people. Dad and Uncle Joe didn't take the services so seriously. They often got into trouble for being naughty and giggling, then Auntie Peggy would have to take them outside.

Dad told me that Grandma, who could have been a Great Grandma, shot a tramp – over in Ireland!"

(Hurdy-gurdy starts up, in the street outside, playing the 'Old Bull and Bush' as the street lights go on, one by one).

On that cheerful note, I think it's time we went home Jacky!

(We both exit, as the Hurdy-gurdy continues to play and the curtain falls).

Chapter Seven

CLIFTON ROAD SCHOOL

The curtain rises on what appears to be a photo of a classroom in the 1950s. But the photo suddenly comes to life!

Don returns as our Narrator, but this time he is dressed casually, and is standing on the right of the stage:

This is my class, ladies and gentlemen, in a Clifton Road School classroom, during a Top Junior Project Lesson, in the 1950s, before we all left for pastures new. Our teacher is Mrs Phillips.

Teacher moves to front of class; there is a gentle murmuring, as pupils discuss their work between themselves.

Don's school photo, Project Lesson.

It was my last year at the school, before I went to St Phillips Grammar School. Mrs Phillips split us up into twos and threes. These projects were 'Our Interests'. I'm right in the back corner, holding my Project Book. You can't see it exactly, but there is a pilot, in his overalls and helmet, on my front cover; because at that time, I was very interested in becoming a fighter pilot. That was my main thing in life. Michael Tuffy drew that cover – drawing is not something that I'm capable of doing!

There's a girl right in the middle there – Sandra: she lived in Woodfield Road. I saw her a few weeks ago! I was doing a show and she came to see me. I've seen her several times since I left school.

On my first day at school I was given a bottle of milk, with a straw. I'd never seen a straw before in my life, so I put the straw in the bottle of milk – and blew! The milk went all over me. And this Mary Yarwood ran up to me, put her hand up her dress – and from inside her knickers she pulled out the biggest handkerchief you've ever seen – and mopped me down… I always remember that!

(Don exits as the curtain falls)

(Shirley takes centre stage, near the front, addressing the audience)

Many of the people in our book went to Clifton Road School, like Don, playwright David Edgar; some of UB40 and several other celebrities.

The Wareing's back garden, at 65 Brunswick Road, backed onto the playground in Clifton Road School, so they often had to throw balls back! Harry Senior had been a pupil at King Edward's Grammar School.

(Jacky Curtis enters).

My second cousin, Jacky Curtis, from the previous show, remembers Clifton Road School, from the late fifties onwards:

"We came from the Moseley Road, up Clifton Road. We turned left down Hertford Street – and there was an old caste iron privy/urinal, by a bridge – all in Staffordshire Blue brick; just before the railway line. That would lead into Brunswick Road. I remember Clifton Road School being on the corner of Clifton Road and Hertford Street, ladies and gentlemen.

"We used to walk past it and we definitely got off the bus and came up Clifton. The cinema was on the corner. We didn't go up as far as Lime Grove. A railway line goes over the bridge.

"They changed the usage of the schools at some stage. There's a factory at our family end of Brunswick Road. It's still there, but probably manufactures something else. Some of my family attended Clifton Road School. We have a book that was awarded to Grandad Upton's brother, Uncle Jim, which makes him Great Uncle Jim, to both Shirley, and myself.

"It's Book III of the St George History Readers. The opening page reads:

Council School Clifton Road, December 21st 1911. Presented to John J. Upton, by R.W. Jones, Teacher.

"It was published in 1902, by Thomas Nelson and Sons – a real slice of history. Great Uncle Jim was christened John, but he preferred people to call him by his second name, James. When he passed away he left a substantial amount of memorabilia to me, this being just one example. We were very close and I treasure his memory to this day. And to think that it was awarded to him three years before the outbreak of the First World War! He also won *Gulliver's Travels* and *Robinson Crusoe*, but he gave them to me when I was too young to appreciate how special they were."

Jacky, I understand that you started off in Colmore Road School, which is just up from Kings Heath Park, then went over the road to Camp Hill. However, most of our other relatives attended Clifton Road School, which was a very traditional one – late Victorian. In addition to Don attending the school, some pupils became famous sportsmen. Anthony E Pratt, who invented the famous board game, *Cluedo*, was born in Brighton Road. There's a whole list of well-known people who went there, ladies and gentlemen.

My grandfather, George Upton, Jim's brother, also won school prizes. The Upton men appear to have been good scholars. Sylvia, my Uncle Dennis Upton's wife (sadly they're now both deceased) told me that one of Grandad Upton's sisters, Great Aunt Emily, ran a Post Office. Before she died, Sylvia showed me a bronze-coloured medal that had been awarded to Grandad George Upton, Nellie and Emily's brother, at Clifton Road School.

It's a Birmingham City Department of Education Medal, 'Awarded for four years excellent attendance to George Upton.' It's in a box, decorated with the City of Birmingham Education Department Crest.

"My Dad, Jim Curtis, said that the Uptons were 'Church of England'. But not high church," Jacky concludes, then exits, stage right.

During a visit to *Balsall Heath Local History Society* in Malvern Street, I discovered that Clifton Road School opened in 1878 as a Board School, following the Education Act of 1870. I asked Val Hart, of *Balsall Heath Local History Society*, why the current address of Clifton Road School is in Brunswick Road. Val was Deputy Director of *St Paul's Trust*, before she retired.

She explained that the existing Clifton School is actually in St Paul's Road, because the school moved out of the old building. But the Junior School is around the corner from there. "The school that you took a photo

Two postcards sent by Field Post, by my Grandfather, George Upton, during the
First World War, to his sister, Maggie Upton. She was in service to a spinster lady,
in Boscombe, Bournemouth.

of in Brunswick Road is Clifton Road Primary – it opened about eleven years
ago," Val continued. "Originally they were two separate Board schools: the
Infant school in Hertford Street and the Junior school in Clifton Road.
Then they moved to new buildings: the Infants moved out first – and they
got a new building, which is in Brunswick Road, but eventually the two ages
combined into one new building."

What are the old buildings in Clifton Road and Hertford Street used
for?

"The Infant School has become St Paul's School, which is a Secondary
School for pupils who have difficulty with mainstream schooling; the Junior
School is used for training of various kinds and Early Years Learning."

Chris Sutton, the Development Worker for *Balsall Heath Local History
Society*, has just popped in for five minutes. He explains:

The original Clifton Road Junior School, now used for various kinds of training and Early Years Learning. Photographer Shirley Thompson.

"Clifton Road School started as one the Chamberlain and Martin Board Schools, which were built by the architects *Chamberlain Martin*. The original Board Schools started in 1833, but Clifton Road School was much later.

"My Grandad came here and his sisters. They lived in Runcorn Road, from 1905-1935. Their surname was Francis – my maternal line. My grandad lived there with his parents. I remember, as a child, walking down Runcorn, from Moseley Road, really excited, because I was going to stay with them."

In Chapter 16, Chris, we'll meet Ken Malin, whose family also lived in Runcorn Road. When you came to work for *Balsall Heath Local History Society*, at the Centre, did you have any idea about your family connection, to the area?

"None at all. The big thing for me was when I built a wall in my back garden years and years ago – then found out that my family were bricklayers! As you know, you often find that you follow in your family's footsteps anyhow, without necessarily realising it at the time.

"The front entrance to the school is on St Paul's Road," Chris continues. "Hence you get this humorous thing of Clifton Road School being on St Paul's Road! And St Paul's School on Clifton Road."

Chris is also manager of the *Smethwick Heritage Centre*. Although he must leave us now, to attend a meeting there, he'll be back later, in Show 17.

Meanwhile, Don returns, seating himself at the table:

"I've just remembered Shirley, there was another boy who attended our school – he was another friend who I met again years later, after one of my Little Theatre shows. He was a year older than me – he was tall and thin – about 6ft 2. He said how much he'd enjoyed the show. He said, 'Do you remember me? I'm Stanley Bassett.' And I was so pleased to see him. That was just earlier this year, surprisingly."

What was life like, as a schoolboy, in the Balsall Heath area, during the post-war years Don?

"I had a variety of friends who went to Clifton Road. There was also one on Coleville Road. That was Kenny Coombes. He had a telly. He was one of the first people to have one and occasionally I used to go down there and watch things on television.

"We played in what we called 'The Little Park'. It was on the corner of Brighton Road. On this map it's called Balsall Heath Recreation Ground. It was just really a green patch but we used to go down there and play football: loads of us, particularly in the holidays. There were bomb sites everywhere – they were our playgrounds – which was very dangerous! When you think about *Health and Safety* now, they were completely unstable! We used to climb up and walk across the beams of bombed houses. The stairs were gone, so we were up where the second floor would have been; the beams were relatively wide, but the drop – I presume we'd have died if we'd fallen!

"And then there were Air Raid Shelters of course, and holes where shelters had been, which filled up with water! It's a wonder any of us survived.

"I was born around the time of the last major air raid on Birmingham – there was only one raid after I was born, in March 1943. They were trying to get the *BSA*. I obviously don't remember it, because it was just weeks after I was born. But apparently, according to Mum and Dad, they rushed down the shelter with me. Then my Dad, who was an ARP Warden, went down there with his stirrup pump.

"An incendiary bomb landed on the roof of our house... and slowly burnt through the roof... right in the corner of what became my bedroom, then subsequently went down and burnt through the corner of what was our living room. I remember this sort of ring in the corner, you know the way that people used to decorate in those days? At least once a year; so my father would re-decorate the room and paint the ceiling, ladies and gentlemen.

"Then gradually, over about six months, this mark slowly reappeared. It was ever so peculiar – they never got rid of it! We had a three-bedroom house and my bedroom was the middle of the three. It was a terraced house, with a very narrow garden. It had a flat window at the front. There were bay windows on the other side of the road.

132, diagonally opposite us, was where the Beasley family lived. Micky Beasley was at Clifton Road with me; I think he was a year younger. He was one of the people killed years later, in the Birmingham Pub Bombings. Apparently he was standing right by the juke box and the bomb was underneath it. They put bombs in two pubs. The IRA bombings – in November 1974.

"When I moved up to the Junior School, it wasn't a separate building. There was a central hall and everything seemed to lead off that; but then there was an upstairs. So many people have said this, but I remember going back to the school as an adult and thinking: 'this can't be the same school – it's too small'. But obviously when I was little I thought it was huge!

"The big, forbidden thing, was that they had a big pile of coke; you weren't allowed to go anywhere near the coke – but of course, everybody did. It was behind the gate in the school yard. But it was magnetic – we were drawn towards it! It was really tough stuff. When you picked it up it didn't weigh much – not like a piece of coal. But if you fell over on it you'd rip yourself to bits. And kids were always bleeding – covered in blood and black stuff!!

"One of our male teachers was a Mr White who'd been there a long time – he was an old chap. Then there was a young Mr White – so we had two Mr Whites. There was a Mr Gathergood, who had a beard. In those days there were always rumours about war service, because everybody's Dad had been in the war. People used to brag about their Dads: 'Oh my Dad was a fighter pilot', or a Commando – those were the most prestigious: you either wanted your Dad to have been a fighter pilot or a Commando.

"So it was said this Mr Gathergood had been a Submariner – but a lot of this was folklore. I believe he died, years later, in some terrible floods on the East Coast; for some reason he was there at the time and he was swept away. We had another male teacher who wasn't there for very long. He was very large and very ugly – Mr Rowlands or Rawlins, something like that. He took the top class. There was also a man called Mr Hennessy – a tiny man; he took the football team. He was smaller than the rest of us!"

Twenty years previously, Don, the Junior School was organised differently. Jack Billington, in *Tales out of School*, wrote:

'I went to Clifton Road Infant School. The entrance was in Hertford Street and there were mixed classrooms of boys and girls, until we went to the big school. At about seven years old we were split up and the boys were taught downstairs and the girls were taught upstairs. Now that was in the thirties.'

He writes again:

'We had to be at school at 8.55am to line up and march into the classroom for 9am.' So that was probably the same for you.

Jack continues:

'Prefects took your name. If you were late twice you got the cane. I was late twice but the second time I nipped through the Infants' playground and got in that way. We had two hours' playtime from 12-2pm.'

Don comments: "The lunchtime wasn't that long. But I always used to go out at lunchtime."

Jack elaborates:

'We played football for the first hour – 20-30 of us, playing with a tennis ball, then we had to hurry home before father came home at 1pm. We all ate lunch together but then we had to be back in school for 1.55pm'. They had two 15-minute breaks in the morning and afternoon, the last one being at 3.00pm or 3.15pm and then school finished at 4.30pm.'

"No, we finished at 4pm," Don recalls. "I remember playing football in that playground, there was quite a slope on it; so if you were playing one way, the ball kept running away from you; if you were playing the other way, it kept running back to you!

"Unlike some of the pupils' 1930s experiences, I never went to any other school for special/extra subjects and the teacher didn't use a 'clicker' to get the attention of the class! Writing was still done with a pen with a nib and an inkwell; all books were supplied by the school, but we no longer had Drill in the playground.

"Miss Seal was the Headmistress," Don continues, "I always thought that she looked like a witch! She had a big hooked nose, but she was a most gentle person and very kind to me. When I was in the Top Class I used to go off to see her on my own, from time to time.

"We'd taken an Intelligence Test in which I did rather well, so my life changed after that test. They sent for my Mum and Dad and she encouraged me to read certain Classic books, such as Mark Twain. I used to read avidly – all the time. I went regularly to Moseley Road Library.

"I mentioned my teacher at the beginning of this particular show/chapter – Mrs Phillips – quite a tall woman. For some reason we got off to a bad start – I don't know why – but in the end I absolutely adored her: I thought she was wonderful! She'd been in the air force during the war – a very strong woman and a very good teacher. Her husband would occasionally come in, maybe to pick her up – and he'd talk to me. He'd been a Flight Engineer in Lancasters during the war. That's where my interest in flying started. I had two aeroplanes at one time. I was fascinated by aeroplanes when I was a little boy.

"Every child gets a fascination: my son, Rory, was fascinated by whales and sharks. By the time he was five he knew the names of every shark and every whale! He could tell you what they were, just by looking at the fin. So we all have our little peculiarities. But in those days there weren't that many aeroplanes. I can remember, as a kid, that if I had an aeroplane I'd rush out into the garden. We sometimes made the kit aeroplanes, where I lived, at 131 Ombersley Road.

"While I was at Clifton Primary School, I can't remember exactly how old I was, road signs suddenly appeared, and they had things like Highgate, Balsall Heath and Sparkbrook. So it suddenly appeared that the bottom end of Ombersley Road, which was the end closest to Ladypool Road, became Sparkbrook; it probably always was, but it was then designated Sparkbrook. The top end, beyond Kingsley Road, going up towards Moseley Road, was suddenly Balsall Heath. That happened somewhere around 1950.

"My Grandmother had a Grocer's Shop, *Field's*, in Belgrave Road, almost directly opposite Hick Street – obviously it doesn't exist now. Beyond that there was another sign that said Highgate. So all of a sudden that was Highgate; whereas before the signs, everything had seemed to be Balsall Heath, but now it was split up into different areas.

"By the time I went to Grammar School, when I was eleven, if somebody said, 'Where do you live?' I said 'Sparkbrook.' There were still a lot of bombed buildings around.

"When I was a small boy, before I went to school, my mother, who was very fond of her mother, used to walk with me, every afternoon, to the top of Ombersley Road, down into Belgrave Road – down the hill. The *Belgrave Hotel*, which seemed like a huge building to me, wrapped itself around the corner of Belgrave Road. We walked past the hotel and the alms houses: they were very pretty – beautiful architecture – in a block. Then there were two shops together the first one was *Tews* Newsagents; next door was my Nanny's grocery shop, at 295 Belgrave Road. Her mother's maiden name was Field. Nobody's asked me that for years and suddenly it came back to me!

"There was quite a wide alley to the right of my Nanny's shop, as you looked at it. The two shops were together: *Tews* on the left-hand side and my Nanny's shop on the right. Then there was a wide avenue… there were houses up there.

"Everybody around there was a customer. As I got a bit older, I'd be in the shop, with my Auntie Rene, who was Mom's younger sister, she was lovely: she lived with my Nanny, who was a widow … and crippled in both hips. The first hip replacement wasn't done until 1962. My Nanny died in 1954, so there was no chance of her having a hip replacement. She walked with two sticks and was in quite a bit of pain. We used to go to St John's Church.

"My aunt ran the shop, more or less, for her. It used to kill me, because nobody ever paid! They used to say, 'Put it on the strap!' My Aunt Rene had this book, with everybody's name in, so she just wrote everything down. Then on a Friday teatime it was hysterical – if you were ever there at that time – because there were all these people queuing up to pay – it was ever so funny! And of course there weren't supermarkets then. The first supermarket I ever encountered was in Ladypool Road, when I was eleven, because I used to do the shopping.

"When I went to St Phillip's Grammar School, in 1954, my mother decided she'd get a job. So she got an office job in Town. I remember her coming back ever so pleased because they were going to pay her £5 a week. She said, 'Right – you'll get home before I do, so on a Friday I want you to do the shopping.' She'd leave me a list and I'd go to this big *Co-op*, which was like two shops. It was the first thing that I ever saw that resembled a supermarket.

"You'd walk round and collect everything and then pay for it – which was unusual. There was a shop in Ombersley Road called *Birds*. It was quite an important instrument of society in those days, because Mrs Bird knew everything that was going on, in the whole street! So if anybody was ill, people would visit them; it was a very close community: everybody knew everybody else. And if anybody died everyone would know about it and all the curtains would be drawn.

"But you couldn't do anything wrong, because it was: 'I'll tell your mother Donald!' And you knew that they knew your mother – and you'd be in trouble!

"Because I went to Clifton Road School I had classmates who lived down Brunswick Road. I'd go down there to all of the roads around there. I remember that Brunswick Road had trees – whereas I don't think any of the other local roads did. So that was the difference. Brunswick Road seemed a little bit smarter; the other roads just looked the same. In Highgate Road the houses seemed much smaller – it was the Inner Circle bus route. Then there was our road – then St Paul's Road, which was two roads over.

"The teacher, in this second photo of mine, was Mr Gathergood. The back row, from left to right is as follows: Barry Harris, Alan Pearson, Roger Marsh, Stanley Bassett, Kenny Coombes and Robert Mud – who lived on Ladypool Road.

Next-to-back row: Trevor Yeomans, me, Janet Overton, who was very pretty – with plaits. I can't remember the next pupil; an Irish lad called Norman Geary – quite a character! Malcolm Smith, Jo Best, last 3 – not sure.

Next row: Mary Warwood, Heather Cameron, Angela Bird, Johnny Holmes – they're all in that row. Next-to-front row: 3rd along, Pauline Glover, 2nd from right Ann Coleman.

The children seated at the front include Jean Hood – and three other girls.

"Malcolm Smith lived right next door to the school in Clifton Road; Barry Harris lived next door to him. Johnny Holmes had a younger brother. During the school holidays they went on a fishing trip together – and his

Don's second class photo, in playground.

younger brother drowned – on a canal somewhere, quite sad. Angela Bird's mother owned the shop, half-way down our road. Heather Cameron was very pretty. Ann Coleman always sat next to me – almost right through school: I think she lived in Alfred Street. I was about nine when the photo was taken, in 1952, outside the Junior School.

"Clifton Road was a good school, because, looking at this photograph now, Kenny Coombes went to Moseley Grammar School. Alan Pearson went to King Edward's Five Ways. I went to St Phillip's Grammar School. Pauline Glover went to George Dixon. Angela Bird went to Grammar School too. Heather Cameron went to what used to be Harrison Barrow. So there must have been ten out of the thirty-two children who went to Grammar School, which was about thirty per cent of the class. When you consider that the average for going to Grammar School was about eleven or twelve per cent in those days, we must have done better than average," observes Don.

I've been looking through the Clifton Road School log books. You would think that a school environment would be clean, but when the Public Health Inspectors came in at a certain point, they had to close the school for a few days, ladies and gentlemen, because the walls were filthy!

They also discovered that the school milk was treated with lye from the cows and some of the pupils caught Bovine Tuberculosis! It was quite harsh: I'm going back as far as the 1900s onwards.

As Don leaves, businessman Steve Treanor enters, with his older sister, Josie. They seat themselves with me, at the table, where I ask Steve for his memories:

"I had a bad start to Clifton Road School, because on the first day of school, I broke my arm. It was in the hall – I'd fallen off the Horse. I don't know whether I should have been on it. You can see where I broke my arm – there. I imagine I was off school for some considerable time."

In Don's biography, *Flying High*, there's a *really* funny section about his Welsh schoolteachers. Do you remember any of your teachers Steve?

"No, but up the road was one chap, who was my friend – his name was also Steve. His family had a removal business – *Rainbow Removals,* or something like that. Steve went to school with me.

"We were right at the bottom of Clifton Road on the junction with Ladypool Road. The Infant School was on the corner of Hertford Street and Clifton Road. We were at the opposite end to the school. So we'd just walk straight up Clifton Road. We'd go through the front entrance on Clifton Road; we didn't go through Hertford Road.

"I was about eight when we moved from Balsall Heath, so I'd started the Junior School, which was upstairs. We'd go through the front door. There was a little gate on the front; I don't know if it's still there."

Josie, you went to St John's School in Balsall Heath. Tell me about that.

"We didn't have any posh facilities. We did our PE exercises outside; at one time in navy blue knickers. Regardless of the weather, you were still out there!

"In the playground they segregated the girls from the boys, so we had our own playgrounds. It was an all-in-one school, so we didn't have separate infant and junior departments. There were two Infant classes: you stayed in the first from the ages of five until seven; you were moved up according to age. At seven you moved into the juniors, where there were three or four classes. Then they'd start grading you into A, B, C or D, according to your ability.

"I loved reading; when I moved to the Juniors I was one of the top readers. My Mum and my Gran taught me to read before I went to school. I did a lot before I started school, including tying my own shoelaces.

"In the Senior School they taught you Housewifery," Josie continues. "There was a big house in Balsall Heath. When you were thirteen or fourteen, you'd go there and be given particular tasks: 'I want you to prepare the Elevenses today,' your teacher might say, so you'd make them a cake and a cup of tea. You were expected to host these little tea parties.

"It's a shame that we've lost all of that – and we used to clean the house. It was a privately-owned house, rented by teachers, who actually lived there. Again, going back to Cookery, there were no facilities at St John's. There was a Domestic Science school that we used. Again, you were given a specific job.

"My sister, Alice, went to Clifton Road School, but then she moved to St John's, Josie recalls. "I remember the caretaker of Clifton Road Junior School had two daughters. I used to be friends with one of them, Pauline, but both sisters went to St John's. Their surname was 'Mac' something. There were a lot of 'Macs' living in that area."

As Josie and Steve leave the stage, my cousin, (another Steve), Steve Rogers, enters from the wings, with his employer, 97-year-old Lily Bullen.

Steve is the only son of Audrey, my father Harry's youngest sister. Through pure serendipity, it was Steve who introduced me to Lily Bullen; you met them both in the previous chapter…he just happens to be her gardener! Pouring each of them a cup of tea, I say:

Tell me about Audrey's time at Clifton Road School, Steve.

"She was a very good swimmer. There was a Lido, either in Cannon Hill Park or Calthorpe Park. She didn't like it very much, because a leaf went behind her eye when she was swimming, so she had to have her eye removed and then put back again.

"She was very good at written English; when I used to write something in an English Lesson, I thought that ability had passed down to me. I remember a teacher reading out something I'd written to the class, because of the way I'd put it.

"My Dad was fantastic at Maths: he looked after me that way; my Mum helped me with my English. She was quite imaginative. She used to have to fetch coal in a wheelbarrow, when she was young."

Lily interjects: "The Infant and Junior Schools were joined together; then there was a caretaker's house to the right of the photo. You walked down and there was a big playground. Then there was the Senior School."

I've been researching the Clifton Road School Log Books, so we're looking at a list of teachers, from the 1920s onwards, as you were born in 1920 – do you recognise any of their names Lily?

"I think we've struck gold here, because I recognise the surname Anderton: I've got a feeling that she taught me in the first or second class that

I was in, when I started school. She was a lovely person: really kind; I enjoyed being in her class. Mrs Pocock rings a bell too: I don't know whether she was at Clifton Road or at Tindal Street School, which is where the senior girls moved on to, from the age of 11 onwards. I finished school at the standard age of 14. You left school on the Friday and began working on the Monday!

"My husband, Geoffrey Bullen, was always looking to improve himself. He passed the 11+ but he couldn't go, because his parents hadn't got enough money to get the uniform, but he never gave up. He was always trying to better himself," recalls Lily.

There was a bad bronchitis epidemic at Clifton Road School, in 1925, when you were in the Infants Lily.

January 1926: 'Snow was falling most of yesterday; poor attendance at school. Slight accident in playground with a little boy; Visit of HMI.'

"In the winter, if you'd got a penny to spare – and my mother always gave me a penny – you could have hot milk: the caretaker would make cups of hot milk. Free school milk hadn't started then," Lily explains.

"Going back to Clifton Road Juniors, there was a boy in our class called OD – and every day he had the cane – he was just a little 'tinker'! My husband and I were in the same class – that's how we met.

"After a while, the teacher (I think it was Miss Pocock) was getting nowhere with OD, smacking and caning him, so eventually he had to go to the Headmaster. So the Headmaster caned him for a while, but the day came when the Headmaster got him by the scruff of the neck, brought him into the classroom; moved two children off the desk. Then he laid him across the desk and whacked his bottom with a cane, several times – but never did he cry!! We'd say, 'I wonder if OD's going to get the cane?' or something like that.

"My late husband would be able to tell you far more about all of this, because I'm a very quiet kind of person – I still am. I've been introduced to you, so that's ok; your cousin is my gardener. But I'm a very quiet person; my father was too; my mother was very talkative.

"You just wore your own clothes, but it was always navy-blue knickers… with a hanky tucked in! My husband stayed at the different branches of Clifton Road, throughout his school career, until fourteen. The boys who attended Dennis Road School would have lived in a different catchment area."

Thank you so much Lily – and gardener! And thank you, ladies and gentlemen, for making all of today's guests so welcome. If you or your relatives have any memories of Clifton Road School, to add to ours, do let us know!

The orchestra begins to play, as the audience files out.

Chapter Eight

GOODNIGHT LILIAN

The red velvet curtains are closed. An expectant hush falls over the audience. The theatre is packed. It's a Saturday night – and you can hear a pin drop…

A woman's tearful voice calls from the wings: "For Pity's sake, Harry, I'm forty-three years old. We already have eight children – I won't survive another!"

But, for reasons that we can only imagine, her pleas fall on deaf ears.

Orchestra and chorus, as the curtain rises:

Good night Lilian, the time has come to part

Two young children – left with a broken heart.

Et cetera…

Scene: A large bedroom, on the upper floor of 65 Brunswick Road.

Lilian lies dying, as the music continues. Two small children, standing either side of her bed, sob inconsolably: a five-year-old, blond-haired boy, to her right, standing at the head of the bed; a curly-headed three-year-old, directly opposite him, clutching her doll, stares in disbelief.

It is November 1926, just four months after the birth of their mother's ninth child, Audrey.

The music gradually fades, as Lilian motions to her son, with barely enough strength to raise her arm:

He puts his ear close to her head, as she whispers: "Look after Madge for me Harry. See that no harm comes to her."

Curtain closes. Seated with me at a table, front of stage are Mum, Dennis; my cousins, Carolyn, Pat and Jackie. We each address the audience in turn.

My mother, Eileen Wareing, recalls:

"Mrs Johnson, the neighbour, looked after baby Audrey, while the other girls were at work. Then the two sisters would look after Audrey, when they finished work. Mrs Johnson visited your Dad, years later, with Elsie, when he was in hospital. She was ever such a nice lady. Her husband was the coalman.

"Your Dad had a place where he'd been cut. When they were children, Mr Johnson delivered coal to their house. The kids would run out, while he was taking the empty bags away, to get any lumps of coal that had fallen off. Mr Johnson accidentally hit Dad on the chin, with his shovel!"

Lilian's best friend Amy Cockerill (her married name) lived next door to her, at either 63, or 67 Brunswick Road. They knew each other before they were married.

Dennis comments: "I would say that Dad, Larry, had repressed anger in him, as a result of his dysfunctional childhood, but appeared to be a relatively quiet child. I know it's easy to be wise after the event and I've tried my very best not to judge him. Harry Senior had a very poor role model too. Our great grandfather, William James Wareing, appears to have deserted the family home too – so it was a case of history repeating itself."

And I think that initial separation, of Dad and Madge being cut off from the rest of the family, taken to the orphanage, but then later discovering that all of that suffering could have been avoided, must have sparked a feeling of deep resentment, on both of their parts, Dennis. There seems to have been a considerable amount of repressed anger throughout the family – and no wonder!

Jackie Mason, Madge's daughter interjects: "You mentioned the tree in the back garden of 65 Brunswick Road; Mum loved trees – she told me that she used to climb them as a child. Funnily enough, she also liked to stand under trees. Because the canopy is so big, you feel safe under a tree, don't you? And trees have been there for a long time. And they're always there. It would not be at all surprising to find that Mum would have headed for her favourite tree, when her mother died – for comfort."

Lilian's musical talent, is mentioned on several occasions, during our show: one of her ancestors having, allegedly, been a music hall singer in Broad Street, Birmingham. Reg's grand daughter, Carolyn, comments: "I'm also musical. So is my sister, Elizabeth. I have church and choirs too."

So do I Carolyn… I sang a solo in a musical concert just two weeks ago; our cousin, Jackie, Madge's daughter, played Nancy, in an Amateur Production of *Oliver*. So we have that musical gene in the family… through Lilian. How did Reg and Nellie meet?

His daughter, Pat, explains: "Nellie was courting Reg, so she knew all about his Mum."

Pat, continues: "Lilian died shortly after Audrey was born. She died of dropsy, because the afterbirth was stuck and in those days they didn't know what to do about it. When I had my first baby my afterbirth got stuck, so they had to do what's called a 'manual removal' on me and then I had a blood transfusion – in the early days of blood transfusions. Then I had penicillin when it very first came out. But they gave me such large doses of it that I've never been able to take it since!"

Pat has kindly loaned us her father, Reg's entire collection of personal diaries, including one of Nellie's, from 1925, two years before she and Reg were married. My mother, Eileen told me that, according to Elsie, Nellie and her sister often took bus rides, to bring Reg sandwiches, while he was working, before they were married…she was really keen on him! There is much more information about their courtship and subsequent family, in Chapter 15.

According to Pat: "There's one part in my mother, Nellie's diary, that's written in shorthand, because Mum was a shorthand typist. I've done shorthand but I couldn't quite make it all out. It was about the fact that she was worried that she'd agreed to marry Reg, because he was younger than her. In those days is was a thing that was frowned upon, whereas these days it's more accepted."

We know, from another of Nellie's diary entries, that she visited Reg's mother, Lilian, with Reg, on Tuesday 17 March 1925. Nellie writes:

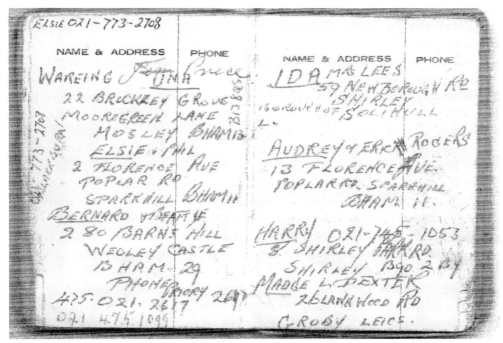

Reggie's Address Book shows the names and addresses of several family members.

'Quite enjoyed myself. We had supper and a huge rice pudding!' She notes that Reg was working nights that week. On the previous Sunday, the two of them had been for their 'usual walk, in Trittiford Park'.

Reg's own diaries begin in 1959 and finish in 1986, shortly before his death. Although his initial education was hampered by the need to help Lilian with the upbringing of his younger siblings, nevertheless, he became a much-travelled and very cultured man; there are many impressive references to Shakespeare, poetry; literary presentations and musical performances, throughout the diaries. After much reading, I was able to select entries, which revealed a fascinating range of invaluable detail.

Pat explains: "Lilian had a pauper's grave – just a patch of grass, with no headstone. It was a great sadness to my Dad – he showed me where it was. He thought the world of his mother. Madge broke his heart too, because Reg promised his Mum, on her death bed, to look after her – and he did. My Dad was a lovely man."

Dennis confirms, "Our deceased cousin David, Bernard's son, told me that Lilian was actually buried at Brandwood End, just down the Alcester Road. This was pre-Internet – I went to the Library and got the index for Brandwood End – I had the approximate date of her death, 1926 – and got the reference from the Curator and he showed me where it was: just a grassed area. Eustace is buried in Brandwood End too, so that would make sense, because he died the following year – 1927, in less than a year."

Just eight months after his mother's death Reg married Nellie Bartlett in Birmingham, on 18 July 1927. Hopefully, Eustace would have been there too, although only four days later, he suffered a fall at 65 Brunswick … and died in Selly Oak Hospital, ladies and gentlemen.

At the old Birmingham Central Library they had the church records for Saint Paul's Road… this was for about 1927, or thereabouts. There's an entry for Reg's christening. Although he was born in 1904, he had to be christened, because he was marrying Nellie in St Paul's. It just shows his name – and his parents: Harry and Lilian Wareing.

Brandwood End is just behind Jacky Curtis' house. What I can't understand is that Eustace had a proper burial, but his daughter didn't. If the money could be found for his own burial, why not Lilian's too? It seems particularly mean.

Pat's given me a photocopy of the funeral cards that were printed for his funeral. You don't have those if you're in a pauper's grave! Maybe someone else in his family provided the money for his funeral? One pauper's grave, after all, is more than enough!

Reg and Nellie's Wedding, 18 July 1927.

According to Dennis, "My father, Larry, started work when he was thirteen, in 1926, at the *Custard Factory,* in Digbeth. Bernard already had a job. Larry wanted Elsie and Una to stay at home to look after Harry, Madge and baby, Audrey.

"But the girls decided to go out to work, so it became progressively difficult to keep Harry and Madge at home.

Dennis continues, "I remember an old lady, in her eighties, who came to Bernard Wareing's funeral; she was Lilian's best friend, Amy Cockerill, née Godsall. By that time she was in her eighties; she had also been a witness at the wedding of Lilian and Harry Senior, before she married, signing the appropriate section of the certificate 'Amy Godsall'.

"Audrey kept in touch with her for many years. Amy told Audrey that she used to meet Lilian at Aston Cross, adding, 'Your mother was a real lady!' Dennis concludes.

We are so grateful that you have come to the theatre tonight in your scores. It is absolutely packed out – even the boxes and balconies are full. There is standing room only at the back.

Word of our family history has spread like wildfire, through the media and also by word-of-mouth.

What follows now is unbelievably tragic, to such an extent that we've decided to release it to you in shorter episodes – this evening's show and tomorrow, Sunday night.

But keep the smelling salts handy ladies!

Things can only get worse – so until tomorrow night, ladies and gentlemen.

The curtain falls as the orchestra reprise *Goodnight Lilian.* The consternation amongst the audience causes such a commotion, it is almost impossible to hear the musicians. Taken completely by surprise by this dramatic turn of events, the crowd are, nevertheless, determined not to miss tomorrow evening's show!

Chapter Nine

LIZZIE AND ME

The curtain opens on the Quayside at Liverpool Docks. Crowds are waving and shouting, as their relatives leave on a steamer, bound for America.

Orchestra and Chorus perform a 10-minute extravaganza version of the 'Lizzie and Me' Musical:

Lizzie and me we're going to sea
Got to get out – there's no hanging about!
Et Cetera...

Brightly coloured streams of tickertape and confetti are strewn all over the quayside, steamers sound their horns – and profuse numbers of champagne corks pop!

On a raised platform, near front of stage, is an interior, 1920s-style setting. Harry Senior is reading about the steamer departure, in his local newspaper, seated in his favourite leather armchair, at 65 Brunswick. His mistress, Lizzie, has been giving him a difficult time...

Half-way through, some of the performers climb the stairs, up to the platform, then dance in a circle, around the Old Man's table. He puts his newspaper down, joining in the dance until they return to the stage.

He continues reading, while Dennis and I seat ourselves at a Bistro table, near right-hand wing. We share a bottle of red wine, and discuss the scene behind us. Suddenly Lizzie rushes on, points to the Quayside celebrations... and starts arguing with the Old Man. Then they both storm off!

Curtains close, leaving Dennis and I in splendid isolation at our Bistro table, lit by one solitary, violet-blue spotlight, creating a slightly surreal effect.

So what happens next Dennis?

"Well, the Old Man's clearly had enough. Lizzie keeps pestering him about America, because she's never going to be welcome at Number 65. It seems like the ideal solution for leaving all the aggravation behind. So he plans to persuade Una and Elsie, the two oldest sisters, to sign over Great Grandmother Lucy Baylis' legacy to him, without them realising what they're signing! He and Elsie have always been close, so maybe he can get round her… and trick her into signing them?"

What puzzles me, is if money had been left by the Baylis Family, for the Wareing Family, why didn't Eustace have some money of his own?

"Well his mother, Lucy Baylis, left a will, which was quite detailed," Dennis explains. "He's mentioned in the will, but he had to pay back some money that he'd borrowed, although there *was* money for his daughter and her children. It looked as if she trusted Lilian but she'd had to bypass Eustace. This was after his son Horace died – Lilian's brother and Lucy's grandson."

Dennis is showing me Lucy Baylis' detailed will: she was Lilian's Grandmother. It says:

'For the benefit of my said daughter, Florence Midgeley, and the other three trusts, hereinafter expressed.'

It also mentions: 'My said son, Eustace Baylis…' Lucy died in February 1900 to give us some idea about the chronology.

"She refers to 'My son, Alfred Lewis Baylis'," continues Dennis, "'with regard to the business, now carried on by me, in partnership with him, under the style or form of *Baylis Lewis & Company* and between my said Trustees – Executors et cetera'.

Shop frontage marks the former premises of Baylis, Lewis & Co. Photographer – Dennis Wareing.

"She refers to Charles Herbert Baylis, who is Eustace Baylis' younger brother. Also in the will, it does rather confirm the fact that there was a lump sum of money – £1,000, left in a Trust Fund, which would be settled on Lilian."

My Mum said that the Wareing sisters wouldn't previously have wanted to be seen anywhere *near* back-to-back houses. But when the family was evicted from Brunswick Road they were forced to live in Lincoln Street, which is at the back of Calthorpe Park. So as you go from the Pershore Road, up to the main road that goes into Moseley, Lincoln Street is one of those side-streets. At that time they were back-to-back houses.

"That was all part of the reason that my Dad, Larry, was very closed about things – he was seventeen when a tragedy befell his father. My Dad was married twice: first to Edna and they had a son named Ralph."

My Mum met Edna. She wasn't too impressed, ladies and gentlemen, because Edna fancied my Dad, Harry and she suggested that they 'Wife-swap'!

"Edna had two children. I don't know whether the eldest was Dad's but she had Dad's name. So Ralph is my half-brother. He moved up to Redcar, in Yorkshire. We went up to visit them, around my 11th birthday," recalls Dennis.

"My Mum is Julia, but everyone called her Sheila. Dad didn't tell me anything, but Mum told me that Ralph was asking Dad what happened when Lilian died. They used to call Harry Senior 'The Old Man'. They never actually called him Harry. But apparently Harry Senior moved a woman into the family home, after Lilian had died. Mum said Dad just wouldn't talk about it. It was immediately after Lilian died. I don't know what her name was. I think she was a barmaid."

Our cousin, Pat, has already confirmed: "I heard that Harry Senior had this woman called Lizzie. She would sleep with Harry Senior, after Lilian died, at 65 Brunswick Road… and they used to put Madge in the other end of the bed with them! Madge told me that. So Lizzie came to live with them and most of the family wouldn't tolerate it."

Madge's son, Gary recalls:

"My father never spoke to me about this, but I know that, before he died, he spoke to my sister, Jackie Mason, about this. Apparently, Mum wasn't interested in sex at all – it was a chore."

She'd grown up with a very warped view of it. Also when Lilian died, as Pat also confirmed, Madge had to share a bed with the two of them, with her sleeping at the opposite end. The family, of course, were absolutely against that: that may well have been the point at which he decided to take drastic action.

So that probably marked the beginning of her warped view of sex – it was something that she was frightened of. In Chapter 11 we'll learn that Madge had even stronger reasons to feel that way!

Have you discovered why Lilian had to sell the new furniture that she'd financed with her war wages, Dennis?

"Yes... have some more wine..." *(pours another glass each)*.

"Soon after Lilian died, and the Old Man moved his woman (Lizzie) into the house, Elsie wouldn't accept that; apparently Una was the only one of the children who tried to accommodate the Old Man in that respect. It was Lizzie who wanted to sell the furniture, but Elsie said, 'Over my dead body. That was my mother's furniture!'

"They started to fight each other over it. So the Old Man threw Elsie out, after she said, 'It's her or me. I'm not stopping under the same roof as your whore!' (Or words to that effect!)

"Harry Senior found Elsie lodgings in Poplar Road," Dennis continues. "When they all moved out later they went to live at 62 Lincoln Road. But then of course he disappears, so maybe Elsie moved back for a while to Brunswick Road, before the bailiffs evicted them? Poplar Road was only across the Stratford Road from Brunswick Road anyway – not far away.

"Our cousin, David, (now deceased) told me all of this. I think he heard quite a lot from Audrey. After Elsie's funeral Audrey told us about the bailiffs moving in. Lincoln Street was a back-to-back house; that's why they didn't talk about it," Dennis concludes.

But there's worse to come Ladies and Gents. Tell your friends about it. See you next week. Cheers!! *(Both raise their glasses to the audience)*

Orchestra resumes 'Lizzie and Me' music, as the audience file out, discussing the night's events as they go.

Chapter Ten

BRING MY BROTHER BACK

Curtain rises on an early 20th Century backdrop of Brunswick Road. Number 65 is featured on the upper left – home of the Wareings. Directly opposite is Number 70 – the Upton's residence.

Children are playing in the street; a woman is scrubbing her front step. The sound of a motor engine starting up, then pulling away. A youth of thirteen or fourteen suddenly runs out from Number 65 shouting: "Bring my brother back! Bring my brother back!"

He then runs towards the audience, shouting, "Did you see where they've taken them?!

What are we going to do?!" As he runs back into the house, the curtains close.

A forlorn Larry reappears from the wings… and addresses the audience:
"The Old Man's run off to America with the £1,000 inheritance money, left by Great Granny Lucy, to look after our family. The Welfare have just taken our Harry and little Madge to Marston Green Cottages, 'cause we've been left destitute. We've got to get them back – they'll hate it in there!" (He retreats, sobbing, into the wings).

Dennis, Jackie Mason and I enter, taking centre front-of-stage:
Dennis: "That's my poor Dad, Larry. He would always 'beef things up' that he was proud about, when he was talking to us kids… like Ebenezer Baylis – he was the connection. So he'd refer to things further back, that he was proud about – or Bernard, the solicitor. But he never talked about the 'dark' side of the family history… and no wonder!

"But as I've found out more about him and about what he was like as a young man, he took on a lot of responsibility, at a very young age. Although he was younger than Bernard – and Elsie was younger than Una, it was my Dad and Elsie, who made the decisions. That's what Audrey told me.

"Elsie had a very strong personality – she needed to – to get through all the hard times. Again, according to Audrey, she told me that my Dad Larry

101

and Elsie, should have got Great Aunt Una's house, instead of it being left to Reg. This is Great Aunt Una who was the dressmaker, Harry Senior's sister.

"First of all she and her sister, Elspeth, lived in Gravelly Hill; then she later moved to Rollason Road, Erdington. But she had a major disagreement with Dad and Elsie, so Great Aunt Una left the house to Reg, instead."

"My Dad was around fourteen when his younger brother and sister, Harry and Madge, (Jackie's mother) suddenly disappeared from the scene; we believe that they were in two orphanages, in Birmingham and Liverpool. Harry was around six and Madge was three, when they were taken from Brunswick Road, but things take an even more dramatic turn, in the next show.

"The original plan was that Larry and Bernard would go out to work, following Lilian's death. The girls would then look after baby Audrey. But, as you know, from our last show, Elsie and Una wanted to go out to work."

(Exit Dennis. Jackie and I move a step closer to the audience)

Mum said that Mrs Johnson, the Coalman's wife, looked after Audrey while her sisters were at work. Then they took over each night when they returned home. The Johnsons lived in Brunswick Road too.

Marston Green Cottage Homes, otherwise known as *Birmingham Union Cottage Homes*, opened in 1879 and closed in 1933. There were originally 14 cottages with 30 children in each; 7 cottages for girls and 7 for boys. According to my father, Madge was such a little 'doll' of a girl, that the lady in charge took a particular liking to her, took her under her wing and even let her lodge with her sometimes… which left Dad feeling even more isolated.

One hopes that the orphanage would have been infinitely better than the workhouse – not an Oliver Twist-type situation. Dad had already been split from his family and from Madge, for most of the time, except Sundays.

There's a five-year age gap between Madge and Pat. When she and Dad moved in with Reg, Nellie and our cousin, Pat, Pat was just a little girl. Dad was probably thirteen when he moved in with Reg, in 1934, so Madge would have been approximately ten or eleven.

A beach photograph of the two of them, riding donkeys, with cousin, Pat, and Reg holding the reins, seems to support this theory.

Jackie and I seat ourselves at a table, front of stage, facing the audience.

Aside from your Mum and my Dad, who were very much the victims in this book, there seem to be two 'Black Sheep' in this story, whose behaviour resulted in all kinds of trauma, for younger members of the Wareing family.

Harry and Madge at Marston Green Cottage Homes Orphanage.
By kind permission of Pat Ward.

Madge in a 'Candy-twist' chair. By kind permission of Pat Ward.

Extensive research, over a number of years, has revealed that both Harry and Madge were both very much the victims of circumstance.

One of the main frustrations I have with our family history, ladies and gentlemen, is that, had Harry Senior been less self-centred, all of this neurosis could have been avoided. Because the £1,000 legacy that was left for the care of the children, by their Great Grandmother, Lucy Baylis, would have enabled them to stay at home and be cared for there. She hadn't bequeathed the money to her son, Eustace Baylis, because she didn't trust him with money; he was already in debt to her. So she left it for the care of her Great Grandchildren.

What's also interesting is that my Dad, Harry, couldn't remember his Mum's face. It was only when someone gave him a photo of her (a family group included in this book), years later, that he could see what she'd looked like. He actually said that he thought that, of all four sisters, I most closely resembled her.

When she was dying, she called Madge and Harry in... we can only imagine how Dad and your Mum must have felt Jackie! Of course, as children, they didn't know they would have to go to an orphanage. The problem was that as soon as they went to this place, *Marston Green Cottage Homes*, they were separated and could only see each other on Sundays.

"Mum said she remembered your Dad coming into Reception at the Orphanage," recalls Jackie. "There were plates of cakes there and your Dad would stick his finger in one of the cakes, so that he knew he would have that cake! That was his now – and nobody else was going to have it! She said, 'I missed him. I never got to see him.'"

The photo of them, hand-in-hand, at the orphanage, which you can see on our overhead screen, was taken on a Sunday, because they had to go to church together. I like this particular one, Jackie, because they're smiling – the poor things! Their boots are more visible; and thick socks. It's got that 'my big brother – my little sister' look! And he was growing out of his coat.

"This second photo of Mum, with the candy-twist chair, might have been taken in the Orphanage," observes Jackie.

Our cousin, Pat, recently commented: "It's taken by a Studios, but she's wearing orphanage boots. If it was taken at the orphanage it must have been soon after she went in, because she only looks about three."

Audrey was born in July 1926; shortly afterwards, Lilian died. Because she was the baby of the family, they decided that Una and Elsie would bring Audrey up, but while they were working, during the day, Mrs Johnson, the coalman's wife, would take care of her. As soon as the girls came home each night, they took over. I think it was mainly Elsie who did that, because I understand that she had a lot more initiative than Una.

When I asked Audrey's son, Steven, if his mother had ever talked about those early years, he said he could only remember her saying that she used to have to get coal in a barrow; she was given a halfpenny or a farthing for doing that.

Donkey riding on the beach: Reg, with Harry and Madge and his daughter, Pat (centre of photo). By kind permission of Pat Ward.

I've been trying to solve the chronology of when and where Madge and Harry went into orphanages. It now seems that the first was *Marston Green Cottage Homes* and after their father's return and the dire circumstances that followed, there was also a second orphanage in Liverpool; particularly in view of what your mother told you Jackie.

"Yes, Reg and Great Aunt Una eventually went up to Liverpool, to collect Harry Junior and Madge and bring them back to Birmingham," Jackie confirms.

In Show/Chapter 14, we will discover more about how Madge's early years affected the Dexters' home life.

The Orchestra begins to play; some of the Chorus sing:

Bring my brother back – he'll hate it there
What are we going to do?

as the audience files out into the night.

Chapter Eleven

LONELY IN LIVERPOOL

Lonely in Liverpool
Oh, isn't it a shame?
For we're on the street
And there's nothing to eat
And our Aggie's on the game!

Aunt Audrey, Dad's youngest sister, recalls her father coming back to a pile of debts.
She said that he was only in America for about six months. The bailiffs (aka
'Guns') came round to Brunswick Road; Una, Elsie, Bernard, Laurie and Ida
were living there – and Audrey. So that was everyone except your Dad Harry,
Madge and Reg, who had married in 1927.

But no one knew about this, for many years, until after Elsie's funeral. They
were evicted from Brunswick Road and obliged to live in Lincoln Street, in a
different part of Balsall Heath, opposite Calthorpe Park.

Dennis Wareing, 2017

During this show, ladies and gentlemen, my cousin, Jackie Mason and
I, as a follow-up to the previous show, will be trying to further clarify when
and where Madge and Harry went into orphanages.

It now seems that the first was *Marston Green Cottage Homes* and post their
father's return and subsequent events, there was also a second orphanage
in Liverpool; particularly in view of what Jackie will be telling us.

The Authorities traced our Grandfather, Harry Senior, and made him
fetch Harry and Madge, from the Orphanage – so he had to have them.
Aggie looked after them, up in Liverpool, but Harry Senior used to do long-
distance driving, leaving them with Aggie, while he was away.

Madge and Harry had to scrounge for food, from other people who were
waiting at a bus-stop, close to their 'Digs', on their way home from work. They
would ask them if they could have any sandwiches that they hadn't eaten!

I understand that, when Harry Senior absconded to America with his mistress, Lizzie, and the legacy money, leaving Dad and Madge destitute, Lizzie 'ditched' him halfway through, so they never actually settled in America together. That's why he came back within about six months. It seems quite likely that Lizzie was a barmaid, whom he'd met in one of the pubs he went to; possibly, *the Boot* at Honiley, or some other country area, as he used to travel quite far afield.

"Yes, Mum said that when her Dad went over to America the lady that he went with was under the impression that he had quite a bit of money – he had paid for both tickets, for the voyage," Jackie explains. "She was surprised to find that he hadn't much money, (or at least he *said* he hadn't); so she found someone, during the journey, who was richer."

Dennis discovered that the 'lady' Grandad subsequently married, in 1928, was Mary Ann Budge – Mum said that Dad and Madge always used to call her 'Aggie'. According to the marriage certificate, she was from the Coventry area. She and Harry Senior lived in cottages in Holbrook Lane, in the Coventry/Warwick area. She *could* also have been a barmaid, from his pub circuit. Either way, it seems likely that he already knew her, or met

Harry Senior and Mary Ann Budge's Marriage Certificate.

her very soon after his return from America, because they married in January 1928 and Lilian only died in late 1926.

When he returned, about six months later, there was a pile of bills waiting for him, at 65 Brunswick Road. He'd either spent all of the thousand pounds, or at least said that he had! So, as Dennis has told us, the bills couldn't be paid and the remaining family were forced to move out, by the Bailiffs – something that Elsie never got over!

We believe that Audrey had promised Elsie not to talk about it – until Elsie had passed on. The houses in Lincoln Road, near Calthorpe Park, were of the back-to-back variety... inferior accommodation, with orange boxes for furniture! It's feasible that this eviction corresponds with the 'Old Man' deciding to marry for the second time.

Harry Senior drove a lorry regularly, between Liverpool and Birmingham, so he and Mary Ann moved to digs, in 7 Moor Place, Liverpool, which was far more convenient for him. Ironically, as Grandad was a motor engineer during his early career, the site is now occupied by *Bat Motorsport*, an Automotive Dealership!

Things went from bad to worse, because while Harry Senior was away, Mary Ann (aka 'Aggie') was, allegedly, 'on the game' and would sometimes take Madge with her, while she was with her clients, so Lord knows what happened there! Harry was, meanwhile, left to fend for himself; foraging in dustbins for food and so on.

As they were in 'Digs' at 7 Moor Place, they probably wouldn't have been able to stay in their rooms during the day, but would return in the evening: fine for Harry Senior, as he was driving lorries – and Aggie if she was out with 'Clients', but not for children, left to fend for themselves!

The Moor Place district has a modern postcode – L3 5XA. It's in the Riverside district of Liverpool; not far from the River Mersey and Lime Street Railway Station.

Although we can't be absolutely certain about which orphanage took Madge and Harry, 'under its wing,' following an even more unexpected twist of fate, (see next 'show') we *can* estimate it would have been between April 1931-1933/34. Also, the two main orphanages at that time were the separate Boys and Girls Orphanages in Myrtle Street, collectively retitled *Liverpool Orphanage*, in 1925.

Funds were being raised from 1930 onwards, for a new building in the Childwall area of Liverpool. The new *Liverpool Orphanage* premises were duly opened in the summer of 1934. Is it mere coincidence that this was around the time when Reg brought Madge and Harry back to live with him?! The

'100-Year Rule' prevents us from accessing any of their orphanage records, until 2027 at the earliest.

Jackie comments: "Mum remembered going to Liverpool. When I was growing up there was somebody local, living in Groby, (pronounce Grooby) who she'd met in Liverpool. It seem likely that Mum was in an orphanage in Liverpool too, because I'm sure this lady she knew, had been in care somewhere, with Mum."

"This woman was of a similar age to her, but I wouldn't know how to trace her now or even her name, but I know she was definitely from a deprived background."

There wasn't a lot of time between Harry's second marriage in 1928 and the next dramatic event. I suppose it's possible that she was taken into care as soon as that happened, before Great Aunt Una intervened, to provide money for the house where Reg helped to raise her and my Dad.

"I got the impression that she actually stayed in the same orphanage as this girl, and that was one of the things that she was really reluctant to speak about," Jackie continues. "I don't think it was for long. I understood that when their father came home, he was obliged to look after Madge and Harry, as their legal guardian."

"My mother, 'opened up' to me later on in life, about this, when my brother, Gary, had left the house. He only came back for a year, and, because of our age difference, was either away at College or had moved out permanently, so he was not privy to any of this information," Jackie concludes.

Events take a highly dramatic turn in our next show, Ladies and Gents, so it'll be standing room only, next week!!

Chapter Twelve

DRIVE HER OUT BILL

Curtain rises on a Bilston street scene, in Birmingham's Black Country. A 23-year-old lorry driver comes rushing down the street, yelling and screaming for help – his clothes partially ablaze!

Several locals rush out of their houses. One of them returns, with two buckets of water, dousing the terrified man's clothes.

"It's me mate!" he screams. "We've crashed into the bridge. I couldn't get him out … I think he's had it!"

As he sinks to the ground, unconscious, fire engine sirens can be heard, their blue lights flashing. An ambulance pulls up and the young man is lifted, carefully, onto a stretcher.

Shirley comes to front of stage, as the curtains close on the Bilston scene. She places a stool in a central position. With newspaper in hand, she addresses the audience:

A *Birmingham Post* article, dated Tuesday 14th April 1931, describes an inquest, held the previous day, in Wolverhampton. It's headed:

THE WOLVERHAMPTON
LORRY TRAGEDY
INQUEST ON THE TWO VICTIMS
CONCLUDED.

———————

BRIDGE PILLARS A "GRAVE
MENACE TO TRAFFIC."

We are told that a verdict of 'Accidental death' was returned.

The two victims of the burning lorry tragedy, on 18 March of that year, were described, firstly, as 'George *Harvey* Bernard Wareing', my grandfather. We know, from numerous other sources, including his Marriage Certificate, that Grandad's correct name was George *Harry* Bernard Wareing, two of his sons having taken his two middle names as their Christian names. So this could simply have been a journalistic error – or maybe, following his second marriage, he decided to change one of his names, ladies and gentlemen!

The second victim was 'William Davies (23) the driver of the lorry, of 65 James Turner Street, Winson Green, Birmingham.' Grandad's address is given as 7, Moor Place, Liverpool, which is how we were able to locate the lodgings that Madge and Harry shared with their father and Mary Ann Budge, his second wife, otherwise known to the children as 'Aggie'. The article continues:

The badly-charred body of Wareing (please … this is my grandfather you're talking about!!) was found beneath the lorry wreckage by members of the fire brigade, after the vehicle had collided with the central pillar of the LMS Railway Bridge, at Monmore Green.

Davies escaped from the lorry, but died in the Royal Hospital, on Friday last. In returning their verdict the jury were strongly of the opinion that the pillars of the bridge were a grave menace to traffic on the road and ought to be moved. They suggested that while the pillars remained there, they should be better lighted.

After hearing the medical evidence, Davies's statement, made when the inquest on Wareing was opened, was read over to the jury. This was to the effect that when the lorry approached the railway bridge there was a back-fire or a 'spit' through the carburettor. The petrol tank in front of the lorry then burst into flames, Davies (in the statement) saying that he was blinded and, as he was unable to see where he was going, he crashed into the bridge. He initially attempted to get his mate out, before saving himself, but could not, as the cabin door was jammed.

The significance of the lorry having one door only, was also considered:

The owners of the lorry were *Southern Roadways Ltd.* The Area Manager of the company, Cecil William Mayhew, explained to the foreman of the jury, that there was one door in the cabin on the left, which is where Grandad had been sitting. It was that side that struck the pillar. The gear lever and the driving wheel were between him and the opening, through which Davies made his escape. Mr Mayhew added that lorries were now being fitted with two doors… too late for poor Grandad!

The man who extinguished Davies' burning clothing was John Cross of Bilston Road, Wolverhampton. Davies had apparently run some distance down the road, before John reached him. It was decided that the pillars should be better lit; although each pillar had a green light, there had been several previous accidents there.

Mr A.C. Skidmore, the Coroner, declared that 'It was no use trying to invent a theory as to the cause of the accident, if there was no evidence!'

He questioned whether the lorry driver made a mistake and hit the pillar, or whether the fire occurred first, which was quite possible. Although Harry Senior was described, at the time of the accident, as a Furniture Remover, we know that he regularly drove a lorry containing all kinds of goods, between Birmingham and Liverpool.

My mother, Eileen, recalls: "Harry Senior would probably offload the goods at Liverpool Docks. I know he was asleep at the time – they took it in turns to drive."

So… that Tuesday night, Harry and his young co-driver, William, (who was driving) had set out from Birmingham at 11.30pm with a load of electrical equipment, weighing fourteen tons, bound for Birkenhead. No doubt Madge and Harry would have been expecting at the very least, a fleeting visit from their father, at their digs in Moor Place, once he'd off-loaded the goods!

The Inquest was originally scheduled for May 4th, to allow time for Davies to recover from his injuries, as he was the only person to have witnessed the accident. In the event of his death, within three days, proceedings were brought forward quickly.

Despite Grandad's callous attitude towards his wife and children, it's nevertheless, of some comfort to know that he was probably fast asleep at the time – hopefully he would have died within seconds – before he could register what was happening. We know that the 'Old Man's' behaviour towards those who depended upon him, had been, at times, appalling – but, surely, no-one deserves to die that way!!

And his two young children were, once again, to see the inside of another orphanage!

The 'Old Man's' father, William James Wareing, the manager of a Pen Factory, in the Jewellery Quarter, had set the pattern: he left Grandad and his sisters when they were in their teens; in Una's case, just into her twenties.

We found WJ's new address in London: Dennis tracked down his marriage certificate. He married a widow, 41-year-old Jane Pilgrim, on 10 September, 1907, at Southwark Registry Office, declaring himself to be a 'Widower'. So, it seems, allegedly, that he was a bigamist, because Sarah was still alive! That was just a year after Harry Senior and Lilian were married.

Jane and William had been living in close proximity to each other, before they married, in West Square, St George's Road. William's occupation was Perfumer's Clerk; Jane had no employment. By May 1917 the couple had moved to Carshalton, Surrey, William being described as a book keeper. He died that same year, from Natural Causes: an aortic aneurism, having outlived his son, Harry Senior by eight years.

Back garden of 65 Brunswick Road, possibly taken shortly after the 'Old Man's' untimely death. See page 116 for the names of the Wareing Children.

His deserted wife, Sarah, lived much longer and was eventually buried in Key Hill Cemetery, in the Jewellery Quarter. Her mother's family originated in Bacup, in Lancashire.

As with most research, the more deeply one delves, the more unanswered questions emerge, or to paraphrase a once-popular song, "The more I find out the less I know!"

Our Great Grandfather's life is a classic example: Dennis and I, who have worked together on much of the 'Brunswick' research, wondered why William James ran off to London with a woman, who had suddenly appeared on the scene, deserting his wife of many years.

Dennis eventually found the answer – which came as a total surprise. All will be revealed in a later show (chapter)!

Dennis found the dates from the 1931 Index, recording grandfather's death. He was looking for HB Wareing. Wolverhampton Registry Office, produced *Harvey's* Death Certificate, so perhaps his second wife called him Harvey? We're not sure... another surprise!

In the programme for this show, you'll find a really special 65 Brunswick Road photo, which Mum found, only recently. I've had it enlarged, but it still needs treatment, to eradicate the lines. It shows all of the Wareing children in a back garden... an absolute *gift* for our show! Judging by the age of the various family members, it was probably taken just after the death of their father.

But in view of what Jackie has said, about the two children spending some time in a Liverpool orphanage, and her actually meeting the woman whom Madge knew in that orphanage, it seems highly likely that between Harry Senior dying on 18 March 1931 and Reg taking them in, the equivalent of Social Services, (probably someone from the Welfare Department) had become aware of the two children's plight and moved them into a Liverpool orphanage, in the interim.

At least two years later, Great Aunt Una helped Nellie and Reg to find a suitable house in Leicestershire, thus enabling them to take care of Madge and Harry. Reg and Great Aunt Una subsequently travelled up to Liverpool, to collect them from the orphanage.

On the back row of the back garden photo, we have, from left to right, Reg, Ida and Larry (Dennis' father, aka Laurie). Next to him is Bernard and his eldest son, Kenny, identified him from the photograph; in front of Ida are Madge, Audrey, Elsie, Dad and Una.

So both of our Wareing grandparents suffered tragic, early deaths... and Harry and Madge, once more, faced an uncertain future....

The management would like me to remind you, ladies and gentlemen, that books of gilt-edged tickets for all the remaining *Brunswick* shows, are still on sale at the Box Office – a far cheaper method than purchasing them individually!

Orchestra and Chorus – 'Drive Her Out Bill':

Chorus:

Time to go, don't be slow,
Drive her out Bill.
Take our load, on the road
To Birkenhead Bill.

You can drive – look alive!
Take her out Bill.
Through the night, 'til it's light
While I sleep Bill.

Final two verses are also sung – (not included here).

Chapter Thirteen

TO LIVE AND LOVE AGAIN

The curtain rises on an Oliver Twist-type orphanage scene, in a large, austere-looking hall. It is boys only, as they are segregated from the girls, at this Liverpool Orphanage.
The boys are making and repairing various items, at a set of 6 large tables, spread across the hall.
Our theatre orchestra and the chorus (dressed as members of the Orphanage staff) stage a short, introductory performance, of the following song:

> *TO LIVE AND LOVE AGAIN:*
> *Strike the hammer, hit the nail,*
> *Polish, mend and bind.*
> *Work until your mind is numb*
> *No happiness you'll find.*
>
> *Turn a corner, look around*
> *It surely must get better?*
> *A ray of sunshine – something fine...*
> *A parcel or a letter.*

A dinner gong sounds. The boys file out, silently, for a meagre meal.

My mother, Eileen and cousins, Dennis, Pat, Carolyn and myself enter from both sides. We seat ourselves around the table, facing the audience, addressing them directly whenever we speak. As usual, the author's words are the only ones not contained within speech marks. Madge's daughter, Jackie, is the last to arrive, seating herself at one of the table ends:

So, ladies and gentlemen, will there be any escape for Madge and Harry? Or are they condemned to orphanage life for the remainder of their childhood?

"We know that when Reg was getting a promotion to Inspector and moving out to Leicester, Great Aunt Una helped them find the house. So that would give us the date for when they went up to Liverpool, to collect the children," Dennis explains.

"Great Aunt Una asked Nellie and Reg," my mother, Eileen, interjects, "if they would look after Madge and Harry. That's when Una and Reg went up to collect them – a while after their father died. The house was on the Narborough Road, Braunstone.

"Great Aunt Una had a tailoring business, with Elspeth, in the Great Western Arcade, Birmingham. The two sisters used to send clothes to the children, once they'd left the orphanage; she made your Dad posh clothes – like an evening suit. Your Dad's sister, Una, is named after her. Reg was sixteen years older than your Dad, so he was forty when Harry and I got married," Mum concludes.

My cousin, Pat, takes up the story:

"As Harry was growing up, like a lot of boys do, he went a bit wild! But then he met your Mum, Eileen and it absolutely changed him."

I understand there was a reason that Dad left the house where he was living with Reg and Nellie?

"They fetched him out of the orphanage and he came to live with us. But one night, a few years later, he came in a bit late; I'm not sure what would be counted as late really.

"He sat at the table and said to my mother, 'Where's my supper woman?' Then he caught hold of her wrist and twisted it. So my father packed his stuff into a carrier bag, put it on his back… and he had to go!" Pat remembers.

"Later on, when your Dad was in the Airforce," Mum continues, "Madge picked up with some married man, and she went and lived with him and his wife! When your Dad came home on leave, he fetched her from the house, because he reckoned the man was after her… and his wife. He took Madge to Les Dexter's parent's house – and they got married later.

"Madge was disturbed, but they reckoned it was as a result of all of these earlier experiences. Elsie used to say what a beautiful little girl she was. You can see on my wedding photograph (she was one of the two bridesmaids) how pretty she was. She had two children: Jaqueline, who's here with us now, and her brother, Gary," Mum recalls.

Dennis elaborates: "When Great Una died she left the bulk of her estate to Reg, having originally promised a substantial inheritance to my Dad, Larry and to Elsie, as they'd both taken care of her brother's younger children, when he deserted them.

"It was something to do with Ida – Laurie and Elsie had defended something that Ida did – they took her side – which upset Great Aunt Una. Dad talked about it, when he'd had a drink. Una had some select pieces of furniture."

Yes, she collected them. Mum gave me one of them, when Dad died. I've still got it – a wooden set of shelves. It's the kind of unit that you'd keep ornaments on, as opposed to books.

"I've got one of her antiques too, it's a china cabinet – because she left it all to Dad after clearing the house out. So he went with a van and brought a load of stuff back home. I've got several pieces of silver that were hers – all sorts of things. I used to go through what he had," explains Pat.

"Great Una's tailoring business was in rooms, above a shop. She made dresses for girls who were going to be presented at court, because there'd be Prince of Wales feathers in them. And she used to send me snippets of the beautiful materials that she'd used, to make dresses for my dollies."

"Great Aunt Una was a very strong character too... like Elsie," comments Dennis. "I didn't know who Dad was talking about at the time, but he used to say:

'You can't speak to me like that!' I think that must have been a throw-back to the way he'd been treated by an aunt; he'd say it to us when he'd had a drink, but I think he was reliving something from his past. Someone had quoted that phrase to him – someone in the family. I think it was Great Aunt Una who'd said it.

"Each of the Wareing children were different characters, so they were affected by their family background, in different ways," Dennis observes.

The date of Great Aunt Una's will is 18 April 1945. It mentions Elsie, Dad and Nellie Wareing, Reg's wife. Una lived at 41 Rollason Road Erdington, at the time of her death. She remained a spinster. It's interesting because she's named the people she left legacies to.

There are various female friends and work colleagues. There's also a Miss N.E. Wilson. Una's sister, Elspeth, married Sidney Wilson, so N.E. was probably Elspeth and Sidney's daughter. Then: 'To Mrs Elsie Blackburn, of 2 Florence Avenue, Poplar Road, Sparkhill, the sum of ten pounds and my grandfather clock.

'To my nephew, Harry Wareing, of 2 Florence Avenue, the sum of twenty pounds.' So it looks as if Harry was living with Elsie and Phil, just before he married Eileen, in August 1945.

Great Aunt Una's mother, Sarah Wareing, William's deserted wife, whom we mentioned in the last show, had a mother – Betty Tattersall from

Bacup – an old Bacup family who'd lived there for centuries and owned quite a bit of land. Also, the Lord family were ancestors – mill owners with cotton factories in the area.

Sarah's there for a few years, but then by 1911 she's in Kidlington, Oxfordshire, where Elsie was born. They moved up there from Cowley. Sarah lived in Kidlington until the age of 84 (1858-1942).

It's interesting to know that she was a 'character', because we haven't got any photos of her. When she moved from Birmingham, she passed the business on to her daughters, Una and Elspeth. Una's business address is listed in Kelly's Directory from 1909 onwards, as being in Dale End, (although they actually lived in Erdington). She is listed as a Dressmaker.

The lights suddenly dim, throwing the table into darkness. Musicians are playing behind the curtain. The curtain rises on a second scene… a typical, mid-1930s parlour:

A young Pat Ward is playing the piano; a fair-haired youth is the violinist. A petite, auburn-haired beauty sings a haunting refrain, to the left of the piano:

Down in the forest something stirred.

So faint – Et Cetera…

The trio continue, with several more lines of this evocative love song.

Then the stage lights dim for a few seconds. When they are switched up again, the musicians have vanished! The lights over the table focus, once more, on the speakers:

"Madge was a very attractive woman," Pat recalls, wistfully. "And she had such a lovely voice, as well. She had it trained. When we were at home, Harry enjoyed playing his violin. Was that me at the piano? – How times have changed. It seems like only yesterday!"

I knew that Dad had started learning to play the violin when he was three, but I had no idea that he continued playing it. We never *once* heard him play.

"Oh yes, we had a violin at home for years. I don't know what happened to it. It probably went down the well. Reg filled the well in later."

You're telling me all sorts of things that I didn't know!

"That song, *Down in the forest something stirred, it was only the sound of a bird,* was a Music Hall song," Pat elaborates. "The words were by Harold Simpson and the music was written by Landon Ronald. I can still see their names, on the sheet music – thank goodness my long-term memory is still working!!"

Jackie interjects: "I know that Reg sent for my Mum at that time; he was working on the Midland Red buses. He was promoted as an Inspector, to Leicester."

Dennis found the following record on *Findmypast 1939* – a national register, taken on the day that war broke out, for 56, Kingsway, Leicestershire:

Reginald. W Wareing; 12 November 1904; married; Omnibus Traffic Inspector.
Nellie C. Wareing; 20 January 1901; married; Unpaid Domestic Duties.
Harry N. Wareing; 20 December 1920; single Grocer (on Co-op mobile shop).
Madge C. Dexter; 1st January 1923; single; Shop Assistant (Store Department).

It's unclear why Madge has used her married name, as she didn't marry Les until 6 years later!

"As far as I know my Dad, Les Dexter, had met Mum when she was working in a factory on the Narborough Road, which was pretty near to the Midland Red Bus Station," Jackie explains. "Dad was working for a local branch of *Jones & Shipman*, this end of Leicestershire. He had gone to look at a job or a machine at the factory where Mum was working and had been knocked out by her beauty. He struck up a conversation and took her out."

I understood that she went to live with another guy, who worked at the factory – and his wife. Prior to that she'd been living with Reg and Nellie, but couldn't get on with Nellie. Madge thought that Nellie just regarded her as some kind of skivvy; Dad, I think, was usually more compliant, because he was just glad to have a home, after all the upheaval of his earlier years.

Pat explains: "Great Aunt Una heard that Madge had gone to live with this couple and was concerned about the nature of the relationship, so she asked your Dad to go round (because he and Madge had always been close) to rescue her, as it were, then bring her back to live with Les's parents, because she was practically engaged to Les by that time, although he was still away in the RAF."

We have a photo of your grandparents' house: you took me to see it, didn't you Jackie – when I visited you in Leicester?

Madge was rumoured to have been in a 'menage a trois' with her co-worker and his wife in Leicester. I'm also wondering if Lilian might have had a similar relationship with the Midland Red manager, Reg's biological father. Especially as his wife agreed to take Reg with them on various family outings – which was very broad-minded of her! It's just a thought. His natural father also helped with his promotion to Bus Inspector, the reason for Reg eventually moving to Leicester.

"I can believe that she would take notice of Harry because she loved him a lot. And the feeling was mutual, not least, because of all the traumatic experiences they'd shared. Dad used to come home on Leave, when Mum was living with the Dexters," Jackie continues. "My Grandma took her very much under her wing – looked after her. And Dad would write to Grandma to ask how Madge was. She'd say, 'She's a bit thin, but I'm fattening her up!' Grandma's name was Celia May, but she was known as 'May'. Granddad was George. Dad and Mum got married in 1945, on 31st August."

My Mum and Dad were married 23 days before that, on 8 August. So that's another coincidence (or was it?)…only three weeks before Les and Madge's wedding!

"My Dad, Les, was one of 7 children; Dad was the youngest. Auntie Bertha, his sister, was the next youngest; Mum and Auntie Bertha struck up a close relationship – almost like sisters," explains Jackie. "My cousin and I have that kind of relationship too. Bertha was about seven years older than Madge, so she took her under her wing. Bertha was seeing a chap who was a major in the army.

"Mum had a job at the local branch of *Jones & Shipman*: there was one in Ratby. She was working on a machine. The Americans were based pretty close in Leicestershire, It was a munitions factory, so some of the Americans would leave Madge silk stockings, on her machine, when they came to the factory on business. They would ask her out, but she'd never entertain it.

"One night she and Bertha went to the local pub and there were a whole load of Americans in there. That was the *Bull's Head* in Ratby. They followed her home but my Auntie Bertha said, 'Back off. She's not interested! She's engaged to my brother!'

"My Mum welcomed that very much – she needed somebody to say no for her. She'd never had a Mum to look after her."

On the subject of Lilian's musical talent, Madge was so enthralled with stories about her Mum's singing voice that she had her own mezzo-soprano voice trained. I believe that she sang with a local band for a while, in Leicester. Also, that you played Nancy in *Oliver*, Jackie, although you reckon your voice isn't as good as Madge's?

"Dad was also interested in music," Dennis interjects. "He'd watch classical concerts on TV – sit and study them. He loved Celtic harp music too."

Carolyn explains: "Reg and Nellie had a shop in Leicester, on the corner of Monica Road, in Braunston, Leicester, not far from what's called the Kingsway, going out of Leicester towards Enderby. When Dad came off the buses, they managed to buy a three-bedroom house in Braunston. This was with Nellie, Reg, my Mum as a little girl; then they took Madge and Harry in to live with them in the house, in Peverell Road."

I think that must have been at least four years after the death of their father, Carolyn, so this would have been 1934 at the earliest. This ties in with what Jackie said about her mother going back into Care after her father's death.

Dexter Family photograph: Les and Madge Dexter; Jaqueline (Jackie standing in front of them. Gary to the right. By kind permission of Gary Dexter.

"But Madge could never settle there and used to run away, probably because she was pubescent and didn't want to be helping out around the house, which is often the way with teenagers," continues Carolyn.

"When Madge and Harry were living with my grandparents, Pat, my Mum, was younger than Madge – certainly pre-teens… maybe eight or nine. She idolised both Harry and Madge – who was a bit of an independent, free spirit by then, wasn't she Mum? She'd seen a few things. So Mum was broken-hearted when Madge left. But also resentful.

"Eventually, my grandparents moved out of that house and bought a shop. They let the house to Nellie's youngest sister, Ethel and she lived there with her son and daughter and whatever husband she had at the time. Ethel lived there for many years until shortly before her death. She was still paying the same rent that she had when she moved in! She was doing war work during the war. Peter, her son, moved in to the shop and lived with Mum and my parents. So Pat and Peter became incredibly close, like brother and sister.

"My Nan died, just after she knew that we'd got another little boy. So this photograph that we're looking at of my Gran, Nellie, Reg's wife, must have been taken in 1972. This is the back garden of the thatched cottage in Norton Green that you went to.

"So, seated left to right, we've got Nellie, Una and Jim Price, and Reg, standing in the back. There's a little dog, a whippet, belonging to Una and Jim: we know that they married quite late, like Elsie really.

"George Bartlett was Nellie's father – Reg's father-in-law. According to his Birth Certificate he was born 23 September 1872. Registration District Bromsgrove. Place of birth Feckenham. Nellie Wareing (Bartlett) had a cousin called Caroline, known as Carrie – forever! And Nellie's second name was also Caroline," recalls Carolyn.

Pat, do you have any other memories of Madge?

"Well they came to us when I was only a baby really. To me, she was my sister, because we were brought up together. When she was eighteen she went to work in a war factory, which was only just along the road from us, on the Kingsway, which is a very long road.

"She got in with rather a questionable group of people, including a man who had been a doctor, but had been struck off the list, which in a way tells you a story as well. So we had terrible upsets and Mum and Dad got the Welfare people in, to try to talk to her – and all sorts of things.

"One night she crept back in, I don't know what time it was, and she was packing her clothes. My Dad's hair went white overnight: it broke his heart! So Madge went to live with a man and his wife, who worked at the same factory as her…. that was the doctor who'd been struck off. I don't know, but I did wonder whether she was pregnant and he was going to do an abortion for her."

Jackie, interjects: "My mother often gave the impression of being flirtatious, whereas in reality, because of her past history, she was very scared of intimacy of any kind. She had a great need to be liked."

We're told that one of Lilian's relatives sang in Music Hall in Broad Street, Birmingham, but we haven't yet been able to discover who she was. According to Jackie, it was when Elsie told Madge about that, that she decided to have her voice trained.

"Yes, she still lived at home with us, when she had her voice trained," Pat recalls. "Madge used to sing with a little band, in *Lewis's* Restaurant, in Leicester. She got hooked up with a bloke in that! I only heard her sing at home."

We seem to be a family of singers: Carolyn is, I am, Madge was and Jaqueline. It seems as though that musical gene has been passed on to us from Lilian.

"Yes, and Elizabeth sings too – one of my other daughters," Pat remarks. "It's certainly not a Wareing gene, because we haven't got any in us!"

That's a really positive talent of Madge's, in contrast with much darker aspects of her personality. For example, Madge ripped up most of their family photos, so I'm giving copies of some of mine, to Jackie. Madge had a phobia – linked to having children and family. Probably directly linked with losing Lilian when she was three.

Nellie, Una, Jim and Reg. By kind permission of Pat Ward.

"From the age of twelve, I used to look after Madge," Jackie recalls. "Our roles were reversed!"

"That doesn't surprise me," comments Pat. "The sort of thing she would do was suddenly shout from the bathroom, 'Nellie, Nellie, come here quick!' 'Why, what's the matter?' 'I've got one leg bigger than the other!' That was Madge – she actually thought that she had."

The account that I heard was that Madge didn't like Nellie asking her to do any chores. She used to say that Nellie was using her as a skivvy. Now Dad being the quieter type, *usually* did as he was asked. He was quite domesticated by the time I knew him.

"She only really ran away that time that I told you about, when she packed her clothes. She never went off for a night, because she sometimes worked nights on this war work, at the factory. Then she came in during the morning. But when she really did run away, I used to go and sit on my bike in Ayleston. I'd watch her come along in this car, it didn't have a top, so her red hair would be blowing in the breeze. The ex-doctor would be driving," remembers Pat.

"Because of the rare occasions that they had cakes in the orphanage," she continues, "when Harry and Madge came to live with Mum, if there were cakes on the table on a Sunday – we didn't have that many cakes – they would stand behind their chairs, with their hand on the cake that they were going to have! It used to annoy my mother greatly."

For the most part, Dad was a caring family man, when I was growing up, but there was another side to him.

"This was something that came up in conversations – the fact that Harry had a bad temper – I did know that," acknowledges Pat. "He used to fall out with my Dad a lot. Reg used to say, 'The trouble with you is that you're just like your father!' So he sat hard on him, to try to prevent that side of him coming to the fore."

This photo that we're looking at, with Madge and Pat, in the back garden, would have been taken at 56 Kingsway Leicester.

"Or, before that, it could have been Peverell Road, in Leicester," interjects Pat. "Looking at the houses in the photo, that's the most likely location of the two. We lived there before the Kingsway."

Dennis, wasn't that interesting about Ida, the music teacher? Because although she was an 'in-law' it shows that there was a musical-cultural circle within the family.

"Yes, this also links in with my father, Larry. If there was a piano concert on TV, he would always sit down and really listen to it, as though he could follow it. Also, with the theatrical side, I went to tap-dancing lessons and then to ballroom dancing lessons, until the other lads at school found out and started to take the mickey out of me! But I used to organise theatrical shows for myself and my sisters."

My sister, Caroline and I used to organise shows with the neighbourhood children and then perform them on a grassy area at the top of Shirley Park Road; sometimes in each other's back gardens too. We'd even sell tickets! I'll tell you more about it in Show 15.

"I did mine here – in the house," replies Dennis. "We'd perform them for my parents – on a Saturday afternoon. They were mostly musical things, so we had a very basic record player and we had some 45s that were given to us. We had a few of our own too. From the 50s – like *Does Your Chewing Gum Lose its Flavour* et cetera. I used to mime to them.

"I designed costumes for us to wear as well, for myself and my sisters. I put them together from old dressing-up clothes. This was between the ages of 6 and 11.

"Dad used to say, 'You've got it!' As though it was something that was in the family. I think he was talking about this theatrical/musical gene. This is quite funny, but when he'd had a drink in the bar (he never drank at home), of the *Three Horses* pub or the *Country Girl*, he used to sing a line from *Oh Danny Boy*. But then he'd stop – that was all he sang! He had a tenor voice," Dennis recalls.

When I was a teacher, I used to produce all kinds of musicals, pantomimes and plays. We did *The Wizard of Oz* the one year, with staff and primary school pupils, playing the parts, I was the scarecrow and our deputy head played a rather 'camp' wizard! I was in an Amateur Dramatics Group as well, Dennis. I still sing solos now, with the Choir that I belong to.

"I also used to make cardboard, Victorian-style theatres, from shoeboxes," Dennis adds. "I used to draw the characters – copying them from library books – and put them on sticks. It was a Box Theatre. The characters' voices were largely me, but I think I might have roped my sister, Lilian in, to do some of it!"

Madge's son, Gary, joins us – taking a seat alongside his sister.

"Sorry I'm late – the traffic was awful! I've just been listening, offstage, to what you've been saying, about Mum. That's really made me think, because I can never remember my mother being bubbly and enthusiastic, like that!"

And yet she'd have to have a certain amount of confidence, to perform to an audience, at lunchtime sessions, with a band, Gary.

"Absolutely!"

The family members from the table, descend in two groups, down steps on either side of the stage, to reserved seats, in the second row of the audience.

Gary, meanwhile, moves to centre stage, near the front, announcing:

Ladies and gentlemen, you'll find the second half of our opening song, at the back of your programmes. Please feel free to sing along with us.

Show closes, with everyone singing the second half our song:

When life is grim and skies are grey
And hope is hard to find
I dream of family, far away
To lighten up my mind.

Learn to live and love again
And escape from this place we will!
Learning to love and live again
When the world is quiet and still... etc.

Chapter Fourteen

STROLLING DOWN
THE PROMENADE

Our theatre audience has more than doubled by this time, as word of the 65
Brunswick Show spreads far and wide. While the crowds enter for this 14th Show,
a brass band is playing a medley of Music Hall Favourites. Such is the liveliness
of their playing, people are virtually marching to their seats!
Suddenly the music changes to a new song, written especially for our show.

(Orchestra and Chorus, from behind the curtains)
Strolling Down the Promenade:
Strolling down the promenade on a sunny afternoon
Strolling down the promenade in the lovely month of June.
I take my seat on a nearby bench and I watch the world go by,
Though life is grim I can raise a grin – and pretend that all is well.
Just for a while, I can raise a smile – for Fate is stepping in…
Etc.…

Curtains swing open, onto a beachside scene, with singers dressed in a variety
of Edwardian seaside costumes, and dancers in full flow!
The performance lasts a good ten minutes. During the Finale, some of the
Chorus, accompanied by brass instrument players, march down the steps on either
side of the theatre, with audience members joining in, as they parade down two
sides of the theatre, returning via the middle aisle.
Tumultuous applause from the exhausted audience, when the performance finishes!
(Curtains close). Shirley emerges from the wings, to address the audience:

My father's framed World War II medals, which, until recently occupied
'Pride-of Place' on the wall of my mother's flat, revive many memories.
(*Reading from the frame*):

The inscription reads:
1275148 LAC
H N WAREING
74 SQUADRON

From L-R his medals are: 1.GRJ 1939 – 1945 Star; 2. The Africa Star. 3. France & Germany Star; 4. George VI GBR Medal; 5. GVI India Empire.

But what, ladies and gentlemen, is the story behind the medals?

Harry joined the RAF at the age of 19, having been in the Cadets. When he was on Home Leave the family continued to have 'Jam Sessions': Dad still played the violin.

Harry joined the RAF Cadets, because he wanted to go off and see the world, which may have been a bit naïve, because they were the first to be called up if a war started!

Whilst war was in progress, my mother, Eileen, decided to treat herself to a seaside holiday, as a relief from all of the austerity.

(Curtain rises again, on a seaside promenade. An attractive, auburn-haired young woman is relaxing on a bench, gazing out to sea.)

There were thousands of GI Brides who went to America after the war. That's Mum, seated on the bench. She'd just become engaged to an American GI sergeant, named John Sinzheimer.

By pure chance, Dad's eldest sister, Elsie happened to be passing at that precise moment, with her husband, Phil Blackburn.

(A young couple appear and start talking to Eileen. Eventually, they sit alongside of her; the conversation continues for some time.)

Elsie remembered Mum as a small girl, when she used to visit 70 Brunswick Road, directly opposite the Wareing's family home at Number 65. Talk about a small world!!

She introduced Eileen to her younger brother, Harry, when he came home on Leave.

Mum broke off the engagement to her American GI.

(Curtain closes again. Shirley moves closer to front centre stage, still addressing the audience.)

There's a bench in Malvern, where Mum and Dad used to do their courting; it overlooks a church. It was such a favourite spot of theirs that Dad's ashes are scattered nearby – and Mum's will be too, when she passes. There's a Gloucester side and a Worcestershire side to the Malvern Hills.

According to my sister, Julie, who helped to scatter the ashes, there's an avenue of trees further down – and adjacent to the spot where the ashes were scattered. She confirms that it's not actually by the bench where our parents used to sit, but it's on the Worcestershire side.

Young couples, during the post-war years, worked hard to establish a new life for their young families, from out of the ashes.

On the opening page of this evening's Programme, you will find Mum and Dad's wedding photo, dated 8 August 1945. It's particularly significant, because the majority of people in the photo feature in our book. Below, we've detailed the names of the guests, so that you can identify everyone!

My cousin, Pat Ward recently commented: "Marrying Eileen was the making of Harry. He was becoming a bit wild!"

Please welcome, once again, to the stage, ladies and gentlemen, their two children: Madge's son, retired Head Teacher, Gary Dexter and his sister,

Mum and Dad's Wedding photo. By kind permission of Eileen Wareing. Back row: l-r: Edna, Larry Wareing's first wife; two girls from work; Charlie Turner (Mum's cousin: Auntie Dot's son); Ernest Blunn – (Auntie Emily's husband); Uncle Les; Auntie Gladys; Iris Turner (Dot's daughter); Jim Curtis? Front row: Peggy Curtis (Mum's cousin); Auntie Nellie (51 Brunswick); Auntie Emily. Seated: Auntie Ida and Elsie (behind them), Auntie Maggie; Phil Blackburn (Elsie's husband); 1st bridesmaid, Rita Lees (Uncle Bernard behind her); Bride and Groom: Harry and Eileen; 2nd bridesmaid, Madge; her future husband, Les Dexter; Grandad George Upton; Uncle Jim; George Blunn (Emily's son); seated far right: my grandmother Irene Upton; her mother, Danny (Annie) Varney.

Jackie Mason, (his former Assistant Head). It's interesting that brothers and sisters, living in the same family, often have a different perspective on their home life. And when there is a significant age difference between two siblings, as there is between Gary and Jaqueline (aka Jackie); in the next chapter, that also applies to Julie and myself.

With hindsight, it took a lot of inner strength to cope with such a traumatic existence. I'll leave you in my cousins' capable hands.

(Gary and Jackie seat themselves on a bench at the front of the stage) Jackie takes a deep breath, then begins:

"Mum used to imagine that things were coming out of the fire. At one time they actually 'Sectioned' her, with schizophrenia – she went into an Institution. But it all seemed to date back to her extremely dysfunctional upbringing.

"As I had to keep looking after my Mum all the time, I developed a trait, which I can't rid myself of, whereby I keep apologising. I had to do that, to keep Mum feeling safe and on an even keel. When she was in hospital one of the nurses pointed it out to me. She said, 'I've never known anyone who apologises as often as you do!'

"In the course of my teaching career, I've studied Detachment Theory, which seems to be particularly relevant in the case of Harry and Mum. It applies where a child is moved from the main carer and the more fluctuation there is in that situation, the less able a child is able to cope emotionally, in that situation.

"So one of two things happen: either anger, whereby children become quite violent, but they can't understand why; or children who close in and become very quiet, so that when you do actually get some kind of physical contact with somebody, they can't cope with it. They're waiting for things to go wrong. They don't trust the situation.

"But then you get children, like my mother, who are very much damaged because they have no boundaries regarding how they're supposed to react, because they haven't had parents there to explain that the stressful situation won't last for ever. That was my mother's situation, in a nutshell.

"At times she'd spiral downwards – there was no convincing her that she'd come out of that. But at other times she was totally different – almost childlike. There was a case of a child whose Mum had to go into hospital when he was two. Because she was in there for quite a long time, that child shut down. He was given a Teddy to comfort him, but actually, that was the only thing that he related to. It damaged the relationship between him and his Mum. He never forgave her for leaving him – it was a very powerful feeling! But it's a well-known aspect of research that the more you remove children from their home environment the more the boundaries change for them and the less stable they are.

"My husband, Laurence and I were married in the same church where Mum and Dad were married, in Ratby. There are a lot of Roman place names around here. It's from Ratsi Cori Tanium, which is the Roman tribe which occupied this region. They took over Leicester. We've got the Jewish Wall Museum – there's a bit of wall where the Jews used to go to sell their wares to the Romans. It's a fascinating city.

"So Ratby is Roman in origin: you can tell by the way it's set out. Groby (pronounced 'Grooby)' was a Roman Spa, but in Ratby they found a Roman fort. In fact, when Dad was digging the garden, he turned over the soil and found a Roman coin. Do you remember, Gary? He gave it to you; you took it to school and swapped it for a Vic Biro!!

"Mum had a great affinity with the church. She was christened, confirmed and married there. That's another security thing. She'd help clean the church and arrange the flowers, but as her health deteriorated she couldn't do that.

"I went to the local C of E School and later Training College, so religion was very important for both of us. In fact, the vicar who married us I'd known since I was a child: he was the one who used to come in to do the school assembly and various things. But Mum knew him particularly well.

"I'm still like that myself. I studied RE at college and funnily enough, it's an integral part of the job I'm in now. I live in an incredibly multi-cultural area – but I love it! At the moment it's Thorp Junior School: I've been there since January 2016. So I've always worked as an RE teacher, in some capacity or other; it's almost like a need.

"My husband is totally non-religious; my Dad was a Methodist, as were all of his family.

"Religion is a way of identifying with Mum too. I'm also very superstitious. We have a house in France in Limousine, it's just up from the Dordogne. We've had that for about twelve years. That was a renovation project as well. It's a fantastic place – and everything stops when you get there. But it's very close to Breve, which happens to be the centre for St Anthony.

"He was a monk who had a particular affinity with young children. So I very often go to Breve. A friend of mine hasn't been well, so I'll go into the cathedral and light a couple of candles for her. I definitely feel an affinity with the spiritual world – one of my friends is a spiritualist. I don't think there is a divide between spiritualism and religion," observes Jackie.

We're looking at a photograph of Great Aunts Una and Elspeth and Harry Senior.

"Great Aunt Una made an outfit for my Mum, out of dark green velvet. Every time Mum put it on people would stop and stare at her, because of the contrast with between her hair and that green velvet. It was ironic that Mum couldn't sew, but she always had it done for her," Jackie continues.

"Mum often felt that she was being abandoned. Whenever there was a change in her life, which she felt was for the worst, she couldn't cope. So she'd shut down. One of the worst examples of this was when I went to Teacher Training College – in fact, she was sectioned.

"I took on the role of mother at an early age – a case of role reversal. I was twelve when I began running the house. Prior to that we had an Off Licence and General Stores in Ratby. It was on the main road: everybody knew it. My Dad's family owned the house next door.

"But we lost so much money in there – I remember Dad saying – because Mum would give things away to people. They'd go in with a hard luck story and she'd give them sliced ham, bacon or packets of cigarettes. I wonder whether that is a throwback to her not having anything – herself? It was always people who were less well off. I think it made her feel more secure within herself – that she could do that.

"There were these two sides to her – so that would be the childlike side of her: she wanted people to love her. People did – but they were obviously taking advantage of her too. Especially as it was an Off Licence too. You could take your jug and have it filled with ale.

"It became the norm. My cousin lived in the house next door. We were talking recently and he remembered that we had to get out of the shop, because we were running out of money. My cousin remembered that Dad was running the shop, but he was also a Works Manager. The place where Dad and Mum originally met was *Ratby Engineering* – a different place but a similar job. But he was so busy; he was trying to make ends meet wherever he could. He had his fingers in lots of pies – quite clever. Very much an entrepreneur, but scratch the surface and he was a very soft-hearted chap. Is that how you remember it Gary?"

"My earliest memories differ from Jackie's, because, being substantially older than her, they are whole family memories and I have to look at a hierarchy. What dominates those early, extended family memories, is a matriarchal grandmother," Gary recalls.

"I was living at 144 Station Road, with my grandparents and then with an auntie and uncle too, because they came to live with us. I can't remember sitting, being cuddled by my mother... at all. What I *do* remember is being cuddled a lot, by my grandmother, Celia May Dexter.

"Mum and Dad were at a Dance, just prior to when they were engaged, or when they already were... they definitely weren't married yet. An American Airman came up and asked Mother if she'd dance. She went up to dance with him, but I think Dad thought he was getting a little bit too close. So he went up and hit him! Dad was possessive as well; certainly in the early years. And Madge needed to feel loved, so maybe, in the early years of their relationship, she would like Les to be possessive: maybe it was symbiotic?

"I remember my Dad being out at work, a lot. He also went out every Friday night, but I used to be in bed before he came back. Whether I was being protected because of Mum's situation I don't know; but I do distinctly remember my mother packing her clothes into two bags and taking them over to the bus stop, directly opposite the house. Then standing, waiting for the bus to Leicester," Gary continues.

"My Dad came back, hotfoot from work, going over and talking her into coming back, leading her back across the road. Somebody must have phoned him; I don't know who it was, because I was never told. I was about eight when that happened, so it was about 1955.

"She wanted to get away; she was in a place where she didn't want to be – and she wanted out! To be quite honest, I don't think it would have mattered where she was. She was a lost soul looking for something that didn't exist.

"So my memories are more of the extended family; mother was always in the background. When we moved next door, my relationship with my mother started to develop: she had to deal with me; I had to deal with her. Because we'd moved into a shop and my Dad applied for a licence to sell alcohol, the place should have been a gold mine. But in the end it wasn't because mother used to have more than a tipple or two... and she was giving stuff away.

"Part of my job was to come home from school, clear the bottles out from behind the counter, put them out the back and then give my mother a break, by serving in the shop. I used to do that from an early age. I was about twelve when we moved into the shop. People used to send their kids anyway, but I'd be on my own – serving! There was no one looking over my shoulder, watching me.

"Anyway, ladies and gentlemen, this particular day I'd come home; hadn't done the bottles; somebody had asked me to go and have a game of football with them, because I used to play with the local lads… we'd get together, down in Big Brook Field; there was a little brook and a big brook in Ratby.

"I'm not sure whether my mother had been drinking or not," Gary remembers, "but when I got back she was absolutely livid – that I hadn't moved the bottles. She took one of my football boots and threw it at me: fortunately I ducked – but it smashed through the window!

"I was only ever hit once by my Dad, but when he came home, I was about fourteen at the time, he looked at the hole in the window and just smacked me around the back of my head… and knocked me over … that's the only time. I never, ever saw him hit my mother.

"To be fair, I can remember Mum being angry with me, but only a few times: not continually angry. When Linda and I got married she wasn't in the wedding photos: she was there, but always in the background.

"According to Shirley, although the Wareings got together on a number of occasions, Mum is hardly ever in the photos. I think she may actually have been there on one or two occasions. She must have been so lonely! She had definitely started to drink.

"I don't know where Jackie was at the time, or whether she knows about this, but I came home from school one day; I must have been about fifteen – and she was spark out on the settee; the shop was still open – there might actually have been a customer in there! I think I may have dealt with it, but I closed the shop up.

"I put her over my shoulder and carried her, upstairs, then went next door to get Auntie Bertha, to come and undress her and put her into bed… she'd been on the sherry! My aunt contacted Dad.

"This must be my earliest memory. One of the pictures that she burnt was a picture of her, holding me, in the street, in Church Gate, Leicester. I remember someone, not sure whether it was a man or woman, came up to us and said, 'Oh what a lovely little boy! Can I take a picture?' I didn't like that idea and I turned away. Mum picked me up and held me – and cuddled me – that was very unusual. I was about five at the time.

"This is anecdotal: When we went to Aunt Mari's funeral, in 2015. She was Dad's brother's wife – (Aldwyn Edward Dexter). A woman came up to me and said, 'You're Gary Dexter aren't you? Well I knew your Mum.' I said, 'That's very nice. What do you remember about her?'

"She said, 'When she first came to Ratby, she was working at the Co-op… everybody liked Madge!' Now, this was amazing for me, because I've always thought of my mother as the retiring type. This woman had been a

Wareing Family Celebration: husbands and wives. By kind permission of Carolyn McCoy. From l-r: Bernard and Beattie; Reg and Nellie; Jim Price and Una; Phil Blackburn and Elsie; Harry and Eileen; Eric and Audrey; Phil Lees and Ida.

customer of hers. She said that she used to love going into the Co-op because Mum was always friendly and always had a good word to say about everybody! I'm assuming that it was just after she'd married my Dad… maybe within the first year – so we're looking at 1945/46.

"This same woman said, 'I saw her in later years… and she was like a different person!'

"Well that really made me think, because I can never remember my mother being bubbly and enthusiastic, like that. And yet she'd have to have a certain amount of confidence, to perform to an audience, at lunchtime sessions, with a band. And when she heard about Lilian's ancestor being a music hall singer at the Royal Music Hall in Broad Street, Birmingham, she was enthusiastic enough to have her voice trained.

"You see, Jackie's whole thought about this is that the Dexter side of the family actually supported mother, so what would have happened if she'd not met Dad – and been surrounded by those people?" Gary continues.

"Dad was not only a very capable entrepreneur, but he also had infinite patience, to manage a situation like that, over such a long period of time. But in my own mind, I'm getting snippets of information, like the one I've just given you, and I'm questioning: what is it about the relationship within the family – if it was a very supportive relationship – that turned a bubbly, attractive woman, into someone who was introverted, and seeking help from someone?

"But as she and Harry both shared appalling childhoods, it's possible that whoever she might have been with, she might have degenerated in that kind of way. No matter how supportive those around her were.

"However, Mum never said this to me, but when I first got together with my wife, Linda and they were having a private conversation, Mum said, 'You know what? When Gary was born, she (my grandmother) wouldn't even let me feed him... She took over!'

"Jackie seems sure that the family was supportive, but I'm not one hundred per cent certain that that was the case. I know that my grandmother ruled the roost. So I'm posing the question: what affect would that have on someone from the sort of background that Mum came from anyway...who is retiring?

"Although Madge was very much in need of a mother figure, because she lost her mother at three years of age, she also needed someone to put her arm around her and talk to her; listen to her and understand her. I honestly don't think that my grandparents were those sorts of people.

"So... I quite honestly believe that there *was* a chance with mother, just after she got married. I think, because of what people outside of the family have told me... Dad's sister, Bertha, saw a different side of her too – they became quite close to each other.

"I think there *was* a chance that, had she been given the right amount of really loving support, I'm not just talking about physical support, there would have been a chance for Mum, to have come out the other side. Had she been in a very strong, loving, family relationship, where she wasn't frightened to be herself, I think she would have stood a better chance. So that's where Jackie and I disagree," Gary concludes.

(Audrey's son, Steve, enters from the wings, carrying a chair. He places it alongside Jackie and Gary.)

"Good evening ladies and gentlemen. Shirley's invited me up here again, to tell you more about my Mum, Audrey, Madge's younger sister – the baby of the family! She lived with Elsie and Phil at 2 Florence Avenue, Sparkhill, before she got married. Then she joined the *ATS*.

"They didn't want her to go, but she was eighteen, so she could make her own mind up. She was a Bat-woman, with the *ATS*, for the Western Commander, so she had a good job there, with him. She was working in the Shrewsbury area – that's how she met my Dad.

"It was in a pub. He had a bad foot; my mother walked in – and trod straight on it!

"He went, 'Oh, oh!!' She apologised, they got to know each other. She probably went up to buy the drinks, 'cause he couldn't walk! He was in *REME*. Mum was born in 1926 and Dad was born in 1922. Four years age difference: the same as Shirley's Mum and Dad.

"She was introduced to Eric's family; in the Lower Road, Harmer Hill, just the other side of Shrewsbury. There were five in his family, but, if you remember, they were also looking after a handicapped uncle. He was a little devil! His name was Ellis and one of his chores was to go up to the local pump, for water.

"They decided to get married, but tell no one. That was a shock to Eric's mother. They just went off and got married in Birmingham, with a couple of witnesses. But it was just after the war and there was nowhere to live. So they went into a Nissan Hut. A bit like Elsie being worried about the bailiffs – my mother was worried, because that was their first place. It was on Sleap Aerodrome, (pronounced Slape). They lived there for about eighteen months and then they got a nice council house in Myddle. I was born in 1952.

"My Mum used to enjoy a party; she used to invite people in like Reg and Bernard, Phil, Una and so on. Especially on New Years' Day, which is when she and Dad got married. My Mum was always singing; I don't know anybody who sang as much as my Mum. Dad used to like that: when there was a programme on, like *Opportunity Knocks*, or something like that, he'd say, 'Audrey can sing a lot better than her!'

"When I've had problems in my life, I've started singing things like *Blue River, Que Sera Sera*. I think I'm a tenor – that's what they said when I tried for the Church Choir – there's another story there! So she was always singing… I'm sure she'd come through in song! Recently I've had a split-up and that one called *Get Along Without You Now* – I've had that one come through when I've been gardening – and I thought: 'where's that come from?!' Audrey was a very bubbly, chirpy person – as you said Gary – your Mum would probably have been like that, if she hadn't had such an unhappy childhood.

"She had a really good sense of humour," Steven continues. "She could be quite funny, without knowing it. A cousin on my Dad, Eric Roger's side used to come and stop with him and Audrey. Mum would do something and she'd have people in stitches!

"But time's run out for this evening – Shirley's only given me ten minutes, but I'll tell you even more about Mum and Dad in Show 18 – don't miss that one, ladies and gents!"

(Shirley re-enters), on cue!

One of the things that keeps bothering me about our family story, ladies and gentlemen, (and I can't seem to shake it!) is if Harry Senior had been less self-centred, all of these disrupted lives could have been avoided. Lucy Baylis had the foresight to plan for her Great Grandchildren's future. She'd have turned in her grave, had she known what was going to happen to them!

Thank you so much for coming... see you next week! And when you arrive home tonight, let's hope it's to a family who are at peace with themselves!

Chapter Fifteen

SISTERS

Spotlight on stage. Shirley seated on stage. Curtains closed.
Early memories: Caroline's only two years old. We're in an upstairs bedroom. It's night-time. We've been fostered out to Mrs Taylor (as we'll call her). Dad's just come to visit. I'm four years old, but I can't stand another minute of this! She makes me wipe my sister's backside – and sends me with money, to the local butcher's. I've not even started school.

She gives us the most vile-tasting oxtail soup and other atrocities. Last time Dad visited, she told him everything was ok. Someone has to look after us, 'cause Dad has to work – and Mum's in hospital, with pleurisy… which sounds really bad!

If we're not careful Caroline, Dad will go home again, thinking everything's alright – and we'll be left to fend for ourselves again, in this hell-hole!

So we scream – shout – make as much noise as we can. Footsteps coming upstairs. Dad's in the room – and we're crying buckets: "Take us home Dad – please … we can't stay here – it's horrible!"

We're with Nanny Upton now. She's been looking after Evie, but she's now got three of us. I'm going to start school at Pitmaston Nursery… less pressure on Nan.

Nan's out with the three of us; Caroline in a pushchair. What a handful!

Evie's run across the road. The rest of us are stranded on the other side.

A huge Alsatian dog, saliva dripping from its jowls, comes bounding up to Evie. Nan's with Caroline and me, on the other pavement… helpless to do anything!

Alsatian jumps on Evie – knocks her flying – she hits her head – crack! On the pavement. She's rushed to hospital with concussion.

Can things get any worse? Dad brought us to stay with Nan, after that awful Mrs Taylor …

And now this happens!!

We're walking through Shirley Park, along the passage by the Rugby Club and out onto Hasluck's Green Road. Once there, we head for the Stratford Road, Hall Green, on this beautiful Sunday morning.

Three sisters, c.1952: Yvonne, Caroline and Shirley.

Through another walkway by Gilbert's Glass… brings us out opposite Redstone Farm Road. Then a network of small roads, leading to Nan's house, opposite the Green at 156, Hazleville Road. It's a magical journey – 'cause the passageways cut out miles – and you're there before you know it.

There's Evie, (Yvonne – the eldest); Caroline, who's about eight now – and me – the middle one – almost ten years old. Julie's at home: she's only two, so her little legs can't toddle this far.

We love going to our Nan's. Big old brown leather furniture; Grandad's brass fire-irons from India – and lots of scrumptious cakes and orange squash – sheer heaven!!

Shouts from behind the curtains: "Don't let them in yet – the show's not starting yet!"
"Have you got the tickets ready Valerie? There's people queuing already!"
"Is everyone in place? Good luck – here we go!"
(Curtains swing back)
Two young girls, one blonde, the other, golden-brown, start to sing:
Sisters, sisters, never were there such devoted sisters, etc.
(We point to each other at the appropriate time!)

Song continues for several verses, followed by other performances, from Shirley Park Road children: jugglers, dancers and comedians.
(Curtains close, when the show ends)

That was Caroline and myself, singing the duet, ladies and gentlemen. We'd rehearsed all of the acts for weeks – on the grassy area at the top of Shirley Park Road – 'til we thought they were perfect.

(Jackie Mason, Madge's daughter, joins me, together with two other cousins, Dennis Wareing's sisters, Caroline and Lilian: the daughters of Larry – Dad's older brother. We seat ourselves on a blue suede sofa, front centre stage):

You know, Jackie, my Dad couldn't even remember his Mum's face. It was only when someone gave him a photo of her (family group), years later, that he could see what Lilian looked like. He thought that, of all four sisters, I most resembled her. But as children, we had no idea how traumatic Dad's childhood had been.

"Mum said she remembered your Dad coming into Reception at the orphanage, Shirley. There were plates of cakes there and your Dad would stick his finger in one of the cakes, so that he knew he would have that cake! That was his now – and nobody else was going to have it! She said, 'I missed him. I never got to see him.' The orphanage photo of them was taken on a Sunday, because they had to go to church together."

That explains why Dad was so possessive, Jackie. Mum remembered them being invited to social occasions with friends, but Dad would say no, because Mum was very pretty and he was afraid one of his friends might go off with her; echoes of the 'finger in the cake' episode!

The most important thing to Dad was to have a stable family life of his own – because he'd never had one. In the end, he had four girls, making a family of six. Most of the time he was a kind family man – and he never deserted us like his father and grandfather had with their families. He tried the police force, then the BSA and finally the Post Office, where he stayed for the rest of his working life. So he was always a good provider and often very tired, because he worked double shifts, to make enough money to keep us all.

But he had smoked cigarettes, since he was about thirteen. He used to hang out of Nellie and Reg's window, when he was smoking, so that they couldn't smell the smoke. As a result of starting at such a young age, he became addicted.

"Well Mum was a chain smoker," Jackie interjects. "In her seventies she had her lungs stripped. It wasn't the actual smoking that killed her, but the stripping of her lungs. I remember the doctor saying, when she was really ill, that the process had caused so much damage."

Cousin Lilian recalls: "Our Dad, Larry, was never an extrovert, but he had his opinions; he'd make them in a quiet way – not shouting or anything."

He sounds a bit more laid-back than my Dad: you couldn't discuss anything with him, if he'd run out of cigarettes. He eventually stopped smoking at 46, but the damage had already been done, health-wise.

Caroline, Lilian's younger sister takes a different view: "Dad had a short temper: when he'd had a drink he'd become quite sarcastic and argumentative – he'd try to cause arguments. I think you were alright as long as you didn't answer him back."

We had exactly the same problem with my Dad. When he hadn't had a cigarette, if you answered him back, he was liable to hit us.

"I always used to answer Dad back. The same applied to Dennis, so they didn't get on. But Lilian kept quiet," explains Caroline.

"I felt sorry for him really: he'd had quite a few disappointments in life. I think Dad and I were very similar because we were normally quiet; Dennis and Caroline were more outspoken. That's why they clashed more with Dad," Lilian elaborates.

My Dad took it out on Yvonne and myself; occasionally Caroline. Unfortunately, because Yvonne (aka 'Evie') didn't have the same reasoning powers as Caroline and myself, she came off worse: she would often 'answer him back', as he used to put it – he couldn't abide that!!

Evie would cower in the corner of our kitchen, her arms across her head to protect her face as best she could: "Don't hit me Dad… I'm sorry!" Then shrieks as he hit her, regardless, not understanding that she didn't realise she'd done anything wrong.

Over the years, this happened quite a lot, when he was out of cigarettes. Finally, I could stand it no longer and started stepping in, between Evie and Dad, when he was about to hit her. But that made him angrier still – and he hit me too!

Until my teens, I went to Sunday School and sang in the church choir every Sunday – went to Choir Practice. God was almost like a surrogate father for me, particularly when I was going through a bad patch with Dad. It was a comfort for me – it helped me to feel loved, like it did for Madge … and you Jackie.

I had a similar experience to yours, of running the house, but for very limited period. When I was about twelve, Mum has a fortnight's hospital stay, so I helped to run the house; cooked the Sunday Lunch and so on; rallying my younger sisters to help with the washing up!

145

But there *were* some happy moments with Dad: outings to the seaside; buckets, spades and donkeys; cycling with him to the River Cole, a couple of miles from our house, to catch minnows and sticklebacks – keeping them in jam jars; picnics on the Lickey Hills. He also enjoyed playing card games with us – and Cribbage. His favourite saying, during that game was, "It are me box!" Making him sound like a crazed Long John Silver, finding the pirate treasure.

During World War II service with the RAF, he'd spent time in the desert with 'Cha Wallas', who brewed up tea for the men. So he'd often exclaim, "Let's have a 'Cuppa Roochee'!" – (phonetic spelling, because I've no idea what the correct spelling would be!)

There was one particular pastime, where I would catch a glimpse of the real Harry, behind the strict façade…. when he and I tended our back garden together. I was quite a 'Tom Boy'!

Amidst rows of runner beans, lettuces, spring onions and beautiful flowers, I'd look at across at him and he'd smile – such a warm smile – and I'd see the young Harry as he would have been, if cruel Fate hadn't intervened.

He had another saying, which might have come from someone in the family. When I'd been particularly helpful he'd say: "You're a good lad for digging!" And I'd feel so proud: just for a while his love and sense of fun would shine through – and I was no longer afraid of the 'other Dad'.

Many a time, when we were out in that apple orchard of a garden, I'd ask him: "Am I a good lad for digging Dad?" And when he said "Yes," I'd feel a glow of pride and happiness: surely this was how it was *meant* to be? I was desperate for him to love me!

My cousins, Caroline, Lilian and Jackie now leave the stage.

Julie and Caroline, my two younger sisters, enter from the left and right-hand wings. They join me on the sofa. Caroline, is twenty-three months younger than myself – we have two Carolines in the family: a cousin and a sister.

Julie was born in 1957, so she's eight years younger than me.

(With a few exceptions, we've just used one set of speech marks, for both sisters, at the beginning and closing ones at the end):

Caroline, what are your memories of life with Dad?

"He worked at the sorting office of the Post Office in Birmingham. Dad did 'shift' hours and I remember him anxiously waiting for the preparation of his sandwiches by Mum, before catching his bus from Shirley to Birmingham.

We used to assist my Dad with getting cigarettes (10 Park Drive) from the Tuck Shop in School Road, Shirley, which was a short walk from our

Sisters Four, at Yvonne's house, l-r: Shirley, Yvonne, Caroline and Julie.

house, at 8 Shirley Park Road. He never had the money to keep a stock of them and seemed to buy them when he had run out. He would be a bit bad-tempered when he needed the nicotine. I remember one incident when he threw one of our dolls across the room, which upset me. I don't remember the detail, but I always imagine that he would come home from work, possibly hungry and tired, to a room full of toys – and possibly he would be craving for nicotine – so he let rip!

I never went to Dad for advice. If, as a child, I had something worrying me, I would go through it with my mother, when I returned from school. Part of the reason for this is probably that he was away at work such a lot. I don't think I ever had any respect for my father's intelligence, not realising at the time that I had the benefit of grammar school education – my father had no such help when he was growing up. It has been interesting to learn, through Shirley's research for this book, that both my Dad and Grandmother's families were intelligent.

Sometimes, on Sundays, the whole family would walk from our house in Shirley, to Hall Green, to see my 'Nan'. (Shirley's also described how we three older sisters sometimes made the trip ourselves).

The start of the whole family trips was always a bit 'fraught', as it seemed to take a long time for us all to leave the house and Dad didn't like hanging around.

Dad was tall (5ft 11 inches) and he seemed to walk quite fast – probably because my legs were a lot shorter and it was difficult to keep up with him! He had a black 'push-bike', which he used to keep in the outhouse in the back garden. I don't particularly remember him riding it though, but I did watch him mending punctures sometimes (probably mine!)

I have fond memories of him teaching me to ride a bike: holding on to the back of the saddle and running with me. I don't remember having stabilisers on my bike, before I learned to ride it. Neither do I remember going out on my bike with the family – only a ride to Stratford-upon-Avon and home again, with my sister Shirley, when we were quite young. We feasted on soggy tomato sandwiches!"

I must tell you a funny story about my own bike-riding episode with Dad, Caroline. He'd bought a shiny-green two-wheeler bike, but could only afford the one. So he told Evie and myself: "Whichever one of you learns to ride it first can have it!"

He didn't have much time to teach us to ride it, because he was always working 'Double Time' at the Post Office, so, unbeknown to my family, I asked a neighbouring friend if I could practise on her bike.

So… Dad was about to give me what he thought was my first bike-riding lesson. Starting off down Shirley Park Road, he walked slowly with me, holding the bar behind the seat. As we got faster I yelled: "Let go Dad – let go!" He did so reluctantly, but then I shot off, at full pelt, down the street – returning to him, triumphantly, a couple of minutes later – beaming all over my face… mission accomplished! Back to you Caroline.

"We used to have holidays at the seaside, staying in caravans, sometimes on Pontins Holiday Camps. These were mainly in the south-west of England; we travelled on coaches from Digbeth Coach Station in Birmingham, sometimes changing at Cheltenham. We played football and cricket with my Dad.

There was a family holiday, I remember (Shirley was married at that time and not on this holiday) when my father was bad-tempered with my mother – it later transpired that he was suffering from a stomach ulcer – and I remember being anxious that Mum and Dad would separate."

Author's note: He was so 'stressed out' at the time, he actually believed that Mum was trying to poison him!

"He looked after our garden in Shirley Park Road," Caroline continues, "growing apples and runner beans; I enjoyed being in the garden with my sisters and Dad. (He was able to guide my husband, John, and I on what apple tree to buy, later on). He shared an interest in flowers and shrubs with Mum. When my parents bought their own house in Rainsbrook Drive, Shirley, during their retirement years, they enjoyed developing their garden there together.

Dad had a go at DIY but wasn't very good at it – I suppose he hadn't had the benefit of a father to teach him.

When I was about 14, I think, Dad bought a second-hand car; he used to enjoy driving very much. He subsequently had a few different cars and driving became his favourite hobby. When he retired, at the age of 65, Mum and Dad enjoyed going on many car trips.

He assisted me when I was learning to drive, going out with me in his Wolseley 1500, which we nicknamed "Jumbo". He was proud of me when I passed my driving test.

I would have loved to have had an intelligent conversation with my Dad on current affairs or politics. He was very shy in company and I felt as if I never really got to know him.

There was an incident when Mum and Dad were living in Rainsbrook Drive, when neighbours had been very noisy in the garden – however, he found it very difficult to talk to them – to sort out the problem. He sometimes said strange things: when there was a fault with the TV he reckoned it was the neighbours, fiddling around with the socket on the other side of the party wall!

He didn't like going to see the GP with any of his medical problems: he had a couple of brothers who had serious illnesses and I think he worried that he could have the same problem.

I know Dad had a prejudice against "black men": he told my sisters and I not to bring one home! Sometimes when I had got dressed and made up to go out for the evening, he used to tell me to "Watch it," but didn't go into any detail. I'm sure he was referring to being careful with sexual relationships with men, but he didn't have the confidence to go through this with me.

He used to be jealous if any other men talked to my mother. I know now, ladies and gentlemen, that was due to a lack of confidence.

At my first full-time job, at the age of 18, I used to sit in front of my boss – the Regional Manager for the Midlands branch of the Woolwich Building Society – and take shorthand. He smoked a pipe and was a very calm, intelligent person. I remember when I told my boss I had become engaged to my husband, John, he said, 'As long as he makes you happy,' which was such useful advice. He gave that advice in the way a father would, but that was something my father could never do. I was also happy to have meaningful conversations with subsequent male bosses – I suppose I was looking for the fatherly figure in them.

I would have liked to have heard from him about his time in the Middle East during the Second World War (Mum has a framed collection of his military medals, which Shirley described in Chapter 14); I know he told Mum about some of his experiences.

When John and I used to visit Mum, I enjoyed sitting next to him: I think that fact that he was tall and, in later life, quite cuddly, helped. It was always me though, who started the conversation; I used to particularly ask him what road trips he and Mum had been on.

So, I was very fond of my Dad, but never felt he provided me with an all-round fatherly upbringing. I understand now that this is because he didn't get a normal upbringing himself."

Thank you Caroline. Now, we lost our older sister, Yvonne, to Ovarian Cancer, in November, 2008, just before her 62nd Birthday:

"As children, I remember Yvonne doing a lot of reading on her own, in her bedroom. Shirley and I used to go out and play – most memorably we organised singing, like you've just seen, in friends' back gardens, where we performed popular songs of the time, such as the title of this chapter: 'Sisters, Sisters, never were there such devoted sisters!' Yvonne didn't join in with these," Caroline recalls.

"In the early 1970s, Yvonne and I lived together for a while in a bed-sitter flat, adjoining a smart house in Ulverley Green Road, Olton. I was 19 and Yvonne was 23. At the same sort of time we enjoyed a two-centre holiday together, starting with the Tyrol, in Austria, with which we both fell instantly in love – with the mountains, the pretty villages and the people. We were amused when we watched the leder-hosen clad young Austrian men, smacking their thighs and dancing!

We were whisked away on a coach to Rimini, on the Adriatic Riviera, for the second week, which was like the Blackpool of Italy (even in 1970) and we pined for Austria. The only way to cheer ourselves up was to go on day excursions, to places like Florence.

We were so inspired to return to Austria and learn more about the people that we enrolled for German night-school, which we continued for three years. It was so nice to share this interest in foreign languages with Yvonne, who was also very good at French. We booked another holiday in Austria, this time for a fortnight, to Alpbach in the Tyrol; we were with another two friends and we enjoyed lots of mountain walking, rewarding ourselves, on our return to the hotel, with scrumptious, huge Austrian sickly gateaux. Although this time together was only a few years, they were precious years for me, which I will never forget.

I was a member of Solihull YHA and used to go away for weekends with the group. On a few occasions, Yvonne came with us; however, she was quite nervous on some of the scrambling-type of walks we did in the mountains: we had to help her negotiate some of the less straightforward walks.

Yvonne was shy and lacking in confidence, whereas Shirley and I were much more outgoing and sociable.

So, apart from the brief time with Yvonne in the early 1970s, I regret I never really got to know her well. At family parties, I would like to sit next to her and find out what she had been doing. Her daughter, Heather, would very often be sitting next to her at parties. Heather blossomed when she met her present husband, Gary, and it was so nice that Gary and Heather arranged to get married, after Yvonne had been diagnosed with terminal cancer, so she was able to witness their happiness.

By contrast, I feel that I know Shirley and Julie much better than I ever knew Yvonne."

Yvonne, and I recorded the following tape, on 13 November 2008, shortly before her death. This was the only possible way to include her in our future family book, when I eventually found a 2-year 'window' to write it! I apologise in advance, if anyone finds this slightly odd, but it was vitally important to include her in this Family Book. Before researching this book, I was totally unaware that two of Dad's sisters, Una and Ida, had also died of ovarian cancer.

Though Yvonne is no longer *physically* with us, we will *never* forget her.

(*The tape is played over the Sound System*)

S: As you know, Yvonne, I'm eventually writing a special book about our family, to include you. One of the things you've particularly asked me to do, is to make others aware about how ovarian cancer can take you unawares; if we can at least do that, maybe it might help others.

Y: Bill said to me, 'Well you wouldn't go' – but I didn't know.

S: If you were talking to other women about this, what would you say?

Y: You need more publicity about it; other people don't seem to know. It creeps up on you. We went to Whitby in September and I got so breathless, doing the walk that we normally do. Whitby is one of my favourite places; I like Yorkshire in general.

Although Heather and Iain have been to Yorkshire with us, in the past, it was just Bill and I this time. We walked across the North Yorkshire Moor.

S: Is that when you first started noticing that you were getting breathless?

151

Y: Yes. I'd started to put on weight, but didn't know what was causing it. I went to the doctor, just before Christmas, 2006.

S: So that's almost two years ago.

Y: That Christmas I couldn't keep any food down – I kept being sick.

S: Aunt Sylvia told me that she'd read quite a bit about it. It's known as the 'Silent Killer'. That's why it's so important that I write this for you. As you say, if we can save a few lives. So we will do that.

Y: Thank you. I've written the names of some of my favourite songs on that pad. One of them is 'It's a Beautiful Day', (sings it): "It's a beautiful day –ay –ay, don't let it slip away –ay –ay." That's by U2. It's a single – 'Bitter-sweet Symphony'.

S: I thought we'd have two really comforting hymns: 'The Lord's My Shepherd' and 'Love Divine All Loves Excelling', because the last verse is about how you're going to a peaceful place.

Julie and Caroline are going to say something at the ceremony and I will do as well. We're going to try to keep people cheerful, by celebrating your life. Talk about all the things you've done in your life – and about your family and so on. And make it a really happy service, do you know what I mean?

We'll get the music you like … and we three sisters will tell people about you, and about how much we love you. We'll get you a really good vicar; I'm in touch with someone who knows all of the vicars in the area… Tom Pyke at St John's Church, Bromsgrove: he did Pat Roach's funeral.

Y: Oh did he?

S: We'll do everything just right for you – and Bill, Heather and Iain won't have to worry, because Julie and I will help them to sort it out. It's important to me that you know that.

Y: We don't know when it will be, do we? I've been trying to eat, but it's not that easy.

S: I think you're doing ever so well – you're really really brave. I love you lots.

Evie's last letter, written in the Hospice:

I don't want to leave my beloved Bill, Heather, Iain and Mom. I could write a story if I had time and the strength. But my lungs are being crushed, so that I can't keep anything down. Consequently, I'm constantly starving.

Shirley and I both love books, music and nature; Caroline and I love languages.

Some of the music I love: Jupiter, from the Planets Suite; It's a Beautiful Day; A Bitter Sweet Symphony; O Lucky Man; Enya; Kate Bush and the Beatles.

I'd like to have visited places such as Italy and France. Tenerife was lovely at the time.

Some of my relatives were from Worcester and Birmingham.

*　　*　　*　　*

Now Julie, you're eight years younger than myself. By that time, Dad had mellowed considerably, along with his temper, so you had none of the traumatic experiences that we three older sisters had to endure. I'm so pleased that our audience will know about your far happier memories of Dad.

"Right – well I was about twelve years of age when my three older sisters, Yvonne, Shirley and Caroline, had all left home. It was strange at first, ladies and gentlemen, to be the only daughter left living at home, but Dad and I would play cards sometimes, when he wasn't dozing off in his chair, after working his various shifts at the Royal Mail Central Sorting Office, in Birmingham City Centre. He had been working there since I was born, after having several jobs previously, which had only lasted a few years.

It must have been hard to settle down into civilian life, after serving in the RAF during the 2nd World War. Dad had driven various vehicles during the war, but hadn't continued to drive, as he couldn't afford to run a car.

Julie and Mike Vincent's Wedding Day, 1980. L-r: Uncle Dennis and Sylvia; my husband David and I; John and Caroline Palfrey; the bride and groom; Bill and Yvonne Wilson; Eileen and Harry; Elsie and Phil Blackburn; my cousin, Michael Upton (Dennis and Sylvia's younger son).

He caught a Midland Red bus to work and back, but in about 1968, he started to have driving lessons. He bought a used Vauxhall Victor Super, so that he could practise his driving skills, with the help of Yvonne's boyfriend, Bill, who she later married. He passed his driving test on the fourth attempt and changed his car to an Austin 1100.

It was good to be able to go on holiday by car, instead of catching a coach from Digbeth Coach Station, as we had done previously. Dad worked very hard doing overtime, so that he could afford to take us on holiday. We had some lovely holidays in the South of England, staying in chalets and caravans on the coast. I remember one holiday when we went to Christchurch in Hampshire, staying on a Pontin's Holiday Camp called 'Wick Ferry'. It was a windy place and Dad bought me a kite: we had lots of fun, trying to keep it flying.

In later years after I left home to get married, in 1980; Mum and Dad came to see me and my husband, Mike, at weekends. When we started a

Following Yvonne's unexpected death, we're in Yorkshire, c.2009, to scatter her ashes, in a favourite spot of hers and husband, Bill. Back row l-r: brothers-in-law, John Palfrey and Mike Vincent. Seated: Michelle Vincent (Julie and Mike's daughter); Caroline and Julie. Photographer Shirley Thompson.

family, Dad would drive Mum over to see the children. They were very helpful, especially when I went back to work, when my youngest child, Andrew, had started school. Dad would drive to our house to pick up my children, Michelle and Andrew, in the school holidays and take them back to his house, while I was working.

My children enjoyed the games he played with them, especially when the weather was nice enough to be in his lovely, flowery garden. Dad was a keen gardener and we still have plants in our garden now, which were cuttings from plants of Dad's. My husband, Mike, learnt a lot about gardening from Dad.

We went on holiday with Mum and Dad, to Swansea, in 1986 and hired two caravans on the same site. Dad enjoyed making sandcastles with the children, on the beach; taking them for a paddle in the sea and searching for crabs in the rock-pools.

We spent every Christmas with Mum and Dad. They always came to our house, so that the children could stay at home, to play with their new toys. Dad enjoyed playing with their new toys too!"

Thank you Julie – plus my cousins and other sisters. Don't miss next week's 'show with a difference'…

We'll all be 'down the pub'!

Chapter Sixteen

BALSALL HEATH NEIGHBOURS

By this sixteenth show, the theatre is packed to the rafters – standing room only!

The curtains swing open to rapturous applause for the opening number, by the orchestra and Chorus:

> *BALSALL HEATH NEIGHBOURS*
> *Once we lived in Balsall Heath*
> *Our memories, thoughts and more*
> *Was it Balsall Heath, or Sparky Brook?*
> *We never were quite sure.*
> ***(Orchestral interlude)***
> *But now we've all come back again*
> *To tell you all about it*
> *Such characters and tales to tell*
> *You really shouldn't doubt it… (et cetera).*

As the musicians leave the stage, a pub scene is revealed… it's a private party, co-hosted by Don Maclean and Ken Malin.

In these days of virtual reality, we've conjured up a Virtual Pub, just round the corner from 65 Brunswick Road! It's the Crown, on the corner of St Paul's Road and Hertford Street. This pub no longer exists, but was once the favourite drinking place of my Grandad, Harry, and Eustace, my Great Grandfather. It's mentioned by several other people in our 'shows'.

Five tables have been reserved, as follows:

Table 1: The Malin Family: Bill, Ken, Irene, Tony, Dianne and Hazel, all brothers and sisters. Table 2: Don Maclean, Frank Miller and Lily Bullen. Table 3: Steve and Josie Treanor (brother and sister). Table 4: Pat Stevens and Kate Cook. Table 5: Trevor and Lorraine Williams.

A pianist is playing quietly in the background. Each person has a drink and the atmosphere is lively and convivial… they're all enjoying themselves!

The Crown Pub, *on the corner of Hertford Street and St Paul's Road by kind permission of the Balsall Heath Local History Society. We have resurrected the pub, for this chapter and the next!*

We're just using speech marks at the beginning and end of each person's memories, unless they're interrupted.

Ken Malin stands and raises his glass: "I'd like to thank you, ladies and gentlemen, for attending this special evening to celebrate our memories of Balsall Heath. And in a pub very near our old house, in Runcorn Road, number 180 something – (it *was* a long time ago)!

If I may, I'd like to start with my own family, the Malins… and a bit of a history lesson!

The development of Balsall Heath and the Inner City area of Birmingham, started in the late 1800s/early 1900s. It was born out of the idea that industry was starting to develop; people were coming off the land and suddenly wanting to find employment, in a city like Birmingham.

The first city development must have come in and around the Inner City areas, particularly Balsall Heath, where a lot of back-to-back houses were built. These houses were cheap – built particularly for the working people.

My father told me the story of a big house in Edgbaston, belonging to the Nettlefold family, which was part of *Guest, Keane & Nettlefold*. It was owned by Mr Guest; he had a lathe in his front room.

The Family Malin, Ken's 60th Birthday: Back row l-r: Bill, Ken and Irene. Front row: Tony, Mum, Emily, (now deceased), Dianne and Hazel. By kind permission of Ken Malin.

Mr Guest started developing screws and bits-and-pieces, which he eventually manufactured. So that was done in the front room of his big house in Edgbaston. We had a sideboard that was taken out of a big house on the Moseley Road. It was owned by a Tea Company and the sideboard was used in their office, as storage for books, accounts and everything.

Moseley was already a well-developed area, with quite a lot of wealthy people living there. But Sparkbrook and Sparkhill was the in-between area. My theory is that these were the second or third generation, but they were very intelligent people. They grew up in the city and there's an important link in this area, of people who were quite famous; well educated in the Arts and all sorts of things.

Basically, you have to look at Birmingham as a big, productive factory area. A lot of the families were brought up to be production workers. But our families were determined to bring us on a bit further, educate us, so that we became professional people.

If we look at the present day, 2017, you'll find that happens in any immigrant society. Because the parents come over here; they're prepared to do any jobs. We've already seen this with the Irish community, who started off in the Balsall Heath area; a lot came over during the war. Then they've moved out and their children have become business/professional people.

I was born in Milk Street, in the Parish of St Martin's, in the city centre, but by 1937 my family had moved out to Runcorn Road – which came under Sparkbrook. My earliest memories of living there date from when I was four years of age. When Mum and Dad moved in we only had one room; there was an elderly lady living there: she had the front room downstairs and one bedroom upstairs. By 1939 Mum and Dad had four children, living in that house.

At the time, just after the War, Runcorn Road was a beautiful place to live in. People didn't lock their doors. I used to walk up the street, to different houses; I didn't know the people but they'd say, 'What's your name?' 'Oh, my name's Kenny. Can I see your tortoise and give him a bit of lettuce?' 'Yes, come in. Have a cup of tea and a biscuit.' I got to know a lot of people round there, who were friendly, lovely people."

Don Maclean interrupts: "I was born after you Ken, in 1943, and I couldn't agree with you more! The audience may recall that my Gran owned a corner shop, *Field's*, which was like a centre of the community; everybody knew everybody else. It was very funny, because the downside of that was that you couldn't get away with any mischief, because they'd say, 'I'll tell your mother – Donald!' And the thing was, you knew they really would!"

"Well Don, I can remember when I was still four years of age, being friendly with one particular boy in Runcorn Road. We used to walk down to the shops in Ladypool Road, on a Sunday morning," Ken continues. "This boy told me to go to the shop and ask them if they'd got any broken cornets. I was only four, so I didn't really know any better!

I'd go in the sweet shop and ask them if they had any broken cornets. The shopkeeper would say, 'Hold on a moment. I'll see if I can find one for you.' She used to put a little bit of ice-cream on it. So I had two of those, took them out, and I kept going back time and time again.

It was a little sweet shop, right opposite Runcorn Road, which has long since gone. In fact, during the war it literally closed down, because of the sweet rationing. The last time I went in, she said, 'No I'm sorry Ken. You've had all the broken cornets!' So, feeling quite dejected, I went outside the shop and sat on the kerb, which we called the gutter.

Unfortunately for me, a sports car coming along Ladypool Road, from Brighton Road end, decided to pull up on the wrong side of the road. A young man was driving it, with his girlfriend and she wanted an ice-cream. I was sat on the kerb and he pulled up a little bit too close to me. His front wheel ran over my leg and this caused a lot of excitement in the road. My father and uncles were all having a drink in the *Clifton Arms*, on the corner of Clifton Road. Somebody told them that a boy had been knocked down. They all rushed out.

This gentleman picked me up, and the person who owned the Radio Shop, just down the road in Ladypool Road, had a car. He drove my Dad and me to Birmingham Accident Hospital. It was the old hospital, called the Queen's. Fortunately, because I was very flexible, nothing was broken. I'd got a nasty scar on my left leg, which they stitched up, and I could go home.

I used to ask my mother for a penny, to go and buy a cake. So I'd got down Runcorn, into Ladypool Road, to a cake shop called *Baines's*. I'd buy a Cream Puff for a penny. That's what it was like. Ladypool Road in particular was a beautiful shopping centre. There were lovely shops down there.

During the day, there was a Fruit Shop that I remember very well, called *Pollards* and a shop called *Westwood's* further down. There was a *Home and Colonial Shop* in Ladypool Road. *George Mason's, Tripacee's Cake Shop* and a Cooked Meat Shop called *Jules* – mother used to get our cooked meat there.

You've got to remember that nobody had a fridge in those days, so the women shopped daily, for all the groceries. But Ladypool Road was one of the best shopping centres in Birmingham. You could buy everything down there and there was a cinema called *The Olympia*, which was a real 'fleapit'!

A much more expensive one, the *Carlton*, opened later, in Ladypool Road; the *Clifton Cinema* on Moseley Road. There were three cinemas in the area: the *Olympia* in Ladypool Road; the *Clifton* and the *Carlton* in Brighton Road.

Now, just before the war I can remember my mother taking me to the Welfare, down at the bottom of Ladypool Road, where I had all of my teeth taken out – I'd be about four-and-a-half! My teeth were rotten: I ate too many sweets and my father used to give me a lot of honey. But I can remember coming back from the Welfare, with all my teeth out. I was crying. My mother took me into a little store called *Peacock's* at the bottom of Ladypool Road and she bought me a cup of tea and some biscuits, which I could dip into the tea – and just suck them!

I started school in September 1939, at Dennis Road School. I can remember the speech the Headmistress gave, that day. She was retiring and she said that it was a very sad day, for two reasons: firstly, she was retiring from school, after a long, long time. The other one was that war had just been declared. 'No one knows where that will take us.' She gave every child in that school a present, because she was leaving. I had a little tiny Blenheim Bomber: a little zinc toy.

After that I went on my own. It was a nice easy walk: down Runcorn Road, across Ladypool Road, through the Little Park; then I was in Dennis Road.

There was an epidemic of diphtheria in the early 1940s and I caught it. It could have been brought on by the disruption of things in the war. I was a 'carrier'. Mother wanted my father to get the doctor, but we had to pay in those days. Eventually my father fetched him: he lived up in St Agnes Road, Moseley. He was well into his seventies and had just retired, but he came out of retirement because of the war. He said that I had tonsillitis, so I was treated at home, although he never gave me anything at all for it!

But it's a terrible disease. I can remember it vividly, because I had a raging temperature and my Aunt Rose, who lived in Chesterton Road, was sent for. She and my mother were bathing my head and trying to get my temperature down. My Aunt Rose put some vinegar and brown paper on my forehead – and it actually worked! After several minutes it evaporated, because I was so hot!

I infected the other three children with diphtheria: my brother Brian, my sister Hazel and my brother Bill, who was only fourteen months old. One by one they were taken into Little Bromwich Hospital. The doctor had cleared me and said that I was well enough to go back to school.

Mother went to visit the three children in the Isolation Hospital; any visitors had to wear a rubber cape. My mother said, 'Well, you've got to stay here and Mary and Sarah will look after you…' – two Irish girls who came to live with us at the start of the war. She gave me a penny to go down to the shops. I bought a pound of plums and ate all of them!

I fell asleep on the settee. The next thing I knew, I was in Little Bromwich Hospital, which is now Heartlands and I was being pumped full of needles all over the place. I was virtually better, because mother and auntie had got me over diphtheria at home. My brother, Brian, who was very similar to me, was caught at the right time, so he got over it very quickly. But my sister, Hazel, and my baby brother, Bill, were desperately ill – they're both seated alongside me now!

My sister Hazel, had galloping rhythm of the heart, didn't you 'Haze'?

My brother Bill was in a cot, right opposite where I was sleeping in the hospital. They brought two priests in to him, the one night. The nurse said, 'He won't live 'til morning.'

She took me over to my brother and I leant over this little tiny baby. I was saying, 'Bill, Bill – it's me – Ken.' He gripped my little finger, really really tight. I told the nurse and she said, 'My God – there's life in him!' And he's still alive today – in his late seventies... Give 'em a wave Bill!

We had an air raid in the hospital. The nurses had to get every child out, this was in 1940, and get us into the air raid shelters. Just prior to that, at the beginning of the war, we were all evacuated, to Pershore.

Mum took four of us over to Pershore. We all assembled at Tyseley Station, with our carrier bag, tied round our neck, and our bag of biscuits. We went to this barn, on a Pershore Farm. There were about twenty or thirty families in there. Conditions were very primitive. There had been no bombing at that stage, Mother decided that she wanted to go back home, so my father fetched us and took us back home.

But no sooner had we got back home when our friend, Hitler, decided to seriously take an interest in Birmingham and we had probably the longest air raid in Birmingham's history. It took place in November 1940: a 13-hour raid. It started at six o'clock on the night, and it went through until seven o'clock in the morning!

We had a shelter in the back garden, at Runcorn Road, but it was constantly filling with water, because we were below the Water Table. So when the raid started, my mother threw us under the stairs!

I can remember, we were all screaming. The bombing had started and mother was lying on top of us, shouting, 'We're all going to die!' The thing that saved us was that my Aunt Irene, who was only a teenager at the time, working in a Munition Factory, befriended a young Air Force man. She was bringing him home to see her sister (my mother, Emily) that very night.

They started off, dodging bombs and goodness-knows-what, running up Ladypool Road, when the bombs were falling. They came to our house and the front door and all the windows were blown off. So they threw themselves on top of us and, in some respects, it calmed us down a little bit.

But we were very heavily bombed, in fact, that night, an aerial torpedo landed on White Street, blowing the whole street to pieces. On the other side of us, in Brighton Road, a landmine dropped, blowing up several big houses. Runcorn Road, which was in between the two, caught the blast from both.

Frank Miller, whom you'll meet again later in this show, recalls taking shelter in an alley, as a six-year-old, with a friend, when a low-flying German 'plane, flying parallel to Ladypool Road, machine-gunned the streets. He later learned that a civilian had been killed two streets away – probably in Brunswick Road!

We eventually got up the next morning, when the raid stopped. There was a lot of disruption in the whole area. The water mains had been destroyed and I can remember queuing up on the morning, with my father and the rest of us, at a standpipe in Ladypool Road, collecting water in anything we could find. We were extremely lucky to get through that! The following night, they came back and started bombing again.

I believe this had a permanent effect on my mother's nerves and, to some extent, myself and my brothers and sisters.

My father, who was a lorry driver at the time, working for a Birmingham company, put us all in the lorry. My mother asked him to collect her mother and sister Rosie too, so he was driving around Birmingham, collecting various people – with the bombs dropping!

He had the cab full of all the little children and the women. I was sat on the back with my Uncle Fred. We were driving down Cheapside… I remember seeing all the factories blazing. It was that hot, the steel girders were melting! We drove along parts of Pershore and Calthorpe Road. The *ATS* girls were on the searchlights, while the guns were firing. It was a really hostile place to be!

But my father kept driving and once we got up through Moseley, then reached Hall Green, the bombing was finished. We drove out along the Stratford Road to Hockley Heath, where my father started going round various houses and places, knocking doors, to see if they could accommodate us.

We came across a big farm, owned by a Mr Eaton. He lived on his own but he'd got a big farm and bungalow. He said, 'Come in – all of you.' He had a massive lounge, with a great big wooden fire. There was a ladder going up onto a mezzanine floor. He told us children that we'd be sleeping up there, which was the loft of the bungalow. He threw up some blankets and all ten of us slept up there for the night. We didn't give a damn where we were sleeping, because we were all safe.

The next day about ten or twelve of us all went to the school in Hockley Heath. I think it's in School Lane – it's still there. We ranged from four years of age to about twelve.

To me, it was exciting! It was just a part of life: we just got on with it. We never thought: "Where are we going, or what are we going to do?" We went from moment to moment.

Imagine the predicament that the teachers were suddenly faced with: trying to teach all this influx of children. We were there for two or three days. We were all walking home one day, about ten of us, in Hockley Heath. There was this plane coming down and my cousin suddenly shouted to all of us; it threw us into the hedge. It was a German Messerschmitt and it dive-bombed us. We could actually see the pilot, laughing!

I'm not sure whether it machine-gunned us or not, but Freddy, who was the oldest of the family, about twelve, threw us down. The German plane was hotly-pursued by two Spitfires. Certain members of the family stayed with Mr Eaton, including my grandmother, who Mr Eaton fancied. She said she wasn't going to marry again, because my grandfather had died.

Mr Eaton used to go out shooting in the morning, so we all had rabbit stew! My Aunt Rose was quite a good cook. She decided one day that she was going to make Spotted Dick, but she hadn't got anything to wrap it in, so she wrapped it in one of her stockings! She put it in the big saucepan and boiled it, so we all had Spotted Dick for pudding, after rabbit stew. At Christmas (we must have gone out there in November or December) my grandmother stayed up all night, basting the turkey over a fire, on the open spit.

We were still at the farm for Christmas, but we were living in a cottage at Hockley Heath, which was owned by an elderly lady living on her own. It was on the Stratford Road – my father talked her into putting us up there. On the weekend he took my mother back to the house in Runcorn Road, to see if it was still standing. It was all boarded up by now.

On this particular day my mother said, 'You and Brian will have to stay here, but play around the cottage. Don't go away, because there's no room for you in the cab.' I asked my father if we could go with him, because we wanted to see the house.

He agreed that we could as long as we sat perfectly still in the back of the open-backed lorry; there was no room in the cab. So we did that and mother did some tidying up in the Runcorn house.

We were driving back to Hockley Heath, along the Stratford Road, with no headlights and very little street lighting. We turned into this long drive in Hockley Heath. As we were driving, very slowly, someone jumped out and shone a torch in my father's face. He said, 'Where are you going?' My father said, 'Why, what's it got to do with you?' He said, 'I'm a police officer.' We explained that we lived there and he said, 'Well, you're not going there tonight!'

I looked up and in the twilight, there was a plane – a Tiger Moth training plane, which had crashed right onto my three-wheeler bike! In the yard of the cottage. So if we'd have been there... I often think, if my children asked me to do anything like that I would always take them with me! My mother didn't want us to go, but if my father hadn't taken us, we'd have been dead. The trainer and the trainee pilot were both killed.

There were airfields close by in that area: there was an RAF Station at Wythall and also smaller places near Stratford. Baggington was quite a big place too.

So that was my experience. I remember also, an incident that happened just at the start of the war. I was watching the Home Guard train, on the Little Park, near Dennis Road School. They were practising throwing hand grenades. At the end of the exercise they'd lost a hand grenade. They were looking everywhere for it. I had very good eyesight at the time, so I knew exactly where it was. I waited until they went, then picked this hand grenade up, put it in my pocket and went home.

My father asked me what it was. He put his hand in my pocket and pulled it out – and turned white. He marched me off to the police station immediately!

Other incidents that I remember very vividly there, were that after an air raid we boys often used to collect shrapnel, which were exploded shells. I collected little milk crates that were used by the Germans for incendiary bombs. They dropped the crates as well, when they finished bombing. We'd have a bucket and take all of this stuff to the police station, for salvage.

I remember quite vividly when the *Carlton Cinema* got bombed. In those days, if you were in the cinema and an air raid started, they brought everybody down off the balcony. A relative of mine, Tom Shepherd and his fiancée, were in the back row, so they were moved forward to the front of the cinema. And the bomb dropped – right on the stage. Tom had his arm around his fiancée and she was stone dead... the bomb blast had killed her. A piece of shrapnel went into Tom's side – and he had it 'til the day he died – which was only a few years ago. But they never removed it because it was lodged close to his spine. There wasn't a mark on his fiancée, but the explosion and the shock of everything, just killed her. A lot of people died that day. The cinema was boarded up until many years later.

As inquisitive youngsters in those days, we used to go into bombed houses and we broke into the cinema – and could see all the blood splattered everywhere! Again – we regarded it as normal – we just had to get on with it. But there was one family where a bomb had a direct hit on a shelter – an above-ground, concrete shelter. All seven of the family were killed; they were boys and girls that we knew... and went to school with.

But it was all about survival at that particular time. And as long as I'd got my Mum and Dad, they were the lynchpin of our lives.

At that time I'd got one sister and two brothers: me, Brian (who was eleven months younger than me) Hazel (eleven months younger than Brian) and Billy, who was the baby. Brian died fairly recently, in New Zealand. Mum and Dad went on to have another part of the family, immediately after the war – including Tony, my younger brother, who was born after the war: two more sisters and another brother; it was like two separate families.

From Runcorn Road we moved out to Trittiford Road. I went to Billesley School for a while and we didn't have a shelter in the garden; we had a Table Shelter in the front room. This was a wonderful area for the children to play… in the Table Shelter.

When my parents thought that the war was coming and we were living in Runcorn Road – and they had four of us – they decided to 'stock up', with flour, sugar, butter and tea. They took all of the clothes out of the wardrobes and stored food in them… everything.

But in those days people would come round to the house and say, 'Have you got a bit of sugar that you could let us have?' Mum would let them have a bag of sugar, so it didn't last long. And we never realised how short things were going to be. There was a lot of bartering went on. If you had a small family, but they were working and you'd got sugar and jam; we could get cigarettes, because they rationed on the basis of how much you spent in the shop: so you could have ten or twenty cigarettes.

We used to take five or ten cigarettes round and exchange it for a bag of sugar. People were very nice and they would help you, but it became so difficult. At the beginning of the war if anyone came home on leave, we had a party, although we hadn't got much. Everybody in those days had got a piano, so we all started singing around the piano: all the wartime songs – 'Bless Them All', 'The White Cliffs of Dover' and so on. Then Uncle Fred would go off to Camp; he went abroad to the Middle East; Uncle Bill went to India and then various others were stationed in this country. But we never saw some of those for four or five years… we'd grown up by then.

Some of them had babies or young children when they left; when they came back, they didn't know their fathers – they cried when they picked them up. My Uncle Bill came home and his daughter, Pauline, who by then was five or six years of age, didn't like him at all. It was rather upsetting, but of course, they soon got over it.

Uncle Bill brought us presents home, from India, he lived in a place called Hick Street, in Balsall Heath. He brought us a leather football home;

for my mother, a leather handbag with camels on it; he was my mother Emily's brother… a Griffiths.

My son, David continues to run the family business; my eldest daughter is the TV Presenter/Newsreader, Joanne Malin; my youngest daughter, Rachel, also works in various aspects of the Media.

But now let me introduce you to a very special lady, at the next table, Lily Bullen, who's 97 years young. You've met her in earlier chapters. She's lived in Balsall Heath for far longer than any of us here," Ken concludes. "Tell us about your memories Lil – no need to get up!"

Lily recalls: "There was a little sweetshop in Brunswick Road, on the corner; two doors away there was a coal yard, where people used to be able to go and fetch the coal.

Then you came further up and there were nicer houses, with an entry and a big house at the top of the entry. I know that, because my auntie used to live there. I think that 65 Brunswick Road might have been like that, with a big bay window. The three branches of Shirley's family lived at the Hertford Street end of Brunswick Road. If you continued on, that was a third part of Brunswick Road.

Shirley's grandfather George Upton's sister, Nellie Curtis, married Stan Curtis, so she was the mother of the family…. the Curtis family lived at 51. By a strange coincidence, Stan was my husband's friend. There were loads of sweetshops. As you turned left at the top of Brunswick Road there, you came cross Hertford Street," concludes Lily.

Don Maclean begins: "As I explained in earlier shows, I grew up at 131 Ombersley Road, and was born in 1943.

In my Nan's shop window, various wares were shown. Then there was a door, to the right of that window, as you looked at it. You went in through the door and the counter was to your left. The window was the width of the shop; the width of the door was where the customers would stand. The counter was then to their immediate left, as they walked in. Then there was a small gate, which stopped them going any further. Beyond the gate there were three steps, on the right, which led up into my Nanny's living room. That had one window, but a great big aspidistra, in a brass pot. So the light in the room was minimal!

"If you didn't pass for the Grammar School you went to Dennis Road School, which was almost opposite the *Carlton Cinema*," Don recalls. "I used to go to Cubs at Dennis Road School, for about three or four years. I ended up a 'Senior Sixer'. That was on a Friday night. Interestingly, in those days, everybody wanted to be in the cubs: there was a long waiting list to get in.

They had two cub packs in Dennis Road, both run by the same Scout Leaders: one was on a Tuesday and the other on a Friday.

There were thirty-six boys in a cub pack. You learnt your semaphore signalling and how to tie knots. The younger boys never went camping; we used to have days at Yorks Wood, which was some scouting area in Birmingham. I can't recall where, but we used to be taken off for a day and did various things there. Hopefully they'd bring back the same amount of kids that they took with them!

They talk about grownups not joining clubs like Rotary now and Round Table, but kids aren't joining clubs so much either. So much entertainment takes place at home that we've become unbelievably insular!

We were talking about family. The other thing is that we don't know our neighbours, but when we were kids we knew everybody – who lived in every house up the street! You'd go and play with the kids, in their gardens," Don recalls.

"Let's take a break for the Buffet now. After that, it's over to my good mate Frank Miller, who'll draw our evening to a close."

30-MIN BUFFET BREAK

Frank Miller, with his parents, Polly and Frank, at the Clifton Road Coronation Street Party 1953. They ran the General Store, 'Millers', at 70 Clifton Road. By kind permission of Frank Miller.

"Right, ladies and gentlemen: I was born in 1933, in a hospital in Loveday Street, Small Heath. We moved to Lordswood Road and then from there to 7 Ladypool Road in 1934," Frank begins.

"My father, Francisco, was born in Hay Mills; did various jobs until he was nineteen, then he worked on drawing steel tubes from the blast furnace for nineteen years, at Reynolds Tube: a very hot job! He then had various jobs in factories, until he moved to the Rover, at Tyseley.

He moved to Yorkshire during the war, then back to Tyseley, until about 1949. Various jobs, then he became ill in 1952, from which he never quite recovered.

He continued working until about 1958, when he had a cycle accident; he didn't work outside the shop again; had a heart attack in 1962; hospitalized but recovered. He was a devout catholic – and he would never miss Sunday Mass. I used to take him to various churches, because he wasn't able to get there. He died on 3 March 1972.

My mother, Polly, was one five children, born in Glovers Road, Small Heath. Her father was killed in an accident when she was eleven or twelve. She was the eldest of the five children and she helped her mother to keep the family together, because with no widow's pension at that stage, they would have been taken into care.

She took an early School Leaving Certificate at the age of thirteen and started work, to keep the family together. She eventually worked at the *Singer Works* on the Coventry Road, just below the Holy Family, in a supervisory role. But in 1931, when she got married, she had to leave work, because married women weren't allowed to work at that stage.

At the beginning of the war she got a job, working in a butcher's shop, called *Newman's*, on Stratford Road, Sparkbrook, near Walford Road, where they used to make their own meat products.

When we moved to Yorkshire she took another job in a local shop. We came back to Birmingham in May 1945. She returned to *Newman's*. She'd saved £400 and, in 1947, bought a run-down shop in Clifton Road. As she often said to me, 'Work never killed anyone!' She took over the shop, and, with a lot of help from Dad and myself, she built the business up. She coped through Dad's illnesses.

I left home to get married, at the end of 1959. Mum carried on the business with Dad. I eventually persuaded them to retire, which they did in 1969. They moved into Waterloo Road, in Yardley. Mum looked after Dad for the short time. Although he died in 1972, she stayed on her own. I was an only child, Mum having lost another son in childbirth, when in Yorkshire.

Eventually Mum gave up work at about seventy-five. She used to go into Birmingham twice a week, by bus, to do her shopping. In 1989 she had a fall in the Bull Ring; taken into the General Hospital. Eventually had an operation for a broken thigh and shoulder, but never recovered. She died on 30 November 1989, at the age of eighty-four.

When they bought what was a General Store in May 1947, it was a 'Dead Duck': very dilapidated, with only three registered customers. Sold one-and-a-half loaves a day. But the saving grace was that you had contracts with *Cadburys.* The shop was at 70 Clifton Road. We had a small contract with *Cadburys and Mackintosh.* They supplied us with chocolate-type sweets. Of course they were still rationed, but it did bring people into the shop. Sweet rationing ended in 1951 but Dad worked hard in his spare time, building cabinets for the sweets and also persevered with the rationing, with a little help from Dad's brother, who was also in business in Hay Mills.

The shop was situated just below the railway bridge and a few doors from the *Railway Pub.* Next to the pub was a house, then a Newsagents, then another house; then the shop at 70. Next door to us was a Greengrocers and a row of terraced houses. The store was on the right of Clifton Road, as you walk up to Moseley Road.

From the outside of the shop, which was a converted house, with a flat frontage, you went in the front door and you had what would have been the front room, which was converted into the shop. There was a cellar head, with steps leading down to the cellar, from the front door.

At the rear of that was the main living room, as it then existed; beyond that, a kitchen, and the toilets were outside, through the yard. It was a small yard at the back, with a shed.

The actual shop itself, had been the front room. You went in through the front door; there was a counter on the right-hand side, with a small display case; then a counter in front of you, with a trapdoor through the counter. Just beyond the counter, on the left-hand side there was a fridge, which came in after we moved in: it accommodated ice-cream, when that became available.

Upstairs there were two bedrooms and an attic room, both served by spiral staircases. The attic room became the shop storeroom, so all the tin cases, all the boxes of cereals and everything else, was taken upstairs and then brought down piecemeal, as and when required. Grocery deliveries were once a fortnight and at the peak we were receiving something like a ton of groceries, upstairs! We sold sweets, tobacco, groceries, bread, cakes; obviously drinks – lemonade and something similar: certainly not the full range.

Like Don's grandmother's shop, on Belgrave Road, it *did* bring people together. The biggest change was really brought about by my father and myself, in the late 1940s. We originally had one delivery a day for one-and-a-half loaves. When my father got involved he decided that the bread was no good, so we drew up a contract with *Hawley's* who were in Moseley, three miles away.

Dad was very particular about bread. When the baker brought it on a Saturday, he would feel it before he'd accept it. He would come home from work about 6 o'clock, get changed; go into the shop where different people would then come in for a loaf, so I would pedal off on my bike, to *Hawley's*, to bring three or four fresh loaves. By the time I got back they were usually sold; some evenings I would go twice. I had no front basket, just bags. The maximum I could carry was twelve loaves on one bike-load!

I became well known at *Hawley's*. I'd always be let in through the back door because they were closed at 7 o'clock at night. So that increased the sales. We reached a peak, one Bank Holiday Saturday, selling 350 loaves! The shop opening hours were 8am-8pm, six days a week; 10.30am-4.30pm on a Sunday. We did close on Christmas Day and Easter Day," Frank concludes.

"Thank you Frank. Let's just relax for the rest of the evening folks, with some music from the orchestra," Don continues. "We'll get together same time next week, when the Treanors and some of the others here, will tell you about their memories of Balsall Heath."

Chapter Seventeen

CHANGING TIMES

We're back again at our 'virtual' pub – the Crown – on the corner of St Paul's Road and Hertford Street, for the second reunion – and more reminiscing: this time from Josie and Steve Treanor; Pat Stevens; Kate Cook; former Off-Licence managers, Lorraine and Trevor Williams; Journalist/Local Historian Chris Sutton and Shirley's cousin, Jacky Curtis.
As before, Don and Ken are the co-hosts.

Josie begins: "As you know from our last Get-together, I'm Josie Treanor and this is my younger brother Steve. Between us, we're going to paint a picture of life in Clifton Road, Balsall Heath between 1940 and 1963.

There were ten children in our family altogether. We lived with our parents at 199 Clifton Road, Balsall Heath ... a short walk from this pub. It was rented from a private landlord, through an agency. The house was originally a shop, a shoe repairers.

My father had lots of jobs, of short duration. He wasn't known for his good time-keeping. It was either that, or they'd ask him to do something that he didn't want to do – and he'd walk out! He was a bit temperamental.

We hired out bikes for a very short time, but we found that although we might rent a bike to someone for fifteen or twenty minutes, they'd take it for an hour or more, then they'd come back and throw it in the alley!

The odd teenagers would rent them – not people using them for any kind of work. The house wasn't right on the actual corner, because *Grinnell's* was there – a Haberdashery.

Being opposite the *Clifton Pub*, people would sometimes need a lavatory, so they'd use ours, because our back garden wasn't secure. There was a gate, but often it wasn't locked. Or they'd do it up the wall!

For a very short time I worked with the Hoopers, at the *Clifton Pub*. They had been there for a considerable amount of time. I was in my early twenties and I worked as a barmaid.

Going up from there you have Mrs Giles: now she was a character! She lived next door to the pub. She was mentally, very unstable, but a lovely woman really. She used to make her living from selling second-hand clothes and chopping wood: quite a well-built, strong woman.

She used to come over to Mum's to borrow something. Mum said that when she moved into 199, Mrs Giles had beautiful hair. But since that time it had been cut short and turned grey. She lost her husband during the war; she had a daughter called Nellie, who visited fairly regularly and a son named Charlie. He lived in Rushven Road: between Clifton Road and Taunton Road, where the Little Park is.

Mrs Giles often had breakdowns. When that happened she'd throw her furniture out. One of the things she used to say, although I don't really understand it was, 'I don't want you Treanor!' I think she felt quite close to my Mum. She had three dogs, which she'd bring with her. Mum would give her a cup of tea; she'd drink half of it, then give the rest to the dog, to drink out of the cup! She talked to herself a lot.

Back row, l-r: Mother (Frances); Father (George); Josie. Middle row: George Joseph (aka Joey); Alice (with cat); Robert; Johnny (holding Steve). Front row: Thomas; Elsie; Gloria and Blanche. By kind permission of Steve Treanor.

She was a friend, but then she'd suddenly turn against my Mum. On one occasion when a soldier was passing by, she lifted her skirt and said, 'You've travelled the world, but I bet you haven't seen one like this!'

When we had sweet rationing you'd have so many coupons, depending upon how many people were living in your house; Mrs Giles sold her sweet coupons to Mum.

During one of her later sessions of throwing her furniture out, Dad went over and persuaded her to go in… but she locked the door while he was in there – which was a bit scary!

There was an article in the local press, about our father, George, rescuing Mrs Giles from her house fire. It was an automatic reaction for him – you do what you have to do in a crisis. You see someone in danger. You don't think: 'Is it PC to do this?' If there's any comeback from that, you just deal with it. That fits in with what you were saying last week, Don, about the community spirit in Balsall Heath. I think you get that caring attitude even today: not everybody walks by on the other side.

I was four when we moved here, from Gran's in Selly Oak, but I didn't have any general feeling about the area. You were mixing in, with your brothers and sisters and the people around you, so you didn't think that you were better than the person next door. Like you said Ken, you just got on with it!

My first job, when I left school in 1953, was as a checker at *Birmingham Co-op*, New Street, for six months, where the shopping Centre is now. I worked on the top floor, but it bored me rigid! It was Dickensian; you had a long desk; you each sat either side of this desk. You may know, ladies and gentlemen, that the *Co-op* used to give out cheques, when you paid your bill. Eventually all of those books went to Head Office. All of the figures had to be married up and you had to account for all of those payments, within five shillings. If it didn't, then you had this long list of numbers; you had to go through them individually! I did that for six months, because I was terrified of giving my Notice in.

But there were plenty of jobs about, so if you needed to change jobs, you could more or less guarantee that you'd get it… we're talking about the 1950s and 60s.

Steve remembers the outbuildings in our back yard, but I don't have the same memories as him, because we have completely different perspectives, due to our age difference. There were three sections: the coal house; the lavatory and the 'cubby hole'. They were all attached to the house in one line.

I was the oldest of ten children, so you can imagine that I looked after them a lot. You didn't have any option about that! I'd take them to the

'Little Park' on Brighton Road; we spent a great deal of time there. White Street had a bombed building site: I'd take them to play there, because I resented having to look after so many children!

I left home when I was twenty-one, around 1959. Steve had another four years of living there. At one time I slept in the 'Little Room': when I was at work. From there you could hear the *BSA* Bull Horn, which sounded for the Morning Shift, at 7.20am until 7.25am. I used to lie in bed 'til the last possible moment. The *BSA* factory was on the Coventry Road, in Small Heath, but the sound carried to our house.

My mother got me my first job. We've always been *Co-op* customers: we had milk delivered by a horse-drawn cart. Shirley's Aunt Elsie, during the Second World War, used to deliver milk around the Balsall Heath streets, but I think she used one of the first mechanical floats. Over to you now Steve – your turn!" Josie concludes.

"Our house was on the corner of Ladypool Road and Clifton Road," Steve confirms, "opposite the *Clifton Pub*. I remembers, as a child, often sitting outside the pub.

Josie was born in 1938; then come Alice, Robert, George, John, Gloria, Thomas, Elsie, Blanche, then me – I was the youngest: born in 1955. Gloria is the only one of the ten who has passed away.

Regarding the fire opposite us, Mrs Giles was trapped in the house and my father ran into the house and pulled her out. He got a certificate from the Fire Safety people for that – I've still got that – and the newspaper article.

I remember climbing through the bedroom window, onto the corrugated steel roof – and sunbathing! We played on the bombed building sites in Brighton Road and maybe in White Street too.

It was fun to live in Clifton Road, although I was very young at the time. I was eight or nine when I left, but I still have memories of the street. There were lots of times when there were street brawls. We'd stand in the downstairs windows, looking out into the street, where the adults would be brawling, on a Saturday night – after they'd been to the pub! But they were virtually 'kicking off' every week.

We lived in a large Victorian house, with a shop front downstairs. Upstairs we had Victorian windows, on the sashes, because I can remember Josie, sitting on the windowsill, and cleaning the outside of the window!

We had an attic, where some of the children slept: we'd get the mattress and come down the two flights of stairs from the attic, by sliding down on the mattress!

Mum was always scrubbing the front step. When we came down in the morning, we had the old, red, quarry tile floor. There were loads of cock-roaches. When the light went on, you'd see them scatter! We had a coal cellar too; there was an outside door that led into it. We also had gas meters: I remember the smell of the gas. We had electricity. From the front we went straight into the shop area. But it was no longer a shop – it was just a complete mess! The old man used it to repair bikes. Both of my parents worked at Moseley Road Baths. People often went there to have a bath.

But I remember using the old tin bath, on a Saturday night, in front of the fire; as the youngest I was probably the last in! My brother, John, who had two sisters after him, was always complaining, because they put him in girl's clothes – until he went to school! He'd have the 'hand-me-downs'.

There were three bedrooms and an attic, with four or five children to a room. In winter we'd have the great big thick coats.

The back garden was just a very small yard, with outbuildings, with corrugated roofs. There was a gate leading out of the back yard, onto the street. To the left of our house was Acacia Terrace. We used to play in the back yard, but I spent most of my time in the street – in Clifton Road. When there was lots of rain I can remember floating lollipop sticks down the gutter!

Pat Stevens is going to take over from me next. Then we've got a break lined up for you, with chicken-in-the basket and a Folk Group," Steve concludes.

"Great to meet you, ladies and gentlemen. Trust me to be on just before the food! You'll all be thinking about your Chicken-in-the-Baskets – and not listening to me!" Pat exclaims.

"I was born in Stechford in 1940; moved to Ryland Street in 1945. I was there for sixteen years. By that time I was married to Kenny Hands. We had three children before we moved to Balsall Heath, in 1963," she recalls.

"I then had three more children – I was twenty-three at that time, so I started early! We lived at 166 Mary Street, next to the *Coach and Horses*. There's a photo of the pub on page 36 of the book, *Balsall Heath and Highgate*. We were there for eleven years. So we lived in Balsall Heath from 1963 to 1974.

"When we got the offer of the house in Balsall Heath we were 'over the moon'; coming from a one-room where we were living at that time. So we agreed to have the house straight away. We had six children in all, while we were there and we met some lovely people. I couldn't say anything bad about Balsall Heath people. The author, Val Hart, describes them as having 'hearts as big as buckets' and they really did: they were the 'salt of the earth'.

"My house had no front gate; you walked straight in the front door. There was a small vestibule area; on the right-hand side was quite a large front

Ryland Street 1959. From l-r: Pat Steven's grandmother, Gladys Bagley, tries to get Pat's eldest son, Raymond to smile, while 18-year-old Pat looks on. Jane, the little girl on the right, used to play in the yard: her grandparents owned James the Drapers, *in Ryland Street. By kind permission of Pat Stevens.*

room. Next door was a quite large middle room, which we mainly lived in. From the middle room there was another door, which led into quite a large kitchen. There was also a cellar, which led off the downstairs kitchen. A door led to the outside and a great big conservatory. It was already there when we went.

The outside toilet was in the garden and another 'barn' place: the kids kept pigeons in it. There was quite a long garden, full of dahlias. When you walked up the garden path you could get out at the top, go round and you'd come out into Bath Walk. That's all been closed off now," Pat continues.

"There was no bathroom – just the outside toilet. We used the local baths – on Moseley Road. There were quite a lot of shops; the shopkeepers were very friendly.

There was a big influx of Maltese: they used the café on the corner – the *Ankrila*; there was a post office next door to it… Mary Street Post Office.

Coming back onto Edward Road again, you'd got *Peters*, which was the Fruit Shop, where they sold all fresh vegetables and fruit. Then you'd come to Sabu, who was a real Jamaican character. Everybody knew him. He was always standing on the step of his shop, in a big white overall; a very friendly guy – always calling out to people. Just past his shop was a passageway, with small houses around the back. Then a small Convenience Store, which was run by the Wassalls. I used to pay weekly there into a Christmas club. Also in Edward Road were the Roses – a Jewish couple with a clothes shop up there; he had a son named Michael; I don't know what the daughter's name was.

Crossing over the road there was another big Convenience Store, run by Indians – it was very good. Then there were a few houses, followed by a Dry Cleaner's. Coming down the back walk, there was a beautiful bakery at the bottom: you could get all of your fresh bread there.

My kids used to enjoy playing *Battles*. There were Sikh kids who they played with – and other Indian families. My daughter was friendly with a girl named Bajau. There were some lovely families in George Street. When I had some bad times they would take my children in; I'm still in touch with some of them today. All of the kids went to Tindal Street – a lovely school.

Of all the parks, we mainly used Cannon Hill. We went to Calthorpe Park a couple of times, but I preferred Cannon Hill Park, probably because I went there as a youngster myself. It was a lovely walk… and there was a Boating Lake.

It was a lovely summer's day and I went down there with my friend, Sylvia," Pat recalls. "She'd got three children; I was taking six of mine. She lived in Bath Walk. We started one end of the park and we walked all the way round. I was constantly turning round, counting that I'd still got them all! Brian was the fourth youngest one; five boys and one girl.

This was about 1968, so Brian would have been four. We were walking round and then all of a sudden, one of the kids started screaming. Brian had gone straight out, into the water! I stood there, screaming my head off! There were a couple of guys in a paddling boat, on the lake. They rushed round, trying to rescue him. They turned over in the boat, but managed to get him out of the water and put him on to the side, where they were pumping him, to get the water out of him.

As it turned out it was quite shallow, but I didn't know that. If I'd have known I could have walked in and paddled it. But round the other side there was a First Aid Unit and from there he was taken to the Children's Hospital. They kept him in overnight, just to make sure that he'd got no water in his lungs. It was in the *Birmingham Mail*, but it was a very scary time!

I was a school dinner lady for five years at Tindal Street School. Mr Claridge was the Headmaster that I used to know. I don't know who it was before him. There was a Mr Harris, a Mrs Gulliver, who did a lot of ice skating, but she had a fall, cracked her skull and died.

"Unfortunately, during the 1960s, we were burgled," Pat continues. "When we came home we just felt that something wasn't quite right. We were looking round and I found that all of my photographs had gone. Two or three weeks after that, the police got in touch with me to say that someone had tried to cash in one of my Premium Bonds – I got that back – but not the photos. They knew who it was – a kid of about twelve.

But most people had an open door and I remembered it being like that when I lived in Ryland Street, as a youngster. Our house probably was locked, but I think the lad got in through an open window.

My husband, Kenny, worked for himself; he was a grafter – I *will* say that about him. We had money coming in every week and he looked after his kids. He started Bingo Sessions next door, at the *Coach and Horses*. You paid about 25p for a ticket and your top prize would be a pound. People loved it. That was in the Saloon Bar. It was quite a nice room, away from the bar area, which was always crowded, with people playing darts and so on.

From there, he took it down to the *Bath Tavern*, which was a nice pub too; we had an upstairs room there. I'd sometimes go along, but mainly I'd got to the *Embassy* to play Bingo, which was on Walford Road. I bet a lot of you in our audience enjoy a game of Bingo!

Kenny, was a typical 'Townie'. When I first met him he was a Teddy Boy. I remember going to Don Giles' house, because he lived in Aston, didn't he? Kenny's mother lived in Bromsgrove Street, for a long, long time; from there she moved to Webster Street, in Aston. Kenny came from a large family but he didn't have a very good upbringing. He knew a lot of people in Balsall Heath, but he liked a drink.

The best pub in Balsall Heath was the *Back Tavern* or the *Snackers*, in Mary Street. It's still there now, but it's run by Jamaican people – they've changed the name. People would play Dominoes or Cribbage all day. There was St John's School, at the top of Mary Street – sometimes you'd go to a Dance or a Fete up there. But that's gone now. My son remembers the *Temple* being at the top of Mary Street, which is still there; the Welfare Centre was up there, but not now.

Balsall Heath became a really mixed area, ethnically; some people have mentioned gypsies to me, as well, but I never met any of those. I think it depends upon which area of Balsall Heath you lived in. My life was quite sheltered really.

I was lucky that I was able to go out to work and get a job, once the kids were out at work," Pat recalls, "I worked at the school and then I had a cleaning job at *Gaskin and Nettlefold* on the Pershore Road – for about £2.00 a week. Then I took an office cleaning job in Ladywood and ended up becoming a Supervisor there. When we moved out to Ladywood it was just down the road. Kenny died about twelve years ago, but the kids still think the world of him.

The Coach and Horses used to be over-run with rats! The beer barrels were right next door to the house. We didn't see many prostitutes about, although I believe Trevor and Lorraine are going to tell you something about them, after we've all had our break. Some of them were run by a lot of Maltese anyway. Where we were, we were probably away from it. A lot of it was centered on the *Cannon Hill Pub*, down the road.

There may have been a few fights at *The Coach and Horses*; we'd got a big, strong door, which kept it at bay… and we kept a big, iron bar, just in case! But on the whole, people were very good," observes Pat.

30-MINUTE BREAK FOR THOSE ON STAGE AND THE THEATRE AUDIENCE.

Folk Group performs a variety of songs, including Bob Dylan's The Times They Are A-Changing.

Don Maclean takes centre stage: "We hope you enjoyed the food and entertainment ladies and gentlemen, Now for the final section of this 2-show *Memories of Balsall Heath,* we have our last five speakers, including journalist Chris Sutton who we hope will be writing a series of articles about the two shows, for *the Balsall Heath Gazette,* so be sure to get your copy!

"Chris took a degree in Education – History – from that he was head-hunted by the police. He worked as a Criminal Research Analyst, trying to catch people who'd committed crimes! Nowadays he's a Development Worker, one day a week, at the Malvern Street Centre, for *Balsall Heath History Society,* spending the remainder of his time at *Smethwick Heritage Centre,* where he's the manager.

"And now ladies and gentlemen," Don continues, "allow me to present – Kate Cook (née Rooney)."

"My Balsall Heath years are from 1964 onwards. *Rooney's Jewellery Shop,* my father's shop, was in Edward Road, past the park, a little way up the hill, past the pub: where the shops began. I was very young when my father had the shop, around fourteen or fifteen. Sadly, he died five years later, in 1969," Kate remembers.

"The outpouring of grief at his funeral at the Oratory was unbelievable. The black community who were, and still are, very religious people, had loved him, as he was very kind to those with not much cash.

"He allowed them to take toys home at Christmas, with the promise that they would pay him back over the year: they never let him down. The church was packed to overflowing – not much good to us down here at the time, but if there is a Heaven, their prayers would have given him wings!

"The man he bought the 'Goodwill' of the shop from was a Mr Fred Wattis. I think we renamed the shop 'C. Rooney', but I'm not sure. It was also a toy and fancy goods shop, as well as selling clocks and jewellery. Amazingly, it had once been the *Swan Library* and housed thousands of books in the back! I still have some of them.

"There was a proper flat upstairs and its gardens were full of fruit bushes and trees, which we let the fruiterers help themselves to," Kate continues. "Their shop was next door to our left, up the hill.

"There was a butcher's on the other side; down from us and next to him were Mr and Mrs Marsh – two very nice Jewish people, running a haberdasher's. Below them was an old fashioned tobacconist.

Opposite my shop was a Triumph bike shop; next door to that was Smith's cake shop, with a gulley leading to a garage and more houses.

Further down still were a couple of babywear/toy stores and then a Halal butcher's run by a lovely, but raucous woman, name of Kathleen – (she was married to the largest black man I had ever seen)... before reaching a public house, on the corner of Mary Street, the *Moseley Arms.*

Two or three doors up from my shop was a Co-op. I vividly remember a woman who worked there, being traumatised as she pulled out of a parking space, to go home. She hit a motorbike rider – and nearly killed him! She never got over it.

Just further up the road from the Co-op was the newsagent's, run by a Mr Sohal Singh; further than that is a blur.

I'd drive up to the police station every time the shop was burgled, so don't let anyone tell you that our society was much different back then!

The prostitutes and gay people in our community (I've just been comparing notes about them, with Trevor and Lorraine during the break) opened my eyes to a different world... having their jewellery so tight, I ended up having to cut the stuff off them, so it couldn't be stolen, whilst they were lounging about at Her Majesty's Pleasure!

I believe the bus I caught home to Edgbaston was on the left-hand side, opposite Mary Street, but it's very hazy – I think it went down Gooch Street.

The death of my father makes this evening's reunion highly emotional for me, so thoughts of back then leave me feeling quite sad.

I just remembered something else... the *Pea-Soupers* back in the day. My Dad closed the shop early one Friday afternoon (unheard of for us!). We ended up against the railings of the park, though we eventually managed to get to the Pershore Road. I dread to think how we would fare today, with the speeds they go at! At least the air is clean now – and the view is clear," Kate observes.

"Now Trevor and Lorraine, as former Off-Licence Managers, met people from all walks of life. Here they are to tell you about them!"

"Thank you Kate. I moved to Balsall Heath in 1960, from Ladywood," begins Lorraine. "My mother's friend told me not to move there, because it was a notorious red light area.

"When I moved down," Lorraine recalls, "I had a friend who lived in the area by Clifton Road School – Pat Hewitt and all her family. Her sister, June, got married around 16 or 17 and emigrated straight away. Pat still had two sisters left. Their relatives, the Bowaters, also lived nearby; they lived in Balsall Heath a long time.

I married Trevor in 1965 and moved into *Fosters* wine shop. Trevor had been promoted to manager. Running the shop was a real 'eye-opener'!

"There were many different characters who came into the shop – good and not so good. We lived on a busy crossroad: Cox Street West, Longmore Street and Balsall Heath Road," she remembers. "Across the road was *Pinnicks Haberdashery* – they also sold prams and cots."

"We lived there from 1965 – mid-1970... about ten years," recalls Trevor. "The Off-Licence was taken over by Peter Dominic, in 1968, but as you'll see from the photo, we kept the *Fosters* name on the shop front. We were on the adjacent corner to the *Wallace* pub – Jack Kilbride was the manager at the time; *Rubens* the Bookie was next door.

"When we moved into the Off-Licence, the quality of the drinks, dating back 20 years or so – champagnes, wines and brandies were very up-market; they kept for a long time. There was a trap-door leading down to quite a big cellar and they were kept in there," Trevor explains.

"It had been a nice little family business: *Fosters* was, owned by a guy named Mr Roberts, who lived in Balsall Heath Road – just before Alexander Road. He'd managed this particular Off-Licence for forty-two years. His wife was still alive – because they used to send her pension to me – and I'd take it over to her.

Trevor and Lorraine Williams' Off-Licence, c.1978. By kind permission of Trevor and Lorraine Williams.

"I was interested to hear about Don's Gran's General stores called *Fields*, near Edward Road," he continues. "It had probably been taken over by someone else, by the time we moved in. The main place we used to shop at in that area was a Butcher's called *Coleman's*.

Across the road from us, directly on that corner there, was the Midland Bank – *(photograph appears on overhead screen)*. As you came round the corner there was a Chemist and a Paper Shop next to it.

"The main shopping area in Balsall Heath was Gooch Street, which adjoined Belgrave Road," Trevor continues. "A lady lived on the corner of Alexander Road; she used to board theatricals. Her name was Hilda Averill. She was Thora Hird's sister-in-law.

The theatricals performers would be people like Eartha Kitt; she was appearing somewhere in the City Centre: she used to dance with the fruit on her head – Like Carmen Miranda.

Hilda had these performers as lodgers. She did mention one or two other people. She didn't board when we knew her – she was too old by then... in her seventies. It was the very first house in Alexander Road. The Belgrave Road – Varna Road houses were originally owned by High Society families," he continues.

"On one occasion, about two o'clock in the morning, we heard a smash. Lorraine looked out of the window. They were stealing the sheets et cetera, out of *Pinnicks*! We phoned the police and they came round. Lorraine asked the police not to say who had telephoned them, because we were afraid of reprisals."

"But I think they must have mentioned us," Lorraine interjects, "because when I walked down to the Butchers in Edward Road, the kids from the houses in that road, used to kick the wheels of my children's pram. So I had to change my route! The thieves would have seen my bedroom light go on you see…the store was right by the river."

"By one of the bridges over that river the police found the body of a girl, who had been thrown in there," Trevor remembers. "That was somewhere by Cheddar Road, which was notorious – and Calthorpe Park. Nothing was ever proved but they thought it was probably her partner who had done it.

There were quite a few Travellers in the area, living in caravans, with friction between those living in the houses in Clevedon Road. The police were there at one of the fights in the 1960s.

There was a character named Casey; very smart – one of the 'girls' – probably the only one who drove a car: a little A40. There was a crash one day, outside our Off-Licence: there was quite a bad crossroads there. Casey got out, looked at the car, and then just walked away and just left it there!

"It was quite a community centre! The West Indian lads were characters: there was a guy called 'Yankee'. He was a kind of drug addict: he was always smoking – but he was quite harmless. But then you got the ones who weren't quite so harmless – they'd come in and try to rob you if they could! But I'd got my Alsatian dog there hadn't I?

New girls would come down from Manchester. One character was a girl who did Princess Road. When I say 'girl' I mean prostitute. She was from the Middle East – we'll call her Belinda Delacroix. She lived in Manchester, but four days a week, she'd get a taxi down to Balsall Heath and worked in Princess Road. If she made the money she wanted in three days, she'd go back to Manchester.

She had her own house in Manchester; she'd also got a coal business there too! She told us one day that she was thinking of selling her house. A friend of mine was in business. When I told him that Belinda's house was for sale, he dealt in property, so we took him up there. It was one that she used to rent out. When we went inside we only stopped five minutes, because it was terrible!

She spent more time in Princess Road after that. She was also in the *News of the World,* because there was a small terraced house in Edgbaston Road, with a dungeon in the cellar! She told us about some of the High Profile people who used to go there."

Lorraine adds, "Belinda invited me to her house party in Princess Road, The room where the party was held was poor and sparse. The fireplace looked like there had been a small volcanic eruption: there was grey ash everywhere!

"I sat on an old dilapidated chaise longue," she continues. "The room started to get crowded. I noticed two C.I.D. officers having a drink, but an argument started and they went. While my husband was getting drinks I was spoken to by a few men, so I told Trevor I wanted to leave. As we left, a man came out at the same time, wearing Trevor's coat, although he gave it back to Trevor when we insisted!"

"The *News of the World* described Varna Road as '…the most vile road in Britain'. They kept stealing the road sign for it! It was found all over the place: in Germany, everywhere! They wanted it as a souvenir," recalls Trevor.

"I used to supply some of the clubs too, like the *Ringway Club* on Bromsgrove Street, which was the old *Rainbow Club* at one time. And there was a builders' club on Moseley Road – *Malcolm House* which was in a house, like a block of offices: on the top floor there. It then changed its name to the *Executive Club.* It was a bit seedy: the guy who ran it was Gary Finn. He used to come in our Off-Licence and get his drinks of a night.

We had 'Benny' from *Crossroads* – and Ian Campbell used to come in, with his wife.

Members of UB40 lived in Balsall Heath. Ali Campbell was Ian's son. They weren't far from where we were."

"There was an article in one of the big papers," Lorraine remembers, "about one of the families who lived in the area: the McNaughts – she had 22 children! They lived in Princess Road or Alexander Road. The family did an advertisement on the television for Kellogg's Cornflakes. They were all sitting around the table, on the television, eating cornflakes! There was a large Jewish element in the area too.

"One or two of the 'Girls' had fathers who were ministers! One of them was knocking our door at two o'clock in the morning, with two of her friends. She wanted a bottle of wine, but she was bleeding. Her friend told us that the girl's husband, who was probably also her pimp, had hit her over the head with the cylinder part of a vacuum cleaner! But some of these people had quite respectable daytime jobs. We'd have quite a few people knocking on our door in the early hours. It was sad, because the girls were very friendly. They'd give you anything – basically."

"I don't know whether we should mention about Lorna, (as we'll call her)," Lorraine continues. "She needed someone to look after her little girl; by that time I was no longer working at the Off-Licence. It ended up as more than a babysitting job. I was fostering her really – she was sleeping overnight with us. I borrowed a pram from next door; she came with nothing.

"The one night, I put her to bed; everything was fine. But she was screaming the bedroom down! I brought her downstairs but I could not console her, for about an hour. I think I got in touch with Social Services. They told me that the mother had often left the child alone, in the house, to go out to do her streetwalking.

"Eventually her mother took her back home, but three months later, there was an article in the *Birmingham Mail*. It said that Lorna had left her little girl alone in the house. There were wires running across the floor of the lodging house and she'd put them in her mouth. It was so tragic! Such a sad ending," Lorraine remembers.

"We also supplied the Blues Parties – the illegal parties – in Balsall Heath: ninety per cent of them," Trevor recalls. "Sometimes they'd get raided and the police would take the drinks away. The confiscated drinks used to go up to Kings Heath Police Station, who would contact me occasionally and ask me if I wanted to buy them back. Of course the company I worked for liked that, because we'd get the drinks back at a special price."

"In Balsall Heath Road there was a little shop that closed down, just a year after we moved there," Lorraine continues. "Mrs Kunz was a small Jewish lady, who sold General Groceries. It was in a row of shops, on the one side of the road. There was Mr Gable's shop: he was the Jewish butcher. *Caddies*, a Greengrocer, was next door to the *Wallace* pub; another Jewish shop, that sold ladies fashions, was called *Benmar*, because the owners were Benjamin and Margaret.

"Kate mentioned reporting shop burglaries, just as we had to. The police station was in Edward Road, on the right hand side going up towards Moseley Road, just past *the Coach and Horses* pub," recalls Lorraine.

"A photo in *Balsall Heath through the Ages* page 9, shows Doctor Wand's Medical Centre. Doctor Wand, as I knew him, was in his eighties. I think he'd been in the Practice for a while, but he shared the house with a Doctor Reynolds, who emigrated to Australia. Doctor Reynolds was quite a clever doctor. It was reported in the *Birmingham Mail* that he had flown so many miles into the Outback and successfully removed a bullet from an Aborigine's chest," Trevor remembers.

"My doctor was Doctor Mason, who was in one of the old Belgrave Road houses as a surgery; then he moved to the new surgery on Gooch Street, which was named after Doctor Wand. Doctor Mason died three or four years ago, I believe.

The *Paragon Hotel* on Alcester Street was previously known as the Rowton House for 'Down-and-Outs'. When I went down there more recently, most of the rooms were occupied by Asylum Seekers. I was amazed how many people I saw there, just hanging about outside the building," Trevor remembers.

Lorraine explains, "At the top of Balsall Heath Road that led up to Pershore Road, there was a house where all the Midwives operated from, that was in the 1960s again. It was a large Edwardian house."

"There were still three of the old houses standing; one was owned by a Mrs Leather, who was my cousin's Granny. She had a jewellery business in the Birmingham Market. She was also involved with a Boarding House, I'm not sure where," Trevor explains.

"I worked for *Hawley's* for about six months, in the 1970s, delivering bread, mainly around the Wolverhampton area. *Hawley's* also owned a Dance Hall, going up to Spring Hill, towards the Dudley Road. We went there quite frequently, to the dances.

"In Cox Street West, just a few doors down from our Outdoor, there was an elderly lady: very chubby and jolly; she sold a few sweets and groceries. She was coming up towards her seventies or eighties," Lorraine remembers. "In Gooch Street there were lots of Public Houses, well frequented by lots of people; standing outside and drinking, of a Saturday afternoon.

"This next picture on your screen, is of *Pinnick's*, where the break-in was. You can probably just see the corner of the Off-Licence there. It's the building to the left – the shop on the corner," she continues.

"It was never obvious that the girls that worked on the streets in Balsall Heath were spending money on themselves, or had anything to show for their work; whether other people benefitted from it I'm not sure, but there were quite a few, American-type cars, driving around the area!

"In *Wrenson's*," Lorraine elaborates, "there was a lovely Irish lady working there, in her thirties, with shoulder-length black hair… She was murdered by her husband. I think it was over a friendship that she had with someone. That was really sad: it was in the 1960s. It was a story that went around, so whether it was in the newspaper I'm not sure, but she was very attractive. There was also Yvonne Kerr, who was thrown into the River Rae.

There was a small piece of land, either in Princess Road or Varna Road. An African guy, who called himself Jimmy Brown, was bringing up two of his children on his own – a girl and a boy. Travellers moved on to a piece of land, opposite to where his lodging house was. They stole his son's coat.

So Jimmy went over to the caravan, banged on the door, but no one answered. He put his hand through the window, which damaged the 'guides' in his hand. It was very bad and he was in plaster-of-Paris for weeks. He got his son's coat back, but a few years down the line, his son was on the programme 'Come on Down'. He won a car, when Leslie Crowther was the Presenter."

"Considering the lives that some of them led," observes Trevor, "it's a wonder that many of them survived. We'll call this guy 'Pork Pie'. The other guy may still be running a shabeen down there, and has been since the 1990s, so we won't mention his name! There was a lot of drugs and alcohol yet some people still survive.

Once the shops in Gooch Street started to close, the area started to 'die a death'. People seemed to disappear, but the shops were the most important thing. Once the shops and pubs closed it took the heart out of the area. That was before Belgrave Road was redeveloped, because people already knew that the 'writing was on the wall'.

"It was said in the sixties that there was at least three hundred girls, just working Varna Road alone! Three to six to a house, with three eight-hour shifts going, through the day and night. From what I've been told, they used to be paid about £8.00 a shift," Trevor continues.

"During our period there, the *News of the World* did an article on Varna Road, saying that it was a vile road, known as far afield as Australia!

The *Crown* was a very popular pub; we went there several times. My uncle and aunt lived in St Paul's Road. It was always overflowing with customers. The *Crown* was an old-time pub that has now been converted into flats. But it's the very same pub that we're now using as a 'Virtual Pub' for these two Reunions! And, as Shirley's explained, it was also the favourite drinking place of her Grandfather and Great Grandfather.

"The guy that ran it was an Irish fella," Trevor continues. "He moved to run a pub over by Winson Green Prison. There was always a 'sing-song' in there. My cousin, Johnny Clarke, would usually lead the singing. People in the area would still know him. He had a brother, Steven, who they called 'Sid'; a brother called Michael; sisters called Carol, Joan and Madelaine. They lived in a big house on the corner of St Paul's Road. My Mum's brother, Uncle Bertie, was well known for his beautiful garden, both back and front.

Bertie's garden was well known, because there would be very few people who would grow flowers in that area. There was also the *Brunswick Arms* pub. That's closed quite recently, I believe… and the *Brighton Arms* on the corner. But the *Crown* had the edge on both of those, at the time.

"The lease on our Outdoor was due to end, so the owners decided to pull out," Trevor remembers. "We'd been on holiday, but I went down one night, because the Area Manager was in there, looking after the shop. We'd just bought this house in Bournville, because we knew something wasn't right. When I arrived at the shop there was a notice on the window: 'This shop will be closing in two weeks'. They didn't bother to tell us! Everything was taken over by the Grand Metropolitan Hotel, which is Gilbey's and everything else.

"When we left the Outdoor, we moved to a different area," Trevor continues. "I tried a bit of taxi driving. Then I worked on the Milk for a bit and on the Bread. I worked for a company called *Glarry's* – ladies' fashions. They had about nineteen shops: I was Distribution Manager for them. They had some in Newcastle etc. We were living in Selly Oak.

"After that I went self-employed. Transport – driving myself – still in the Rag Trade. We've got two children: a boy and a girl," Trevor concludes. "Now, over to Chris Sutton."

"If you take a walk around Balsall Heath, there are patches where it's different. The top of Mary Street is quite lovely and a little bit different to everywhere else. It would fit in the Moseley type of area," explains Chris.

"There were lots of back-to-backs in Balsall Heath at one time, but many of them were replaced by terraces, so the character of the housing changed, once the back-to-backs had disappeared: they had been down the Moseley Road, Balsall Heath Road, Sherbourne Road.

The land in Balsall Heath was gradually sold off piecemeal, by the wealthy landowners. For example, somebody over in Worcester died, so they sold the land to build the Ombersley Road Estate, to help settle the death duties.

In the 1980s, I lived in Cannon Hill Road for about three years, just a stone's throw from the park. The last guy who was executed in Birmingham, in 1963, was actually arrested in Cannon Hill Road. He was done for shooting a Newsagent on Lea Bank Road. There are books on *Murderous Birmingham* that have more detail. For some reason, they stop at the murder before that.

"They do Quayle, as the last murderer, World War I," Chris continues. "He killed a girl on a building site. There are things about mugging in

Birmingham; the black community and so on. The Balsall Heath and Highgate areas were featured in the News quite a lot. We have a list of famous people who lived in the area; it's on our website. We have a new name to add: the actress Peggy Bryan. I think she only made two or three films, but she had a very small part in one of my favourite films – *Dead of Night*. It's a Portmanteau Film, where you have a lot of stories coming together. It's the one where Michael Redgrave has a dummy that comes to life. But, probably scarier, is the haunted mirror sequence.

"In Balsall Heath, you've got the 'triple-whammies' haven't you? You've got the degradation of the housing stock – post World War II… and all the bomb sites; at the same time you'd got all the immigration," Chris observes.

Jacky Curtis joins Chris, front of stage:

"On the subject of the changes in Balsall Heath, Chris, Grandad's brother and sister, Maggie and Jim Upton were both elderly and frail, when they moved from 170 Brunswick Road to Wickets Tower, in Edgbaston.

Auntie Maggie couldn't go out very much, she was unsteady on her feet; but they were on the third floor, so they had a good view – they could see everyone coming and going. She loved watching them. My Great Uncle Jim made great friends with the owners of the shop, underneath the flat. They were both very comfortable there," Jacky recalls.

"Maybe because of the hardships they'd been through, to have something clean, safe and warm, without any effort, was probably wonderful for them. Unfortunately, Balsall Heath's character had changed quite a lot. I wasn't expecting them to like the move, but perhaps their values changed over the years? They could show me the Edgbaston Cricket Ground from the top floor.

"They knew a couple of the neighbours, on the same landing," Jacky continues. "My Auntie Maggie had always served things up beautifully. After she died, Uncle Jim's little rebellion was to help himself to a cake… out of the box!" she quips.

Ken Malin takes the floor again, to bring our 'virtual' evening in the Crown, to an end:

"Ladies and gentlemen, let's drink a toast to 20th Century Balsall Heath, which, I'm sure, will continue to live on – in our hearts and memories!"

Pianist closes with a medley of World War II favourites.

Chapter Eighteen

BEYOND THE GRAVE

You're not awake, you're not asleep
You just control your mind.
A lesson in Trance Mediumship
Beyond the grave you'll find.

James Upton's; life in Umberslade
Larry's visit from my Dad.
Aunt Una's will – a bitter pill
Drives some of us quite mad.

So go the opening verses. In this Chapter (Show), ladies and gentlemen, we're combining all kinds of experiences.

We'll be telling you more about the Uptons, my mother's family. Also Dennis, Caroline and Lilian, Larry's children, recall life with their father – one of Dad's three older brothers.

My Aunt Sylvia, Uncle Dennis's widow, now, sadly, deceased, recalled that when she and Dennis visited the Lickey Hills, he would point out Bill's cottage; that's Danny's brother. Danny was my maternal great grandmother, real name Annie Varney.

One of the houses by Hall Green Church, where Mum and Dad were married, (see key photo of their wedding) was lived in by Danny's brother-in-law, her husband, James's brother – Ralph Varney.

Steven Upton, *(enters stage left)*, my Uncle Dennis's eldest son, Mum's nephew, joins us once again. I feel justifiably proud of Steven, an internationally-known Healer and Spiritualist Minister, who has helped many people during times of illness.

We are discussing aspects of the Upton's family history, with the aid of an overhead projector and screen, (so that you, the audience, can see all of the photos) from our collection… and one very precious Irish marriage certificate.

Steven and I have known each other all our lives. When he was being mistreated by his biological mother, as a very small boy, I would try to cheer him up, by giving him piggy-back rides… couldn't do that now … he's much bigger than me!

It has been said that when someone experiences early-childhood trauma, it *can* release a kind of Sixth Sense power within that person, enabling him or her to help others. Although I can't prove this scientifically, the evidence suggests that this is what happened in Steven's case.

This first photo shows our mutual grandfather, Thomas George, in the back garden of 70 Brunswick Road. He's wearing a fob watch, which was passed on to my Uncle Dennis. According to Dennis' wife, Aunt Sylvia, Grandma Irene was cleaning windows, as a young woman, and all of a sudden she thought to herself: 'I'm pregnant!' She had a *feeling* that she was – and that turned out to be Dennis, Steven's father!

Steven, what are your memories of Nan – of Irene?

"Well I lived at 156 Hazelville Road, from birth, until I was about eight. After that we moved to Arcot Road, Hall Green – one-and-a-half miles away from Hazelville, near the Dog Track. I used to go back and visit Nan every Saturday. We were at Hazelville Road the one day and Sylvia, my stepmother, must have been there," recalls Steven. "I remember a gypsy coming round. If you bought a trinket they'd do a quick 'Tell your Fortune'.

I remember this very clearly, because she said to Sylvia: 'You're going to win a lot of money and buy a house with a big garden, with lots of trees in it.' Shortly after that, they won 'Spot-the-Ball' or the Football Pools – one or the other. That gave them £2,000. In the 1960s you could buy houses for that amount. So they bought 25 Arcot Road. It certainly came true, within weeks of being told that!

Nan was always there. I remember her telling me off once for playing with some of the other children in the street. They were a rough family and she didn't want me playing with them. But at that age, your friends are your friends, regardless of things like that.

Nan did a lot of sewing, because she was a professional dressmaker."

Yes, she used to make dresses for myself and my sisters – we would never have managed dress-wise without her. Mum just bought the material.

"I remember the treadle sewing machine," Steven continues. "Dad was very good at D-I-Y you know. He converted the sewing machine from treadle-powered to an electric one! He could turn his hand to anything like that, carpentry, plastering, concrete. He did a lot of decorating too. They didn't have much money so he had to do things like that himself."

I remember watching him play football, Steven. He was captain of a local team, but I used to worry about the yellow and purple bruises he got – they looked so painful. He'd arrive at our house, with his motorbike and sidecar – and we sisters would take it in turns to go for outings with him. It was a real treat! He was *very* kind.

"Later, he had a blue Austin A35 van. It was FOA, something, something. We went to Germany in that. I don't have an individual strong memory of Nan," Steven continues.

"I remember the front bay window of 70 Brunswick Road – and when Maggie and Jim Upton, eventually moved to their flat in Edgbaston – Wickets Tower – and the heavy, sage-green tablecloth. I've described some of its other features in a previous show.

When I look at the photos I know, internally, that some of it must be memory, I remember having tea with Maggie and Jim, and cakes, when they were in their flat. I would visit them with my father.

But when I was seventeen I joined the RAF, so I spent most of the following decade away. I never went to any of the funerals or anything. I went to see my Grandma for the last time before she died, in a Home somewhere. She was born in November 1899 and died in 1981, aged 81."

Do you remember anything else about Thomas George Upton, our Great Grandfather? We have his Marriage Certificate, dated 21st May 1883, when he married Margaret Neiland (Nealon) at St Mary's Parish Church, in the city of Limerick, Ireland. He was in the 52nd Regiment. The couple lived in Castle Barracks, following the wedding. His Discharge Papers (1886) are printed on parchment!

"He died in about 1951 or '52, so I never knew him… but I've met him since – on several occasions," Steven continues. "I visited with my grandmother and grandfather, last year. I had a good talk with my grandfather. I've had communication with him, on and off, for a number of years, but I went to visit them last year.

"I actually publish old books – and run a book publishing company – *SDU Publications*. Although I've printed a couple of new ones, I specialise in old, out-of-print books; either about Spiritualism: books where I think that the content is valuable and needs to be kept in print.

There was a book of particular interest to me by a woman called Gladys Osborne Leonard. She was an actress, but in 1914 before the First World War, she became a Professional Medium. There's a particular kind of link called Trance-mediumship, which is something that I do. That's when you do it through a Spirit Guide.

So for over fifty years she did sittings through a 'Trance' state and she wrote three books. I decided to reprint all three books, in a single volume, called *The Complete Gladys Osborne Leonard*. For me to buy the three originals, costs over £200, but I'm selling all three in one volume for £20. So it's now affordable, because the information in those books, for people interested in this subject, is very important.

The second book she wrote, was after her husband died, and she learned how to go and visit him. She describes how she did this. So last year I tried the practice that she suggested... and it worked for me," Steven explains.

"So, effectively, it's an out-of-body experience – you go to somewhere else. You're in a state where you're waking up; you're not quite awake and not quite asleep; normally, you would do one of two things: either wake up or go back to sleep, but you recognise that you're in that state and stay in it.

You have to control your mind: hold yourself in that and what CAN happen is that you can then exit the physical body. I have very vivid dreams; this is *not* like a dream – this is for real... and to some extent it's coloured by memories.

I was looking at 156 Hazelville Road but I knew that something wasn't quite right about it – it was very different. Firstly, it was almost in isolation; not with the street. It was a similar property – very familiar – but not like a real house, as Hazelville Road used to be. It was modelled on that, but wasn't it. I would never have gone round the back, to go into the house, I would always go in that side door, I went round the back and my grandmother was stood there. She said to me, 'It's nice to see you, but they're waiting for you inside.'

I always knew the back of the house as having that veranda on it, but there was no veranda on this one. So I went into the house; through the kitchen and into the front room. There were three people but I could

Steven Upton, during a healing session.

194

only see two of them: my father and my grandfather. The third person I couldn't see but I knew there was somebody there. This happened around April 2015.

My father didn't really say anything; he just smiled and acknowledged me, but my grandfather spoke to me a little bit – a slight Birmingham accent – like my father's – no hint of an Irish accent. He said a few things, then after a few minutes he said that it was time to go back. Thomas George Upton did all of the talking. I don't know who the third person was, but I suspect that it wasn't a family member. It was somebody connected with the work that I do, who was facilitating me being there – so in a sense, controlling the events.

I've also had a communication from your father, Harry, in a public service! Very good evidence. That was at Wolverhampton Spiritualist Church, ironically, a short distance from where his Dad, Harry Senior died, in Bilston. I was attending a Medium Assessment, for a Certificate Award. This was in the early 1990s. I'm still in touch with the Medium whom I was assessing. Harry died in November 1993.

The church is opposite Wolverhampton Football Ground. The Medium was Janet Parker. She was being assessed for her Certificate. She talked about a relative named Harry and said that there was a relevance to some medals. Now at that time I'd borrowed your father's medals; I had a photograph of them and took them away for framing. So the medals were very relevant."

Those are the ones that were on Mum's lounge wall: here's a photograph of them – *(overhead screen)*.

"Your father referred to them," Steven continues. "That's very good evidence of what we call 'on-going intelligence'. The Medium couldn't have known any of this. Also, it shows that wherever she was getting the information from, presumably your father, also had knowledge of what was happening now; it wasn't just knowledge about what happened before he died; it's knowledge of events *after* he died.

It wouldn't be unnatural for him to be interested in what's happening to your mother after he's gone. In my entire life the only other Harry I've known, who had anything to do with medals, was your father. They were actually being framed when this happened – twenty years ago. As he had knowledge of events after he died, his intelligence hadn't ceased to exist, on death. That was the one and only communication from him. I'm sure that I told your Mum, at the time."

Tell us more about 're-visiting' Hazelville Road.

"There was a large back garden, but that could have been created for familiarity, so it wouldn't seem weird and strange to me. It's not about where we were, it's more about who they were – and that this experience was extremely real and clear. Because I'm a very lucid dreamer anyway: I can tell the difference between normal dreams; dreams with an emotional content – which have an emotional effect on me and dreams which are an out-of-body experience. I'm familiar with all of this."

How did you become involved with Spiritualism?

"When I was fifteen and still living at home, at Arcot Grove, I was going to school at Moseley Secondary, I had a friend from school, who lived up at King's Heath. I used to cycle up there a lot, during the evenings. I was either going to the Boys' Brigade, or the Air Training Corps.

One Wednesday evening, in October 1971, we came across Kings Heath Spiritualist Church. There were three of us: two friends from school and myself. The church is in School Road, Kings Heath. The church is still there, because I've been back to do services there recently.

We came across the church, literally, walking down the road one evening. They were about to have a service and my two friends wanted to go in. Rather than walk home on my own I went in with them. It was very interesting and, out of the three of us, I was the only one who continued to go back.

At seventeen, when I joined the RAF, I'd been going, on what I'd call a casual basis, for about two years. I trained to become an RAF Police Dog Handler, so that took me away for 11 months' training, so I didn't go to church any more.

Very soon after I finished training I was sent to Cyprus for a year, in 1974, because of the emergency there. When I came back to England in late 1975, I was stationed in Nottingham in 1976. It was very strange – like a repeat experience.

I was with two friends in the RAF, looking for somewhere in Nottingham and we came across a Spiritualist Church! I started going again and it became serious from that time onwards. To the point now where I'm currently Vice President of the *Spiritualist National Union*, responsible for Administration, a Religious Minister, a working Medium, in predominantly Trance and Trance Feeling. I'm a tutor for the SNU so I teach at College and all around the world.

I'm also a Prison Chaplain… that's part of my ministerial work. I can conduct weddings and funerals, but I don't do much of that. I did a wedding eighteen months ago, but nothing last year. The Headquarters of the *Spiritualist National Union* is at Stanstead Hall in Essex. I'm responsible for the Head Office – a Director responsible for that.

We have a Residential College there of a hundred plus beds and I teach there occasionally. I'm away from home seven months out of twelve. Last week America; next week Switzerland. From the point of view of healing I do private appointments, or teach students about healing mediumship – that's what I do predominantly."

Thank you Steven. *(He exits)*. For the second half of our show, let me re-introduce you to my cousins, Dennis, Caroline and Lilian whom you've met in previous shows. Dennis begins:

"My Dad, Larry and Bernard, were very close in age – just a couple of years – but they also worked together at *James Upton's* the printers. Quite a co-incidence, as you've just been talking to your cousin, Steven Upton, Shirley!

Uncle Bernard was a foreman at *James Upton*, which was in Barford Street, Digbeth. My Dad was a baler: sorting through the different types of paper and card, for printing. I remember he would point out watermarks to me, if it was good quality notepaper.

Bernard got my Dad a job there, you see, around the time he met Mum. When we moved from Balsall Heath to here, Umberslade Road, for a few Sundays, Dad used to take me and my sister Lilian to visit Bernard and his family, in Weoley Castle, Barnt Hill. So I remember the younger cousins, because they were our age, Alan was just a couple of years older than me; then Sandra and Brenda. Alan and I looked very much alike," Dennis remembers.

"We went to a Christmas 'Do' at *Uptons*. When we went up to see Father Christmas, he asked if Alan and I were brothers. But then there were the older children the sisters and Ken – we did really know them so well. They were adults – so they were more in the background to us. That's all I remember about Ken's children, until a few years ago, at Elsie's funeral. We only went to Bernard's a few times and I remember Sandra and Brenda coming here once.

"My Dad, Larry, met my mom, Sheila, around April/May 1957. Then I was born August 1958, so at the time Dad was separated from Edna," Dennis recalls. "When Edna found out that Dad had met someone else, she asked my Uncle Bernard to try to get Dad back. Bernard just showed her the door. I imagine the divorce would have taken five years to go through, because they took longer at that time.

My parents got married in 1961 and Edna married a local man, so they were both free to marry then. Bernard was Best Man at my parents' marriage. It's really interesting, seeing the photo of Edna, in your parents' wedding photo.

Dad would never discuss his family, as such; although every now and again, he'd come out with something. So all I gathered was that both of his parents died young, as we've explained in earlier shows," Dennis continues.

"If I asked him anything about the family he would say: 'I don't want to talk about it.' Or he'd say: 'It's all in the library.'

His older brother, Reg's death, is described by our cousins, Pat and Carolyn, in the next chapter. Our father, Larry, was with him when it happened. Reg phoned Dad in September 1986; I'd just come back from a 2-week holiday in Ireland. I went with Dad to Digbeth Coach Station, for him to catch the coach to Gloucestershire.

"Barbara, Ken's oldest daughter, used to come here more often, with her husband, Jim. But then James Upton did a 'Runner'- with the Pension Fund – and went off to Barbados – or somewhere like that, so they couldn't get Bernard's pension. They had to fight for it," Dennis continues. "Dad was still working, so they used to come here. Bernard died in 1975. Dad was the Union Rep for a while, at *Uptons.*

I have happy memories about Dad, digging the garden. We only had a small lawn. He dug furrows in the soil and scattered sweet pea seeds and some root vegetables. We always had some mint in the garden.

He talked about being a chef, when he was a young man. He was a chef at Warwick Castle: whether that was for a special event only I'm not sure. They were filming an historical pageant at the time. An aeroplane flew past, but they carried on filming, so it was like a Medieval Banquet – with an aeroplane in the background!

When we were small he'd cook a stew on a Monday, and then we'd eat it on Tuesday. He'd give us a cup of the gravy before we went to bed: quite greasy really! It was always when *World in Action* was on the telly, so it would have been 8.30pm. He liked cooking.

"Mum's sister-in-law had a farm in Ireland. In the 1960s she used to send a turkey over to each of her siblings in England; she had to pack them specially, to send the over.

The turkey would be delivered a day or two before Christmas Eve, Dad used to gut it. Lil and I would watch him do it. We were fascinated, but then the smell of its innards being removed would make us run away! But he'd do all of that, then leave the turkey hanging upside-down in the pantry, so that it was cold."

He may have learned how to do that as a boy, when he lived at Brunswick Road, with him being one of the older children, helping to look after the younger ones. Maybe he helped Lilian and the girls with some of the cooking?

"Yes – and Dad was an Altar Server, probably at Saint Paul's, because that was the closest church to Brunswick Road."

We've put two photos on the screen: the first one was taken at Umberslade Road, Dennis on the left, Caroline in the middle and Lilian on the right.

"For this photo we had to wait for our little sister Caroline to smile; we were a bit fed up so by the time the picture was taken, we only had half a smile! This was taken at home, at Lunchtime," Dennis remembers, "just after we'd returned to school in September 1966. We were at Raddlebarn School. Our Insurance Man's friend took photos, so Mum said she'd be interested. It was taken against our living room wall, facing the window. I had been smiling, but I was just giving up! It's interesting that we hadn't a full set of teeth between us: we were at the stage where our milk teeth were dropping out," Dennis concludes.

The other photo was taken at Caroline's wedding.

"Yes, my wedding was on 28 August 1993. I married Paul Carroll," explains Caroline. "My sister, Lilian, on the left, me in the middle and my

Dennis, Caroline and Lilian Wareing, photographed during a lunchtime, September 1966.

Mum, Sheila, on the right. It was taken at the Selly Oak Ex-Servicemen's Club. My birthday is the 17 December 1964 and I have two children, Kerry and David. Kerry was born on 4 June 1990; David on 16 March 1993."

"And I'm Lilian Macmillan. I was born on the 29 February 1960. Married to Darren Macmillan. We've been married since 1991. I've got two children: Elizabeth, born on 15 January 1991 and Christopher who was born on 17 November 1992.

"For many years my father didn't seem to have much to do with his family. He was close to Bernard: they used to go drinking together," Lilian comments.

Caroline recalls: "Dad passed to go to the Grammar School, but his parents couldn't afford the uniform. He was normally quite quiet, but when he'd had a drink, he'd open up more about the family."

My Dad was quiet too, but I think most of the brothers were rather repressed by their father. Reg was the exception.

"Dad used to read a lot and he liked listening to concerts and classical music. He was also into politics," continues Caroline.

That probably comes from the Baylis side of the family. Eustace's father, Alfred was a Worcester councillor and Eustace himself became a clerical secretary to the new branch of the Birmingham Liberal Party, after it had just been established in Birmingham.

So Caroline, there's an eighteen-month difference between you and Dennis?

"We were Dad's second family, so I think by the time we came along he had mellowed; when he was younger, he was quite different. When we went to see our half-brother, Ralph, in Redcar, he told us that Dad had a bad temper and that he was very strict with them. But he wasn't like that with us.

"Dad would have been early fifties when he had me. I always remember thinking at school that he was more like my grandfather, compared to the other pupils' fathers. There was quite a big gap – like a completely different generation," observes Caroline.

Larry Wareing, in later years.

200

"So maybe thinking about *your* Dad, Shirley, that he'd mellowed by the time that Julie was in her teens and in his fifties, like Dad – maybe both brothers had mellowed by then?"

"Dad was a Birmingham fireman for many years, according to Ralph; Bernard's sons used to know Dad as 'the Fireman'. But Ralph was quite frightened of him, because he was so strict. He had a difficult relationship with his older son and daughter – by Edna. I don't think he ever had any contact again with his daughter," recalls Lilian.

"I felt that Dad was quite a distant father; whether it was the age gap I'm not sure. He never got involved with anything that we did: it was always Mum," Caroline remembers.

Dad used to take us out cycling, fishing for tiddlers and on various holiday and day outings. Did Larry do anything like that with you?

"No, I don't remember anything like that – he was too busy drinking! Sorry, but… his spare time was spent in the pub," continues Caroline. "Not just at night-time, he was more of a daytime drinker, although he did have a job. If he wasn't at work, on the weekends he'd go out early afternoon and come back late. He definitely had an addictive personality."

Like Madge and my Dad; with Madge it was alcohol as well; Dad only drank at Christmas because he was haunted by the devastating effect that drink had on his family. My Dad died at 72.

"Our Dad was 77 when he died, so he lived a few years longer than Harry," Caroline explains. "He was only ill for the last six months; before that he was strong."

When my Dad visited Larry on that last occasion, what do you remember about that visit?

Caroline recalls: "Lilian wasn't there, but I was. I remember being surprised, because I didn't even know that they'd got in contact. Maybe Mum had done it? But Dad was really pleased that he'd come. And they talked for quite a while, but I didn't listen to what they were saying. That was the first time I could remember meeting your Dad, although I may have done before – and was too young to remember."

This visit must have been in 1990, as Larry was 77; three years before my Dad died.

"We'd been to Reg's 80th, some years before, (1984). He was in touch with Bernard, but not the others – and I don't really know why," Lilian remarks.

Our cousins, Ken, Gary, Pat and Carolyn will be with us for the penultimate show.

Chapter Nineteen

TEA FROM THE SPOUT!

Curtain rises on a Disney-type scenario: backdrop, a wood. Chorus variously dressed as teapots and teacups! As the song begins, the teapots bob up and down, singing a gentle ostinato: "Teapot, teapot, etc." The teacups sing the main song:

Drinking tea from the teapot – straight out of the spout!
First a walk in the woods, when the lights were all out.
Covering a mynah bird… tree spreading out –
Madge feels protected – and Reg travels out.

Et cetera…

Shirley steps forward:
Please welcome to the stage, once again, Audrey's son Steve Rogers. Audrey was Dad's baby sister.

"When Dad took Mum home, for the first time, they walked through the woods, which was the back way to the house and then came down through the back garden," Steve begins. "Mum said it was quite eerie – dark – because there were no lights in those days; but there was a light on in the kitchen.

"She said, 'Eric, who's that man, drinking from the teapot?!' He said, 'Oh, take no notice of him!' But she wondered what she'd got into. If there was a teapot left around, with some tealeaves left in it, he used to drink it from the spout! He couldn't speak much, but he was a nice enough bloke. He was my uncle's half-brother and he looked after him.

Audrey and Eric first lived at the RAF base, at Sleap, Shropshire (pronounced 'Slape') when they married. Then they moved to a new council house in Myddle, soon afterwards.

We lived in Myddle for thirteen years. It was a village community. Coming from the town, Mum didn't like it, because Dad was at work and when I was at school she was on her own.

Dad was a Tool Fitter, at a local company. Mum said that she didn't like that village life, but when she came to leave, everybody missed her. They said, 'What are you going for?'

We were there for quite a long time, but then Eric's father died in the early 1960s, and my parents moved to a refurbished house – 14 Florence Avenue, Sparkbrook, in 1961, when I was nine.

I went to Golden Hillock Junior School – and Moseley Secondary School after that, because I just missed passing the Eleven Plus, but it was just as good really. That was one of the best secondary schools around: Moseley Modern, they called it.

After leaving school, I started off my apprenticeship as an electrician. I was doing quite well – at Hall Green Tech – I was in the top stream there as well. But then, after a few electric shocks, I decided that I didn't want to do that anymore… I also fell off a ladder!

So I was side-tracked into the Butchery Trade, but went into the car industry after that, at the *Rover*. Afterwards I went to Longbridge, for a short period; then an engineering company in Redditch – I learned a bit there."

Like your Grandfather, Harry Senior: he worked for the *Austin* at Cowley, Oxfordshire, Steve, then did other car-related jobs when he moved back to Birmingham.

"But then when I went back to Longbridge I ended up in the Method School – where we did all the models and put them on the track – testing them, in a technical, Fitter's way, to prove that they were viable," Steve continues. "Then we'd take them up and train all the people up on the job. So I was a Trainer-cum-Fitter. I was twenty-five years in the Car Industry.

It was taken over in 2005. You do learn a lot and I've worked for quality companies; you've got the knowledge; I worked on all the wiring at the Land Rover. But after it went down the pan I was just glad to get out.

I'm a Gardener now, ladies and gentlemen. I like it because it's creative. I used to be a Wedding and School Photographer as well. They sent me out to Southam, to a small Primary School. There was a Pre-School Class where there was a set of twins: one of them was kicking my equipment, I said to the Head, 'How do you put up with this?!' She said, 'Oh, I'll enjoy the challenge!' I thought: 'Yes, you will, won't you?!' I did that for about ten years.

Although I'm technically-minded, from my father's side, I'm creative as well. You can actually do a job, step back, and say, 'That's good,' and that's what I like. I didn't really know anything about gardening, when I started, but you never stop learning.

When Claire, my daughter, was about six or seven, Mum took her to the local Mappleborough Green Nursery, to buy something. There was my wife, Linda, Dad – I don't think my son Stuart was there. I've lost Stuart actually.

Mum was holding Claire like this and we were coming to the check-out. If anything went wrong with my Mum, you'd hear, 'Owa!' So she fell over a bale of wire, backwards, with Claire in her arms; held onto Claire, but as she went over, she'd got these French Knickers on – and they were like brilliant red! You wouldn't expect that really, would you? I was really laughing!

When we got through the checkout, she said, 'I'll kill you our Steven, when you get out of here!' But there's lots of incidents like that.

She won a writing competition, run by the *Birmingham Evening Mail.* We had too narrow a fridge to take the turkey – at Christmas – so she put it in the front room... and the cat had it! – And ate all into the breast. She wrote about that for the competition... something to do with Christmas. It was in the *Mail.*

After she got married Mum was a charge-hand at an electrical company, in Baker Street, Birmingham. There was a company there making electrical switches. Mum supervised the work. So both in the *ATS* and that electrical company she held responsible positions. She was very good in that type of job, because people liked her.

She actually took a lesser job, cleaning at the *MEB* Showrooms, on Walford Road, but she'd sell to the customers who were coming in. The manager wanted to send her on a Sales Course, but Dad wouldn't allow it. That was a shame, because she had a gift for that sort of thing. She could tell a good story as well.

I could write a small book about her. I'll give you an example of her being funny without even thinking about it – being naturally funny.

She went to the Butcher's the one day, on the Stratford Road, when she was living in Sparkhill. She bought a frozen chicken and placed it on top of a whole bag of shopping. Came out of the shop, swung the bag and the chicken flew out of the bag, hit the slabs on the ground, Then it slid along the path towards the bus stop. There were five or six people waiting for the bus – and all their eyes followed that chicken! (She told it in a funnier way than that).

Mum and Dad travelled up to Wales, with Bruce, the dog: a Staffordshire Bull Terrier. They decided to get out for a wee, but Eric said they should wait until they reached a gate, because at that point they were in the countryside. They arrived at a gate and climbed over it. Mum pulled up her panties, but then she screamed 'Aah!!' She pulled her pants up again, because she's got a clump of nettles in her nether regions!

There's loads! My parents went fishing in Malvern; my girlfriend and I went with her and the two of them needed the toilet. The nearest ones were in the village, so they decided to look for a suitable spot, where we were. Mum went round the pool and started, before she'd got cover. Then she went, 'Oowa!' and fell backwards, all the way down the bank. And the man who was fishing, directly opposite, got a bird's eye view!!

Dad asked her to look after Bruce, because he was running about everywhere. So Audrey tied Bruce to her chair, got up to do something – and off he went – pulling the chair behind him. We had to catch the dog – then she decided to tie him to a branch. There was a sound of splintering wood and off he went with the branch trailing behind him! That was all on one day. You could have some fun with my mother!!"

Normally, there would be some repercussions, Steve, for a child who is orphaned at birth, then cared for by her sister and neighbours, although she's still living with family members – and not in the awful situation that Dad and Madge found themselves in. Her childhood had a disastrous effect on Madge's life… and Dad had significant issues too. So Audrey, one would have thought, must have been affected in some way, by the loss of her mother at such an early age. Can you think of any evidence for that?

"There were times when I'd notice that she'd be sad – for example, when she was in the kitchen," Steve continues. "And when Bernie went – that was another time when she was really sad. They were both particularly close to each other – and they were both small – although Bernard was a little bit taller.

Yes, there was this sad side to my Mum. She had a cardboard cut-out picture of her Mum, upstairs; like the portrait photo you showed me – she kept that with her – all the time. She told me that she never had a Mum and a Dad – they both died young.

I was Eric and Audrey's only child, although they were talking about adopting another one – and Elsie and Phil were too: they used to take me away on holiday with them to Poole, in Dorset. Una and her husband took me on holiday too.

My Dad was seventy-five or seventy-four, when he died, in 1997; he was born in 1922. My Mum died in 2000. When Dad became ill, they moved out to Paddock Lane, Oakenshaw, Redditch; they had a little bungalow. Dad lived there for four years; Mum for about six, because she lived two years after Dad. So they moved there in about 1994. They loved it, because they had a nice little garden. Dad planted bushes and conifers. He had leukaemia, you see. He developed it. His blood count went down and he had to have blood transfusions. They had a little shed in the garden on one side and a bird table on the other. Like Harry, my Dad loved his garden too.

My Grandad, on the Rogers side, was a professional gardener. He worked on one of these big estates, before he went into the War... His legs were damaged during the war, so he was in Irons. So the gardening side comes through the family as well.

I think they were happy in Redditch – it was just Dad's illness. Mum used to use *Dial-a-Ride* to go shopping in Redditch.

"I've got a daughter, Claire and a son, Stuart Ian Rogers," Steve continues. "The reason I gave him that name is because his initials spell 'Sir'! He joined the army – the Queen's Royal Hussars – QRH – joining at sixteen-and-a-half, which takes some doing! Did his basic training at Winchester and Bovington: somewhere in the Dorset region, where they do their tank training.

Then they sent him out to Germany. He married Julie and had a daughter called Leah Rogers. In a tank there are four jobs: a Commander, Gunner, a Radio element to it; three or four skills that they have to learn. Stuart was a crack shot – so he became the tank commander's Gunner. Then they became trainers and trained the younger recruits. Stuart became a Lance-Corporal.

He was just twenty-four when he died. We both did the Cycling Proficiency Course; Stuart then passed the motorbike course and bought a great big motorbike... a British one. He was riding that at the time of the accident. It was a last blast – he was going to put it away for the winter. So he was driving at full blast in Germany – but he had a 'speed wobble', according to a witness – and hit a tree. He was a really good lad. Claire has two lads: Tommy and Josh, down in Redditch," Steve concludes.

As he exits, my cousin, Ken Wareing, enters from the opposite side.

Ken, your father, Bernard, joined the Navy in 1941, but was invalided out, having been bombed twice! Originally your family lived in Sherlock Street, but when you came out of the shelters your house had been destroyed! Your father was called back, so your parents quickly found a house at 20 Ladypool Road. The only two children at that time were yourself, born in 1937 and Barbara, born in 1941. Tell us about the snow that winter.

"I was about seven years old. The snow was on the ground and the house was absolutely freezing! My father helped us move into Ladypool Road, but he could only stop an hour or so," Ken recalls. "When he left, my mother was crying buckets! There was no furniture in the house whatsoever; it was desolate.

Bernard and Beattie Wareing, at their daughter, Barbara's wedding, October 1971.
By kind permission of Ken Wareing.

My mother, Beattie, left the house – almost immediately, taking us to live with her mother at 32 Sherlock Street. She felt much happier moving back there; her sister was there too. A short time later, the council gave my mother a house, round the corner, in Moseley Street. We lived up a yard: Court 2, 2 back of 9 or 10, Moseley Street.

I hated Mondays – Washing Day. The Brewhouse. I could never be early for school on Mondays. I even had the teacher send a friend of mine back to my mother, to find out why I was late. That was Hope Street School in Balsall Heath," Ken continues.

"My father was invalided out of the Navy, in 1944. He spent many months in Portsmouth Hospital. During that time, they told him that he might lose a leg. He had numerous pieces of shrapnel in both legs. They said they might have to amputate. My father said, 'No way!' and the day he died, he still had bits of shrapnel in his legs. He died in 1973.

Beattie Edith May were my mother's Christian names. I'm not too sure how my parents met. My mother went to St David's School, in MacDonald Street, just off Balsall Heath there. Just after the war, I remember my father was walking up the street with Audrey, Steve's Mum, going to my house. Sadly, Dad and the family became quite distant after that.

I can tell you an amusing story. Ida's husband, Phil Lees, and my father, fell out, after they went out for a drink. Phil came home blind drunk – and Ida, Dad's sister, never forgot that," Ken continues.

"I was the oldest; Barbara next; Pauline was born in 1943; David was born in 1947. Barbara was 66 when she died. Pauline was 67: she lived in London for many years. Brenda was born in 1951 or 2. Sandra was born in 1953/4; Alan, the youngest, was born in 1955. Other than myself, Brenda and Sandra are the only two who have survived.

I was listening to your cousin, Steven Upton, during the last show. My wife, Doreen and myself, have both experienced healing through Spiritualism. The first time we went to a Spiritualist Meeting the church was very full: we could not get in. The church was facing Ward End Park; it's still there today. My wife was given a seat, by a lady who did no more than put the palms of her hands behind her back. She said that there was a lot of pain there. My wife was suffering with cancer at that time, although no one knew that she had it.

But this person put her hand down her spine and declared that there was a lot of pain in my wife's back. The gentleman standing next to this lady wore a necklace with a cross and a ring with a cross, on his finger. He immediately took my wife's arm and gently started rubbing it. After a short time he declared that her pain had transferred to his arm.

Eventually we walked into the church and my wife, that day, was healed. We came back and as we walked over the park, my wife turned to me and said, 'Ken, I feel at peace.' And we went to the church for months, every Monday evening. And I watched my wife being healed. Two or three times she said to me, 'Ken, why don't you be healed?'

Still being sceptical, I eventually went to be healed or cleansed.

The church was full of flowers. John, the gentleman who helped me, said, 'There's a lot of spirit in flowers.' He also said, 'You could be a healer if you wanted to.' But at the time I didn't take it up. That's a story that I can relate and if it does somebody some good hearing it, that's fine. We went for twelve months and my wife felt at peace, each time we went.

Ultimately she died from breast cancer, but that was four-and-a-half years later. I was sceptical at the time, but I certainly wouldn't knock it now. When you're in that situation you tend to clutch at any help you can get.

My eldest is named Gary Robert Wareing. He was born in 1963; Andrew Kenneth is the second oldest, born in 1967. My youngest son, Neil John was born in 1971. Gary lives near Cannock; Andrew lives in Walsall and Neil lives in Sussex. Gary is a site manager for Kirkman Bowland building company; Andrew is a postman and Neil is an electrician."

Do you know anything about Dad's older sister Una, Ken? She's the one person we don't seem to have much about?

"Una married Jim Price… she was the quiet one. But I believe that she had problems in her later years: she suffered with her nerves. She was the oldest one, after Reg."

How about Aunt Elsie, my Godmother?

"She used to tell me off. Every Sunday I'd sit there in Florence Avenue, Elsie and Phil's house, eating my Sunday Lunch. I didn't like my greens – Elsie said: 'You'll eat your greens, because they'll do you good!' So I ate them, under protest! But now I love them."

Our cousin, Dennis, said that Elsie and Una both married late; they waited quite a while. We both thought that probably resulted from their Dad's attitude to women and marriage. He'd sometimes take the two of them with him, when he visited his women; there was one particular caravan area, on the corner of Hasluck's Green Road in Shirley. They probably thought: 'I'm not going to go through all that – I'm not having my husband cheating on me!' We think it hardened both of them against marriage; that's why they probably held back for so long.

"Did you ever see Elsie's mynah bird, Shirley?"

Yes, it was really funny, because the bird copied people's voices!

"Elsie's to a 'T'! It *sounded* like Elsie."

When people came into the room, it would say, 'Oh you are nice!' just as though Elsie was saying it, Ken. She sometimes had to cover the bird up, because it could be really embarrassing!

"That's right. She used to go mad. I wish I could show you the photo I had in Elsie's garden, at 2 Florence Avenue, because she had two or three dogs. She lived there for many years, but eventually moved to 1/1737 Bristol Road South, Birmingham B45 9PE. I used to go to Florence Avenue, every Sunday, for dinner. They even took me on holiday: we went to Ludlow, in a caravan, many years ago.

Over the years, they had a number of dogs. One in particular was Chum. In the black-and-white photo, on your screen now. I'm about eleven years old and I'm standing in Elsie's back garden with him. He was a little spaniel. Sadly he passed away, then along came a lovely little black dog. I'd take her dogs for a walk, around the block.

In a sense, Elsie was instrumental in getting me the house where I'm living now. They lived in a private landlord's house; we rented our house through the same landlord. Elsie's husband, Phil, was very kind and loaned me the £20 Key Money," Ken concludes.

Back on stage is my cousin, Gary Dexter, Madge's son.

"From 1988-1992, I had my first Headship – I was Head of Newry Junior School, an inner city school, off Saffron Lane, Leicester. At that particular point, the school was described to me by the Director of Education, as the most difficult job in Primary, in Leicestershire. So part of my background was dealing with dysfunctional parents and children," Gary explains.

"Later I worked for the last fifteen years of Headship in a nice little village. Within a few years, in discussion with the Governors, following an Interim Deputy Head, I offered my sister, Jackie Mason, the Deputy Headship. That was at the village school: Captain's Close Primary School, in Asfordby; four miles outside Melton Mowbray. She was there as my Assistant Head until I retired. We were very successful – by any standard."

When I worked in 50 different schools, in five years, in inner city Birmingham, Gary, I dealt with a wide range of difficult situations like that, so that's where we're both coming from. It's therefore doubly important to get your perspective on Madge and my Dad's situation, which was a very complex one, built up over many years. I'm told that your Mum loved trees?

"A tree is like a supporting structure: the overarching branches and the leaves … covering her. That's what she was always looking for. I just feel very sad for my mother, because she'd had really, no life. And the life she had didn't match what she'd wanted or expected."

Some branches of the Wareings became professionals and did well for themselves. Elsie and Larry were instrumental in raising the family, following Lilian's death. Elsie used to say that if Harry Senior had been a responsible father, as many of the Wareing fathers were, Harry and Madge would never have had such a terrible childhood.

And yet he started off well, Gary, by winning a scholarship to King Edward's Grammar School, in New Street, Birmingham. He was obviously an intelligent boy…

"But self-centred."

Also, his addiction to drink played a major part in his downfall, as it did with Eustace Baylis, Lilian's father. Two of Harry Senior's sons, Larry and Bernard, were regular drinkers too. My father, on the other hand, wouldn't touch a drop, except at Christmas, because he had been a victim of the consequences of drinking.

Madge's death certificate was registered by Les, your father, at Leicestershire Central Office 24th December 1994. She died at Glenfield General Hospital, Groby Road, Leicester:

Madge Gertrude Dexter, wife of Les Geary (that's Irish) Dexter, a retired Engineering Works Manager. Home address 26, Lawnwood Road, Groby, Leicester.

Cause of death was a pulmonary embolism: a blockage of the pulmonary artery; the blood vessel that carries blood from the heart to the lungs.

Gary seats himself at a table, centre stage, where he is joined by our cousin, Pat Ward, Reg's daughter, and her daughter, Carolyn.

Carolyn recalls: "Grandad was a local Tour Guide in Gloucester – with Coach Parties, between the 1970s and 1980s, after he retired. He gave tours around Gloucester Cathedral. He was quite a scholar."

In the previous show, Dennis told me that Reg went on an organised seaside holiday

"Yes, he'd lost most of his sight by then," Carolyn continues. "My Mum and Dad lived next door to them, because they owned a pair of thatched cottages, on the Green. Because he was going away, my Mum and Dad and a cousin, Peter, the one Mum became very close to, went on holiday too. I know that I drove Reg and Laurie (aka Larry) to the coach. I was the one who got the phone call from the Holiday Centre where he was staying, to say that he had passed away. My immediate reaction was 'You're kidding!'"

And Reg's ashes were scattered on the Malvern Hills, just like my Dad Harry's were?

"Yes, right by the obelisk. We all had a bit of his ashes to scatter there, because he loved Malvern. In the latter years, after my Nan had passed away, before his sight got so bad, he used to drive around, all over the place."

Pat recalls, "After Dad had given up driving, I used to drive him up to Birmingham, whenever he wanted to, to see his half brothers and sisters. Carolyn took him too. A page in Reg's Diary Collection shows most of their names and addresses."

"Una and Jim lived in one of those pre-fabricated houses. We used to go round there; they had an aviary in the back garden – budgerigars. It was a whole estate of those little bungalows," Carolyn explains.

"In my grandad's latter years, after my Nan had passed away, he was still able to drive, although we hit the side of the road a few times! He'd take a primus stove in a tin, his sandwiches, his loose tea and he'd drive off for the day. He'd walk around Malvern. He'd park up there and he had a little collapsible chair. And he would have a picnic. He even took himself as far as Scotland at one time! It was only a little car."

"Then another time he went on an overnight ferry to Norway. He liked to travel. He went to the Channel Islands with a club he belonged to, then he took the ferry to France, from there," Pat interjects. "He was 82 when he died, so it would have been 1986.

"Dad wanted to go on holiday with the Blind Association, because by then, he was practically blind himself," she continues. "He needed help, so he paid for the holiday for Laurie, so that he could go with him, to look after him. They'd been for a drink and when they came out, they got on a bus or a tram – and Dad collapsed. He didn't die at that moment; Laurie got him on the bus (he should have called an ambulance really) but they got as far as the gate where they were staying – and that's where Reg died. Laurie told me afterwards, that he said to him, 'Reg, Reg, you mustn't die now. Pat will tell me off something awful!' It was a Holiday Camp in Paignton. It wasn't a Butlin's."

"I felt terribly guilty," recalls Carolyn, "because the night before they went on holiday, I went there to make sure they'd got everything ready for the next morning, sat on my Grandad's knee, looked at Laurie and said, 'Now you take great care of him, because he's so very special to everybody.' I felt really badly afterwards, about having said that to Laurie, in view of what happened."

Pat adds, "When my Dad died, my husband and I went to the solicitors who had been Great Auntie Una's solicitors. We went there, because my Dad had stuck with them. My Dad had made a new will, leaving everything to me, because my mother, Nellie, had said that if he didn't, she'd come back and haunt him! During that conversation I asked the solicitor if he

Pat and John Ward's children (Reg's grandchildren); Malcolm, Carolyn, Rosemary and Elizabeth. By kind permission of Carolyn McCoy.

knew anything about the fact that my Dad's surname should have been Baylis, according to his birth certificate, but he said, 'I didn't know. But I think we'll forget that, because it could open a whole can of worms!'"

Now Peter is your second husband, Carolyn... how long have you been married?

"Fifteen years. My son, born in 1971, is the one in the bearskin hat, in the photo. My daughter, Charlotte, was born in 1975. My brothers and sisters are Elizabeth, who is eighteen months younger than myself; she's married to Ray Wynne and lives near Carmarthen in Wales, although they've now returned to England. The next one down is Rosemary, who lives in Gloucester. The youngest is my brother, Malcolm, who lives on a farm not far from here; Mum lives with him now.

I have two children of my own. Liz has four: a boy and a girl and then twins. Rosemary had two girls, but then I brought them up."

And you are a nurse, by profession?

"I've done nursing, but then I became a little fed up with that, so I became a chef/cook at a local agricultural college."

In this next photo that we're looking at, ladies and gentlemen, Reg is pushing the trolley. To his right is Elizabeth. Rosemary is wearing a headband. To her left is Malcolm. Two cousins from Leicester, David and Neil, are at the back with a trolley. We think it was taken at Nellie and Reg's cottage, in Norton Green, around 1963.

"This next photo is of Grandad, not long before he passed away. It was taken in the back garden of my bungalow, in a village called Staunton, between Gloucester and Ledbury. That is in the orchard at the back of the bungalow."

Everybody has said the same about Reg – what a kind person he was. He had such a sunny personality and a very intelligent man too.

"Yes, he was full of character; very mischievous. When we were still living in Leicester and he was down in Gloucester, I was eleven years old at the time, he'd turn up at the window of the house in Leicester, in the early hours of the morning. My Mum told me he'd throw stones at the window, to wake us up!

He came up to fetch us because they'd got two baby lambs that wanted feeding. So we'd go straight back down to Gloucester, which in those days probably took quite a long time… just to feed his lambs!

He used to have all the generations of our children down to his cottage, up until he was very ill. He would play with them and bounce them on his knee."

Pat, this photograph shows the caravan where we sisters stayed with Mum and Dad at Ingoldmels. We three sisters are standing in front of it.

"Yes – it was built by my husband, John Ward. Previous to that, my Dad had bought a shell of a caravan, but John built all sorts of things into it, that he'd picked up. Your sister, Julie, wrote to Reg for years. She used to visit him from time to time. I think she thought a lot of my Dad, for some reason."

"Reg probably didn't tell us about his real father, because it was a 'No-no', so why talk about it?" recalls Carolyn.

"I remember my Mum calling me to one side, when we were in the shop," Pat continues. "'Your Dad's going to tell you about the circumstances of his birth – and you've got to pretend that you don't know already!'"

"When I was living down in Somerset and my son was a new-born, they spent a lot of time going backwards and forwards to Bridgewater. I was really hard up at the time. My first husband was a farmer and we had a Tied Farmhouse. Nellie used to send me money, wrapped up in a plastic rain hood," explains Carolyn. "There'd be a fiver wrapped up in it, but she would say, 'Don't tell your grandad!'

"It gave her the feeling that she was doing something to help me, because I was the eldest – and I spent all my time with them – when they were away from the shop. They took me with them, everywhere."

"I'd sometimes look after the shop for them. It was a General Store, like the one in *Open All Hours*," recalls Pat. "His real job, which his father got him was on the Midland Red buses. He finished up as an Inspector."

And my grandad, George Upton (Mum's Dad) knew Reg when he worked for the Birmingham branch of the Midland Red, because George was a bus conductor. What was the address of the house on Kingsway, that Reg and Nellie owned and Ethel later lived in Pat?

"56 Kingsway, Braunston, Leicester. Great Aunt Una helped Mum and Dad, money-wise, to look after Madge. She used to make clothes for Harry and Madge; she made them for me as well. She came over to Leicester in her little car. She wore a very smart hat – very posh! But she'd have slippers on her feet! She'd say, 'Oh Ducky! Nobody can see my feet can they?!'

"And we always had salmon for lunch when she came," Pat continues. "Never any other time. She brought fresh salmon with her. We took her ashes to Bradgate Park in Leicester. There's a stone in there, in memory of the man who gave the park. We knew that once a year they have a service there, although she wasn't really a church-goer. So we took her ashes and sprinkled them on the grass – just by that stone.

The reason being that when she came to see us and my Dad, on a Sunday, he sometimes said, 'Do you want to go out somewhere?' She often asked to go to Bradgate Park – and she'd feed the deer, with Fox's Glacier Mints! They loved them!"

Dad's ashes are scattered on the Malvern Hills too, because Mum and Dad used to go courting on the Malvern Hills; there was a particular bench that they used to sit on.

Harry Senior's sister, Elspeth, was a runner with the Birchfield Harriers. Do you know anything about her, Pat?

"She was very much into physical fitness and she gave me a skipping rope: a lovely one, with wooden handles. I used to go to *Keep Fit* and use that rope."

Mum has one of her medals, because they share the same initials – EW.

"I've got one of her medals too. She changed her name from Elsie to Elspeth."

That explains why she's shown as Elsie on some of the earlier Census records. She got married, although Great Aunt Una never did. She married someone with the surname Wilson, didn't she?

"I think so – I remember talking to him. The two sisters were quite different," Pat continues. "The all-abiding memory of Great Auntie Una that I've got, is of one Christmas. We used to go to my grandma's in Yardley, most every Christmas; my mother's mother – Grandma Bartlett. We went by bus: we got it cheap, because Dad was working on the buses. This particular Christmas we took the bus to a church in the middle of Birmingham – St Martin's, in the Bullring. Great Aunt Una met Madge and me, in her car, and took us to her house in Erdington. I was about twelve or thirteen.

Madge went next door to Una's neighbours – the Broomheads! Great Aunt Una said to me, 'Right, come upstairs, because I've got something for you.' She'd made me a most beautiful dress. I put it on and looked at myself in the mirror. Then she said, 'Aren't you going to kiss me then?' I'd never dreamed of kissing her before, because she hadn't seemed like that kind of person. So I kissed her and hugged her and I thought: 'I bet she's been wanting a kiss and a hug like this, for years!!' And I've never forgotten that."

I think when you have a kind mother, like Sarah Patchett, as Great Aunt Una did, combined with a really strict father, like William James Wareing allegedly was, (or Lilian and Harry Senior as parents) that really confuses the children, Pat – they don't really know how they should behave!

"But you see, I'm not a Wareing. In blood terms, there's nothing Wareing in me. I had the feeling that, although they were Reg's family, and he did his very best for them, my father always felt not quite one of them. Although he could lose his temper sometimes," recalls Pat.

"As you say, there are no pictures of Dad's real father. But when Dad told me about his past and got the things out of his wooden box, there was a magazine, to do with the *Midland Red Social Club*. There was a group picture in it and his father was on that. He showed it to me: his nose was just like his father's!

However, when I got his stuff after he died, he'd got rid of it. So I've just got a couple of letters from him. He never ever admitted to being Reg's father. He just writes 'My dear Wareing'.

But on the other hand he was always there if my Dad wanted any advice – like when he was going to buy the shop. Then Reg would visit him, in the office at the Midland Red."

He must have been quite a young man, Pat, when he fathered Reg, because he seems to have remained at the Midland Red for many years, by which time Reg was a mature man himself.

"Dad bought the shop when I was about sixteen – (around 1944/45); Peter was already living with us when we were at 56 Kingsway, so he moved with us to the shop. He originally came to live with us in 1940. When we moved into the shop in Monica Road my parents then invited Ethel to move into the Kingsway house… and rent the house off them.

I spent years and years crying, over Madge leaving – she broke my heart when she went – but then gradually it passed off," Pat continues. "When we were living at my Dad's shop, in Leicester, she came back once… and *she* cried, but I didn't… so the tables had turned. I was in my early twenties at that time. We lived at the shop after Carolyn was born, until we got the house – just before Elizabeth was born."

Here's a photo of Madge with Pat, ladies and gentlemen.

"Yes, we were going to a dance evening, to do with Reg's Social Club, at the *Palais de Danse* in Leicester. Madge is in a dress that Great Aunt Una made and I was in a dress that my Mum had made. It was taken by *Jerome's Photographers*. A woman slipped on the floor, down to the dance floor that night and broke the heel off her shoe. I can see her now, hobbling away, perfectly elegant, with the heel in her hand!"

How about this other photo?

"They were rosebuds, the frocks we had there. I was always the plain one with Madge – she was the pretty one."

We're looking at another photo of the Wareing siblings, ladies and gentlemen, which Carolyn has found. On the far left, back row is Reg, with all his half-brothers and sisters, including Ida… if only we could find her daughter, Rita!

Other relatives are in the photo, including Mum. Reg would be around sixty; my Dad looks in his forties. I think that must be shortly after Dad was in hospital, with a duodenal ulcer, because he suddenly looks much thinner. So that would be c.1966, making Dad forty-six, so Reg would be sixty-two.

This other photograph, taken at the same celebration, has Gary and Jackie Mason on it too. Our final, really brilliant photo, shows Pat standing in the front and Madge with her. It looks like the back garden of Brunswick Road.

"Yes, that's either Leicester or Birmingham," Carolyn concludes.

Do join us next week, for the Grand Finale to all of our shows ladies and gentlemen….when it will be… PARTY TIME!!!

217

Chapter Twenty

TOGETHER AGAIN

Cast and Chorus, with Don in the centre, dressed once again in his 'Good Old Days' costume, perform our final song, 'Together Again':

> **Together again**
> **After all of these years**
> **Handshakes and hugs**
> **And a great many tears.**
> **Through all of the heartaches**
> **The joy and the fears**
> **We've all come together**
> **To fold back the years.**

At this point, Don invites the audience to stand, link arms and join in with the performance:

> **So join hands together**
> **Let's celebrate too**
> **A family divided**
> **United anew...**
> **Et cetera.**

As the song ends, the cast members take their seats at the tables laid out for our Family Reunion, with a summer garden backdrop.

Muted conversations around the tables, as family members discuss aspects of our Story. A camera pans around each of the party tables in turn, transmitting pictures to an overhead Display Screen, providing audience with a bird's eye view.

Suddenly, there are shouts from the auditorium. An elderly lady is struggling to reach the stage:

"Shirley, hang on there! I've only just read Dennis's letter. It's me – Rita Cotterill – Ida's daughter – and my son Geoffrey. I hope we're not too late!"

Steve Rogers and Gary help her up the steps and onto the stage, with Geoffrey following close behind.

Family Party at Shirley's house, 2016: Back row, l-r: Caroline Carroll; Shirley Thompson (author); Mike Vincent; Dennis Wareing; Caroline's daughter, Kerry, with baby son, Harlen; Lilian Mcmillan; Ken Wareing; Steve Tipton (Michelle's partner); Gary Dexter. Middle row: Laurence Mason (leaning over chair); Jacky Curtis; 3 sisters: Elizabeth Wynne, Carolyn McCoy and Rosemary Towel; David Thompson (Shirley's husband). Seated (front row): Linda Dexter; Jackie Mason; Julie Vincent; Michelle Vincent with baby daughter Harriet (named after Dad); Mum – Eileen Wareing; Pat Ward. Photographer Steve Rogers.

Dennis Wareing and Steve Rogers, same party, 2016. Photographer Mike Vincent.

Rita Cotterill (Ida's daughter) and her son, Geoffrey, Bromsgrove 2017. By kind permission of Rita Cotterill.

Ending: all family members then move in rows, to the front of the stage, with Don at the centre. The curtains close. Don steps forward:

*"So many lives, ladies and gentlemen. So much joy and so much sorrow. And remember, there's a story out there for **every family**."*

Each family groups take it in turn, to step forward, in a line:

(Jackie Mason and Gary Dexter): "Our parents, Madge and Les Dexter."

(Jacky Curtis, Steven and Michael Upton and the author's mother Eileen):

"The Curtis Family – and the Uptons at 51 Brunswick and number 70: Thomas George, the two Jims, Joe, Maggie, Dennis, Sylvia – and all the rest of them!"

(Reg's daughter, Pat, with her daughters, Carolyn, Elizabeth and Rosemary):

"The Baylis's, Wards and the McCoys."

(Rita and Geoffrey Cotterill):

"The Cotterills... Ida's daughter and Grandson...just in the nick of time!"

(Eileen, Caroline, Julie, Shirley; Dennis, with sisters, Caroline and Lilian; Audrey's son, Steven and Bernard's son Ken):

"And the Wareings, of 65 Brunswick Road!"

The Curtain rises again, this time on a Brunswick Road backdrop. Number 65 is featured in the centre, with number 70 across the road. Three street lamps, placed at intervals, glimmer in the dark.

Shirley steps forward:

So Dad – with all this *research* – by myself and everyone involved in the book, I've just one question for you:

"Am I a good lad for 'digging'?!!"

Entire cast exits, via both wings. Suddenly, the whole theatre is plunged into darkness, apart from the three street lamps. There is pin-drop silence.

(A young girl's plaintive voice echoes, in stereophonic sound, across the auditorium; she sobs at intervals):

"Mummy, where are you? I don't ... like it here....

And they've taken Harry away from me – I don't know where he is!!"

(Young boy's voice):

"I want to go home Mummy. I want to be with my brothers and sisters. Please – if anyone can hear me out there –

I WANT... TO GO... HOME!"

LEAVING

I could never leave my Dad,
I don't want him just to go,
Though he's lying ill in hospital
And it's probably touch and go.

They say his poor old heart
Has had enough and so
His liver, heart and lungs
Are telling him to go.

I'm not ready to let go,
Though it's selfish, that I know,
But my heart and mind and soul
Are saying, *'Please don't go.'*

If there really is a God
And he's watching us here below,
Can't he see it's not yet time
That this man should have to go?

contin...

For it's Harry, he's my Dad,
And I really love him so
And it's tearing me apart
That he soon might have to go.

Time is just a drop
In an ocean deep and low
And I haven't really *told* him yet,
Please don't make him go.

Four weeks of time have passed
As the tides *will* ebb and flow.
He just closed his eyes in peace
Fate said, 'Now it's *time* to go.'

God bless you Dad.

Shirley Thompson © 1998

First published in
Anthology of Verse, *A Father's Love*
Triumph House 1998

Appendix 2

SELECTED BIBLIOGRAPHY

Archives and Maps:
Ancestry Archives (see also websites).
British Newspaper Archives.
Clifton Road School Log Books – 1920-1930 inclusive.
Ordnance Survey Maps (1902): Worcester NW; Worcester NE; Worcester SE.

Books:
Balsall Heath & Highgate – Alan Hemming & Val Hart, Sutton
    Publishing, 2003.
Balsall Heath Through the Ages – Val Hart, Amberley Publishing, 2011.
Birmingham Theatres, Concert & Music Halls – Victor J. Price, Brewin
    Books, 1988.
Chocolate Girls – Annie Murray, Pan Books, 2003.
Chronology of the 20th Century – Philip Waller & John Rowett, Helicon
    Publishing, 1995.
Dear Carice – (postcards from Edward Elgar), Michael Fardon, the Elgar
    Birthplace Trust, 1997.
Flying High – Don Maclean and Chris Gidney, Hodder & Stoughton 2003.
History of Barbourne – Claire & Terry Wardle, MTC Ltd 2007.
Pat Roach's Birmingham – Pat Roach & Shirley Thompson, Brewin
    Books, 2004.
Saint Chad's Visitors Guide Book – The St Chad's Association, 2016.
Saint John in the Wilderness – Alan Titterington, 2016.
Tales Out Of School – Val Hart & members of the Balsall Heath Local
    History Society, Brewin Books, 2009.
The Patchetts of Warley, 1350-1900 – by John H. Patchett MA.
Writing it All Down Before It's All Gone – Tindal association for School &
    Community, Bleak House Books, 1984.
Wuthering Heights – Emily Bronte.

Directories & Records:
Birmingham Trades Directory
Kelly's Directory
Registration of Marriages for Birmingham
The Worcester Academies Public School Records

Magazines & Periodicals:
The Balsall Heath Gazette – Editor, Chris Sutton, for the St Paul's Trust,
  Balsall Heath.

Newspapers & Journals:
The Baylis Bugle
Birmingham Mail
Birmingham Post (March 1931)
British Phone Books (Worcester Section)
Derby Daily Telegraph
Leamington Spa Courier
Worcester Chronicle and Worcester Journal – (various articles)

Websites:
Ancestry.co.uk
Find my past 1939 Register
First World War.com
Marston Green Cottage Homes

BY THE SAME AUTHOR

Adrift in Paradise, ISBN 978-1-85858-447-8   £9.95

Auf Wiedersehen Pat, ISBN 978-1-85858-292-4   £14.95

Finally Meeting Princess Maud, ISBN 978-1-85858-284-9   £14.95

If – The Pat Roach Story, ISBN 978-1-85858-209-2   £14.95

King of Clubs – The Eddie Fewtrell Story, ISBN 978-1-85858-406-5   £14.95

My Life In A Flash – Kash 'the Flash' Gill, ISBN 978-1-85858-499-7   £14.95

Pat Roach's Birmingham, ISBN 978-1-85858-252-8   £12.95

The Power of the Pendant, ISBN 978-1-85858-466-9   £5.95

There's More Out Than In, ISBN 978-1-85858-141-5   £5.95

Unlocking the Gates, ISBN 978-1-85858-478-2   £9.95

The Original Alton Douglas, ISBN 978-1-85858-230-6   £14.95

All the above titles are available to purchase at www.brewinbooks.com